GOING TO WAR WITH JAPAN, 1937–1941

JONATHAN G. UTLEY

GOING TO WAR
WITH JAPAN
1937–1941

THE UNIVERSITY OF TENNESSEE PRESS / KNOXVILLE

Publication of this book has been aided by a grant from the American Council of Learned Societies from funds provided by the Andrew W. Mellon Foundation.

The paper in this book meets the guidelines for permanence and durability of the Committee on Production Guidelines for Book Longevity of the Council on Library Resources. Binding materials have been chosen for durability.

Title page photograph: The carved ivory Asian chess set is reproduced courtesy of Dr. Robert Feinberg, Knoxville, from his private collection.

Library of Congress Cataloging in Publication Data
Utley, Jonathan G., 1942–
  Going to war with Japan, 1937–1941.

  Bibliography: p.
  Includes index.
  1. World War, 1939–1945—Causes. 2. World War, 1939–1945—Diplomatic history. 3. United States—Foreign relations—Japan. 4. Japan—Foreign relations—United States. 5. United States—Foreign relations—1933–1945. 6. Japan—Foreign relations—1912–1945. 7. Hull, Cordell, 1871–1955. I. Title.
D742.U5U74 1985   940.53'112   84-11923
ISBN 0-87049-445-7

FOR *Frayn Utley* AND *Carol Marin*

CONTENTS

ILLUSTRATIONS

Photographs

Maps

INTRODUCTION

For two generations, Americans have read about December 7, 1941, the "day that will live in infamy." In trying to explain how the Imperial Japanese Navy was able to launch such a devastating attack on American forces, dozens of authors have cited incompetence, confusion, treason, conspiracy, and lack of imagination on the part of American leaders. Lost in this debate is the fact that the Pearl Harbor attack was not just America's first official battle in World War II but the culminating event in nearly four and a half years of diplomatic maneuvering between the American and Japanese governments. Preoccupation with the attack itself has caused authors to narrow their focus and produce works that have more in common with legal briefs, anecdotal accounts, or detailed chronicling of events than with the history of the period.

Even the more traditional historical studies concentrate on the last few months of 1941 as if those days and weeks held all the crucial decisions. To be sure, many important decisions were made in 1941, but actions taken and opportunities missed during the first four years of the Sino-Japanese War, July 1937 to June 1941, brought Japan and the United States so close to the brink of war that it was almost impossible to keep them from falling over the edge. To understand how diplomacy failed to avoid a war, we must look beyond the final moves and examine the chain of decisions that brought the nation to that point.

David Potter stressed this approach when he examined the origins of the American Civil War. Nations do not choose to go to war, he concluded; they choose to follow a course of action that *results* in war, which is an entirely different thing. To avoid war one must see it coming, but to go to war it is only necessary to take step after step and make decision after decision until the leaders finally resort to war because they have exhausted their other options.[1] Potter's explanation is particularly applicable to pre–Pearl Harbor diplomacy. The Franklin Roosevelt administration's inability to resolve peacefully its disputes with Japan was not the consequence of a single critical decision during the fall of 1941, or even a combination of decisions during that period. The slide toward war took years.

To understand how war came, we must understand the ideas underlying the decisions of the foreign policy managers, their principles and values, their world view and concept of vital national interests. These ideas are not difficult to find. Even as Japanese forces threatened American, British, and Dutch territory in Southeast Asia, the president, the secretary of state, the ambassador to Japan, and numerous officials within the Roosevelt administration explained to anyone who would listen that the threat was more than military. The future of the world depended upon a system which encouraged the free exchange of goods and services. If this liberal commercial order were replaced by a world partitioned into autarchic economic spheres everyone would suffer, not least of all the United States.

But if we understand the policy, and even the ideas that lay beneath that policy, we still do not have the whole picture and we cannot explain why war occurred. Beyond principles and policies it is necessary to examine the execution of policy. Stanley Hornbeck, the ranking Asian specialist in the State Department, emphasized that while principles derive from the temperament, experience, and thought of the nation, and policies are determined by the needs, desires, capacity, and opportunities of the nation, the execution of policy involved decisions by individuals who were "substantially affected by temporary human and material equations." In other words, the action taken is not always consistent with the established policy or with the principles of the nation.[2]

Hornbeck knew whereof he spoke. We cannot hope to explain the road to Pearl Harbor by examining only the principles of Cordell Hull or the policy decisions taken at the highest levels of government. It is even more misleading to assume that an action taken necessarily reflected a high-level policy decision. Rather than a smoothly functioning, harmonious machine, the foreign policy establishment in the Roosevelt administration was a snake pit of influential leaders and faceless bureaucrats working at cross-purposes, striking deals, and not infrequently employing sleight of hand in order to move the nation in the direction each thought most appropriate.

Some of the people who touched the conduct of American foreign relations are apparent: army and navy officers, the secretaries of war, the navy, and the treasury. Others are more obscure: the administrator for export control, the petroleum coordinator for national defense, the assistant chief of the State Department's Division of Controls. A few were buried deep within the Washington bureaucracy: the executive director of the petroleum group of the Chemical Products Division of the Industrial Materials section of the National Defense Advisory Commission. It was the interaction of all these individuals and agencies that moved the United States down the road to Pearl Harbor.

By examining the full span of four years and five months of the Sino-Japanese War, by looking at all the levels and departments of the Roosevelt administration, and by focusing on why the actors behaved as they did, I have sought to explain why a nation that never wanted to fight Japan ended up doing so.

My views on what the Roosevelt administration did, and why, differ from those of many historians, but rather than clutter the text with these disagreements, I have relegated them to the notes. For any flaws that appear in either the text or the notes, I accept sole responsibility. On the other hand, to the extent to which the reader finds my views persuasive, I must share the credit with a wide variety of people.

Wayne Cole and Robert Divine read the entire manuscript and provided helpful comments, most of which I have taken to heart. As I worked on the manuscript, my colleagues at the University of Tennessee, Knoxville provided the collegial support and stimulating conversation that were invaluable in helping me to shape my thoughts. Still earlier, David F. Healy and Norman A. Graebner introduced me to the study of American foreign relations and Waldo Heinrichs proved to be everything a mentor should be.

Beyond these professional contacts, I owe a special debt to my family for helping shape the way I look at world affairs. My parents, Frayn and Clifton Utley, both made their living studying and commenting on international relations and the entire Utley household saw a constant parade of foreign visitors and participated in countless animated discussions of world events. In my youthful debates with my parents and my two older brothers, David and Garrick, I soon learned that if you wanted to be heard you had to say bluntly what was on your mind. I followed that practice in this book in the belief that the reader would rather see candid opinions than artfully qualified sentences.

Moving from the molding of ideas to the actual writing of the book, I owe thanks to two groups. One is the army of archivists and librarians who manage the massive amounts of historical source material and who have the wonderful characteristic of gaining pleasure from going out of their way to help researchers. The other group is composed of the personal friends in Knoxville and Chicago who did not always know just what it was I was doing but who showed an interest in it anyway, and provided moral support.

I owe a special debt to my wife, Carol Marin, who managed to play a dual role: She provided the personal support without which I could not have completed the manuscript; and she applied her journalist's eye to my academic prose with painful but beneficial results.

J.G.U.

Knoxville, Tennessee
May 1984

GOING TO WAR WITH JAPAN, 1937–1941

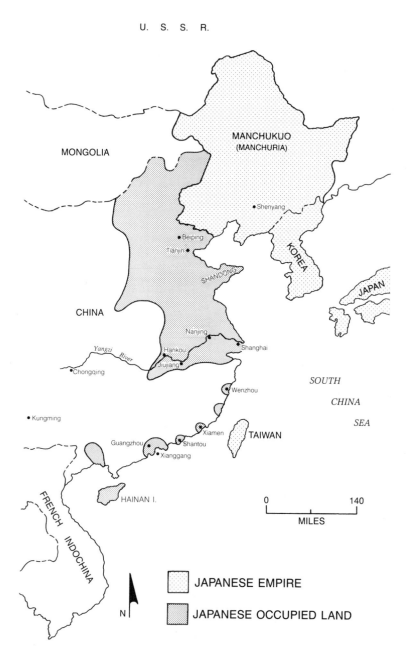

Map 1. East Asia

CHAPTER ONE

CHARTING A COURSE

It did not start as a big war—just a little skirmish between Japanese troops on night maneuvers and Chinese troops guarding the Marco Polo Bridge ten miles outside of Beiping, China's capital. American intelligence had not predicted any trouble and early reports indicated that it was only a minor incident that would probably be resolved on the spot.[1] But each side was more intent upon winning than compromising and the skirmish quickly grew into a test of power between the industrialized and aggressive Imperial Japan and the disorganized and industrially backward but incredibly large China.[2]

None of this was readily apparent when Secretary of State Cordell Hull arrived at his office on the morning of July 8, 1937. Cables from the American ambassadors in China and Japan described an isolated incident best left to the local authorities. By Monday, July 12, however, the situation seemed more serious, and Hull and his chief Asian adviser, Stanley K. Hornbeck, urged moderation on the Japanese and Chinese representatives. Their friendly advice had no effect; the fighting continued to escalate and Hull was faced with the difficult assignment of determining the proper American response. That task would consume most of his time and energy for the rest of the year.[3]

Hull and company brought to their deliberations assumptions

derived from the history of American involvement in East Asia. Of these, the most important was a deep and abiding belief that Japan was not trustworthy, that its recent history was strewn with broken treaties and meaningless promises, and that except for a brief affair with liberalism in the 1920s, Japan was a militaristic state bent upon establishing a self-serving hegemony over East Asia. To this end it had waged war against China in 1894, Russia in 1905, Germany during World War I, and China again in 1931. In the course of these wars Japan had established dominance over Korea and Taiwan, wrested southern Sakhalin Island from Russia, seized German concessions in Shandong, and in 1932 set up a puppet state of Manchukuo in Manchuria. Since then Japan had walked out of the League of Nations, rejected naval arms limitations, and expanded its war machine. Political leaders who dared to challenge these actions risked assassination. The conventional wisdom in Washington was that as soon as Japan felt strong enough to do so, it would try to eliminate all Western influence in East Asia.[4]

In contrast, Americans had a "clean record" in dealing with China. In 1900 the United States called for an Open Door in China with free commerce and investment. In 1915 it denounced Japan's Twenty-one Demands of China. At the end of World War I President Woodrow Wilson tried to get Japan to withdraw from Shandong, while the other Western powers accepted Japan's new sphere of influence. In 1922 the United States persuaded seven other nations and Japan to sign the Nine Power Treaty pledging respect for Chinese territorial integrity. When Japan marched into Manchuria in 1931, the United States denounced the action and said it would never recognize Japan's conquest.

American friendship, however, did not extend to renunciation of the unequal treaty system Western powers had imposed on China in the nineteenth century. American gunboats and marines remained in China to enforce extraterritorial rights and, in cooperation with the other powers, the United States retained control over the Chinese Maritime Customs. The United States and China may have been friends, but they were not equals.

More important, the "clean record" was limited to words, and meant little. The Open Door note of 1900 did not even imply American action should some other power seek to close the door to American commerce. The United States rejected anything beyond moral support for China in the face of Japan's Twenty-one Demands. Wilson was not prepared to sacrifice anything in Europe to force Japan out of Shandong. The Nine Power Treaty contained no enforcement provisions and was coupled with a Five Power Treaty that established a naval arms ratio that effectively prohibited American naval action in East Asia. When Japan conquered Manchuria in 1931–32, the only American action was Secretary of State Henry L. Stimson's refusal to recognize Japan's ill-gotten gains. Such American action, or more precisely inaction, showed that the United States had never been prepared to pay a price to preserve China's integrity or the Open Door there.[5]

By 1937, American military posture reflected this reality. A modest number of troops and a handful of antiquated gunboats protected American nationals from the outrages of unruly Chinese, but these forces were never designed to challenge the Imperial Japanese Army. Naval power was equally ineffectual. The Asiatic Fleet was pathetically weak and of value only in "showing the flag." America's real naval power lay with the United States Fleet, based in southern California. It lacked the fortified naval bases, capital ships, supply train, and experienced personnel to confront the Imperial Japanese Navy in East Asian waters. Only at great expense and with great difficulty could the United States wage a war against Japan in East Asia.[6] As far as the American people were concerned, there was nothing that could justify such a war. In 1937 most Americans were isolationists intent upon avoiding the destructive fury of the next war.[7]

Diplomatic precedence, military realities, and public opinion all pointed Cordell Hull toward one course of action: to issue a statement denouncing Japan's aggression and then quietly abandon China to its fate. But policy is not simply the sum of precedence, politics, and military realities. These factors are weighed by the policy manager in light of his own principles and personality. Cordell Hull's globalist view compelled him to reject a policy of denounce and retreat as shortsighted. He saw the North China incident as part of a worldwide effort by aggressor states to replace the rule of law with the rule of force, an open world with a closed one. Germany and Italy were espousing such a doctrine in Europe, and in Asia Japan was reasserting it. Hull was sincere when he told the Japanese ambassador, "There can be no serious hostilities anywhere in the world which will not one way or another affect interests or rights or obligations of this country." The secretary was convinced that unless the aggressor states were stopped, their new world order would destroy all the progress civilization had given to the peoples of the world.[8]

The immediate questions confronting him were, at what point would Japan be stopped, by whom, and at what price? Within the State Department it was well understood that if it was going to be the United States that did the stopping, it would probably not be over China and it would certainly not be now. It did not take them long to see that rhetoric would have no influence on the course of Asian events and that only a great power's demonstrable willingness to use force would alter Japanese or Chinese plans for war. No one in the department suggested that the United States should be that great power, and Hull himself agreed to avoid "uncalled for or futile protests or gestures."[9]

No sooner had Secretary Hull made that pledge, however, than he publicly proclaimed that world peace could only be assured if nations respected law and the sanctity of treaties and endorsed arms limitation, free trade, and national self-restraint. To gain maximum attention for these "pillars of peace," Hull circulated them to the nations of the world and planned to publish the replies.[10] Such emphasis upon peace through respect for fundamental principles has earned Hull a reputation as an idealistic, well-meaning, and ineffectual secretary of state who believed that words and ideas could restrain armies and navies. The characterization is unfair.

Hull had no difficulty reconciling his appeal to principles and his recognition that words would not deter Japan, because he considered them on entirely different planes. The Sino-Japanese War had prompted Hull to articulate his "pillars of peace," but the statement itself was never part of his diplomatic arsenal and he took care to keep it from being intimately tied up with the Sino-Japanese crisis. Preaching the principles of right conduct would not persuade Japan to alter its foreign policy and Hull knew it. But, he asked, who could stand silently and refuse to challenge "the doctrine and the reign of force and international anarchy?"[11] Enunciation of principles was part of Hull's long-term educational effort, not his short-term diplomacy. He hoped to educate the world, not convert Japan.

Nor was Hull trying to arouse public support for a stronger anti-Japanese policy. Just the opposite was true. When critics denounced Hull's official impartiality as a betrayal of United States obligations under the Kellogg-Briand Pact (in which Japan renounced war as an instrument of foreign policy) and the Nine Power Treaty, Hull sought to placate them by declaring that he had already spoken to that topic in his "pillars of peace" statement. But the secretary stopped short of labeling Japan a transgressor of either the treaties or the principles.[12] Even as the war escalated to include a battle over Shanghai in August, Hull showed restraint.

Shanghai was not a typical Chinese city. It was the fourth largest city in the world and held forty thousand foreigners in its international settlement. Its banks and trading houses were of great importance to the economic life of East Asia.[13] Consequently, reports that Chinese armies were about to confront Japanese troops stationed in Shanghai prompted Hull to intervene more directly than he had since the fighting began. And surprisingly, his intervention proved to be in support more of Japan than of China.

In an attempt to keep the war from spreading into Shanghai, Hull had the American ambassador in Tokyo, Joseph C. Grew, offer America's good offices as mediator if Japan was willing to talk peace. The Japanese replied that they had already offered peace terms to China and if the United States sought to be helpful it could persuade China to accept the Japanese proposal. While the peace terms were likely to be harsher than the United States would like, Grew believed Japan was seriously trying to keep the war from spreading into central China. And if this desirable goal was going to be accomplished, China would have to negotiate with Japan.[14]

This put Hull in a predicament. If he did nothing the war would spread, to the detriment of China, the United States, and world peace. If he asked China to negotiate a settlement with Japan it would be a forceful blow against China's will to resist, tantamount to asking China to appease Japan.

"The urging of such a compromise by the United States would seriously impair the public stand we have taken against war and against violation of international agreements," Nelson T. Johnson warned from Nanjing. On a more practical note, the ambassador argued that "a compromise truce at this juncture would merely postpone the inevitable decision whether China shall be dominated by Japan with resistance. . . . If serious hostilities occur between Japan and China, they will inflict untold damage in China and possibly Japan, but they may correct in China a tendency to rely on foreign aid and in Japan a belief in the profitable results of imperialist expansion."[15] Stanley Hornbeck concurred in Johnson's position, warning Hull: "We should be very much on guard in considering any suggestion that we exert ourselves toward inducing the Chinese to make concessions.[16]

Ignoring this advice, Hull instructed Johnson to urge the Chinese foreign minister not to reject any Japanese proposal but to keep open the "door to negotiations." But the matter became moot as Japanese and Chinese troops clashed in Shanghai and the "North China Incident" became the Sino-Japanese War.[17]

Hull's behavior does not fit the stereotypical view of the secretary as idealistic and ineffectual. Rather, it shows a pragmatic secretary of state. In not asking China to accept Japanese terms but only to avoid closing off negotiations, Hull had disclaimed any involvement in the merits of any Japanese proposal. But to ask China to negotiate was to ask it to compromise. Never before had the United States encouraged China to appease an aggressor. Not during the next four years would the United States do so again. On this occasion, however, Hull believed that a pragmatic approach was better than strictly adhering to the principles of right conduct he had publicly proclaimed.

The expansion of the war into central China produced a rift within the State Department. Activists feared that if the United States did not act, Japan would dominate all of East Asia and bar Western influence altogether. Others saw Japan, Germany, and Italy as bandit nations that sooner or later would have to be faced. A few stressed the need to strongly defend Hull's principles of right conduct.[18]

Stanley Hornbeck was the most outspoken member of the activist school. For a decade he had headed the Far Eastern Division (FE) and had only recently been promoted to adviser on political affairs, an office from which he continued to dominate Asian affairs. He was a pure Asian specialist who took a political science Ph.D. at the University of Wisconsin with Paul Reinsch, former minister to China, and whose first government service was at the Paris Peace Conference as an adviser on Asian questions. So narrow was Hornbeck's vision that he seemed to believe that the sun not only set but rose in Asia. He reacted to everything that happened "in specific relation to the Far Eastern situation and the Far Eastern situation alone." A defender of China and an implacable enemy of Japan, Hornbeck was so rigid that his associates found it difficult to work with him.[19]

Hornbeck's message was simple: Japan had to be stopped, and as that could be done only by force, the United States must build more battleships and strengthen its naval power in the western Pacific.

Diplomatic note writing unsupported by a determination to use force would accomplish nothing.[20]

The opposite point of view was championed by two State Department European specialists, Assistant Secretary of State Hugh Wilson and J. Pierrepont Moffat, chief of the Division of European Affairs. Wilson was a senior diplomat who had served briefly in Japan during the early 1920s but had spent most of his career in Europe. Moffat was a rising star within the foreign service whose primary contact with Asia was through his father-in-law, Ambassador Joseph Grew.[21]

Both these men considered themselves realists, maintaining that principles were important, but not worth a war. Both saw Europe as the most important area for diplomatic action and dismissed American material interests in Asia as so limited that they probably represented less than the cost of waging war in that area for one month. Wilson went even further. Asia was useless to the United States. It had been a mistake to seize the Philippines in 1898 and it would be best if the United States shed itself of that albatross and withdrew from Asia altogether. When he spoke with Hull, however, Wilson argued more pragmatically. Economic sanctions against Japan would not work without cooperation from the Netherlands and that cooperation could not be acquired without an American guarantee to protect the Netherlands East Indies, a guarantee the United States could not give without British naval support. Since Britain was preoccupied in Europe its fleet would not be available to act against Japan. Nor should help be sought from the Soviet Union, for a Soviet-Japanese war would tempt Germany to begin a war in Europe. And peace in Europe was more important than saving China.[22]

Hull heard all those arguments repeatedly. He ran the State Department in a way that encouraged everyone to speak his mind. Rather than surround himself with yes sayers, he would gather his staff in his office and conduct hours of seemingly endless debate on the proper policy. Such tiring sessions sometimes degenerated into bickering and tempers were lost, but the secretary was unflappable, sitting quietly, asking an occasional question and considering every aspect of every argument. Hull was not given to snap decisions.[23]

Temperamentally, Hull sided with the activists; but he subordinated his feelings of righteous indignation at Japan's aggression to the less emotional criteria of national interest. There was neither the naval power nor the popular support for military sanctions. Hull did not believe the United States had the leverage to make economic sanctions effective, and they could easily lead to a military confrontation. Most important, Hull understood that, at the moment, Japanese aggression did not threaten a vital American interest. Japan's invasion of China was undesirable but not intolerable. Unwilling to risk a confrontation for anything less than a vital national interest, Hull rejected the activist recommendations.[24]

Yet Hull was not prepared to simply withdraw from Asia. He believed that unchecked Japanese expansion would eventually pose a threat to vital American interests, and it was important to make Japan aware that the United States could not be discounted "under all circumstances." Thus, the secretary sought a middle road between a policy of confrontation and one of withdrawal. In effect, he split the difference between the bold and cautious schools within the State Department. As long as he was in control of American policy, there would be no confronting Japan and no withdrawal from Asia. The United States would have to acquiesce in Japan's superior power, but it would not be necessary to give any open approval of its actions.

This policy of no confrontation, no withdrawal, and no assent was never drafted into a policy paper and submitted to the president; these were the days before the national security state mentality had developed, and policy formulation and implementation were more informal. It was sufficient that Roosevelt knew what Hull was about and that Hull's staff understood what was to be done. It was a policy they implemented consistently. How consistently can be seen in State's response to Japan's seizure of Chinese Maritime Customs revenues and the Japanese blockade of China.

When in the course of their conquests Japanese troops seized Chinese custom houses, the United States had an issue on which to challenge Japan, since the maritime customs were used to secure American loans to China. But Hull ordered no ringing denunciation of Japan. The diplomatic language was discreet in tone and concentrated on the particular interest involved. State's only apparent concern was the security of loans held by American nationals and corporations.[25] A more troublesome issue was the Japanese intention to search all ships entering China in order to catch Chinese ships hiding under the cover of the American flag or that of some other neutral. As a traditionally neutral power, the United States repudiated such stop and searches, especially when there was no declared war. As there were few American ships involved however, and an incident did not seem imminent, the United States silently acquiesced in the searches and refused to prohibit American flag ships from trading with China. There would be no confrontation with Japan, no assent to Japanese actions (though there would be acquiescence), and no withdrawal from Asia.[26]

The same principles were applied in the way Hull dealt with China. While he treated China as something less than an ally, he also tried not to do any disservice to that beleaguered nation. Hull's staff encouraged the Export-Import Bank to make a planned $25 million loan to China, but when the bank hesitated, Hull refused to apply any serious pressure. Much the same approach was taken toward the giant munitions maker, E.I. DuPont Company, when it decided to forgo sales of TNT to China in order to keep from being "crucified by publicity." Since this left the Chinese government with five thousand bomb casings and no TNT to fill them, State tried to convince DuPont to reverse its stand. But when DuPont directors demanded a letter from Hull stating that "such sales were in the interest of the United States," he let the deal die.[27]

A far more sensitive issue than credits or munitions was that of American nationals serving as advisers in the Chinese air force. Hull could have encouraged the creation of a "Flying Tigers" type of secret air force four years before he finally did so. But that would increase the risk of a confrontation with Japan. On the other hand, the best way to avoid an incident was to order American pilots already in China to leave; yet that action would have the drawback of looking like a step toward total American withdrawal from China. Hull's middle-road policy rejected both alternatives. Instead, the State Department routinely denied passports to Americans seeking to offer their services to China and privately assured Americans already in that service that while their actions were in violation of American law, they would not be prosecuted even if Japan made formal protests.[28]

Though Hull's method of developing a policy avoided any open rebellion with State Department ranks, there were some significant challenges to his policy during the latter months of 1937, particularly from a nervous public and a scheming Britain.

With Hull's support, Roosevelt had played somewhat fast and loose with the 1937 Neutrality Act by refusing to apply it to the undeclared Sino-Japanese War. As a result, China continued to buy war supplies in the United States. But there was a war going on in China, declared or not, and the American people became increasing-

Cordell Hull (right) and Franklin Roosevelt were responsible for determining policy, but they did not always see eye to eye. (File 208-PU-175T-7A, NA.)

ly nervous about America's relationship to it. The Chinese bombardment of Shanghai in August which killed 1,700, including three Americans, and the accidental Japanese shelling of the American cruiser *Augusta,* killing an American sailor, spurred on those Americans who demanded withdrawal from China and invocation of the Neutrality Act.[29]

Hull was worried. Application of the Neutrality Act would, as one department officer wrote, "make it more difficult to sustain any position vis-à-vis Japan in regard to our right to remain on the face of the Asian earth at all." If the United States abandoned its position in China, the other powers would do the same and Japan would be given a free hand in the region. That would cripple Chinese resistance and assure Japan a quick victory. It was even possible that the Chinese, feeling betrayed, would take out their anger on the American nationals remaining in China. So Hull insisted there be no hint of American withdrawal. When the Justice Department contemplated shutting down the United States Court sitting in war-torn Shanghai, State interceded to keep the court where it was and in full operation.[30]

Calming an increasingly worried public was more difficult. Roosevelt and Hull's first move was to announce on September 2, 1937 that all American nationals in China should leave and that those who remained did so at their own risk. Hull wanted to go farther and declare a moral embargo on export of munitions to either combatant.[31] Roosevelt thought his secretary was yielding too much. The president had opposed invoking the Neutrality Act because it would have allowed Japan to buy raw materials from the United States that Japanese industry could transform into weapons of war, while unindustrialized China was dependent upon buying the already manufactured war goods that would be embargoed under the Neutrality Act. Hull's moral embargo, while less binding, would have the same immediate effect. The only concession Roosevelt was ready to make was on the specific issue of the S.S. *Wichita,* a freighter carrying nineteen bombers to China. What made the *Wichita* so important was that it was owned by the United States government. As public attention focused on this ship, Roosevelt reluctantly agreed to recall it, order all government-owned ships out of the Sino-Japanese War trade, and announce that all other American flag ships would engage in such trade at their own risk.[32]

To describe the *Wichita* case in terms of calming public opinion, however, overlooks an important diplomatic dimension. State Department officers worried that if Japan stopped the *Wichita* the United States might be faced "with an embarrassing situation." The United States could not ignore such a stop and search as it had with ships registered to American companies. Thus, by ordering the *Wichita* to stay out of the China trade, Roosevelt was not only allaying public fears, he was circumventing a situation that could easily have resulted in either a Japanese-American confrontation or a humiliating American retreat.[33]

It is difficult to measure the influence of public opinion on American policy, as the *Wichita* case shows, because rarely were policy decisions taken simply to satisfy a concerned public. Roosevelt and State Department officials worried about public opinion and spent some time trying to control or guide it. But they had a clear idea of what national policy was (or should be) and did not intend to let the uninformed and emotional feelings of the populace dictate either withdrawal from China or confrontation with Japan.[34]

On the other hand, a public chary of involvement in Asia was a convenient excuse for avoiding action the foreign policy managers had no intention of taking. Chinese requests for help, for example, could be turned down by referring to the strong isolationist mood of the public.[35]

The same technique worked well with the British, who since the start of the Sino-Japanese War had urged joint Anglo-American diplomatic protests to Japan. Hull tactfully declined such offers, in order to avoid the image of Western powers conspiring against Japan and because he and his staff suspected the British were trying to lure the United States into a position where it would have to defend extensive British investments in Asia.[36]

Thus it was with much skepticism that Hull and staff received a British proposal in late September 1937 for a joint Anglo-American boycott of Japanese goods. To accept this offer would go beyond existing American legislation, anger American isolationists, push the United States toward a confrontation with Japan, and if hostilities resulted, leave the U.S. Fleet to face the Japanese navy without any British support. On the other hand, to reject the proposal would allow Britain to blame the United States for blocking any action. So Hull decided to tell Britain the United States could not accept the proposal because it violated the Neutrality Act and to assure His Majesty's government, rather disingenuously, that if it could suggest some form of collective action that could be reconciled with American principles of neutrality, the government of the United States would be glad to talk about it.[37]

Though Hull won that round, the British found a new opportunity to entangle the United States in the Sino-Japanese crisis when China appealed to the League of Nations. In all probability, the league would shunt the problem to its Far Eastern Advisory Committee, a relic of the Manchurian crisis of 1931–32. The United States was still a member of that moribund body, however, and if it resigned from the committee it would be damned for retreating into isolation and abandoning Asia. If the United States participated in committee deliberations, it might find itself in a more aggressive diplomatic posture than Hull thought the situation justified. All the secretary of state could do was instruct the American delegate to attend but accept none of the responsibilities of the league members and answer no hypothetical questions.[38] The British countered by trying to establish a special subcommittee made up of countries particularly interested in Asia. If the subcommittee consisted of Nine Power Treaty signatories the United States would perforce be a member, and thus be pushed into the leadership role Hull strove to avoid. In consultation with his staff, Hull decided the best way to avoid this trap was to insist that the Asian conflict was of interest to all nations because it threatened the peace of the world and should not be relegated to a subcommittee consisting only of nations involved in Asia.[39] Meanwhile, he would endorse any league statements that denounced aggression so long as the United States was not involved in creating such statements.[40] Hull's strategy of endorsing league talk while blocking entangling actions worked well, for a while.

By October, three months into the Sino-Japanese War, Hull had grounds for cautious optimism. He had just parried the latest British attempt to involve the United States in the Sino-Japanese conflict. There was a reasonable chance his efforts had prevented the league from calling a conference of Nine Power Treaty signatories. Within the United States he had successfully avoided application of the Neutrality Act and had soothed those who demanded stronger action than he thought reasonable. Many American nationals had left China, thus lessening the likelihood of an incident, while an official American presence preserved American rights. Hull could not be happy with the situation, since a war still raged in China and peace was not in sight. But he had carved out a policy that would permit the nation to wait for better times: for the war to end, Japanese sanity to return, the balance of power to shift. Hull could also be pleased that he had devised this policy with little interference from either the president or other departments. On October 5, that changed.

Franklin Roosevelt did not like Hull's Asian policy. He might accept Hull's arguments, but he never really believed them. Frustrated by a policy that let Japan get away with blatant aggression, Roosevelt lashed out at Japan in a speech delivered in Chicago, the heartland of American isolationism. Most of this "Quarantine Speech," as it became known, was standard internationalist fare, much of it drafted within the State Department: "The present reign of terror and international lawlessness . . . [means that] the very foundations of civilization are seriously threatened. . . . International anarchy destroys every foundation for peace. . . . The situation is definitely of universal concern." But there was also a new tone in this speech, a "sting in the scorpion's tail" inserted by Roosevelt: "The peace-loving nations must make a concerted effort to uphold laws and principles on which alone peace can rest secure. . . . When an epidemic of physical disease starts to spread, the community approves and joins in a quarantine of the patient. . . . War is a contagion, whether it be declared or undeclared. . . . There must be positive endeavors to preserve peace."[41]

Roosevelt's speech did everything Hull had sought to avoid. It exacerbated Japanese-American relations by engaging in name calling, it pushed the United States into a leadership role among the Western nations, and it made a league-sponsored conference of Nine Power Treaty signatories inevitable.[42] The speech also caused problems within the State Department. Hull had resolved the activist-versus-noninterventionist debate generally in favor of the noninterventionists, but this new presidential leadership reopened the debate and gave the activists a powerful ally. In effect, the Quarantine Speech represented the beginning of a contest for control of American foreign policy. Roosevelt wanted something more dynamic and assertive; Hull was content to follow the established policy.

The president's idea of a "quarantine" probably included economic pressure against Japan consisting of boycott, embargo, and some form of long-range naval pressure. But Roosevelt tended to think in broad, sweeping terms and to avoid concrete, detailed plans, so when he arrived in Washington on October 8 he had few specific instructions. The conference should include more than just Nine Power signatories, it should be held in Brussels rather than London, and

The Roosevelt admnistration split over how to respond to Japanese aggression. At the Brussels Conference, Stanley Hornbeck and Norman Davis (left and center) wanted to confront Japan while Pierrepont Moffat (right) thought China did not warrant such action. (Standing are Charles Bohlen and Robert Pell.) (File 306NT-120136, NA.)

Norman Davis should be the chief American delegate—beyond those points, there was no presidential direction. As a result, proposals within the State Department ran the gamut from Hull's suggestion that the conference be used as a platform for moral preachments to others contemplating sanctions. It was the old debate between activists and noninterventionists all over again.[43]

Stanley Hornbeck argued the activist case with a proposal he somewhat deviously labeled "constructive." Japanese expansion, Hornbeck maintained, came from a variety of cultural and economic factors. If the powers desired to restore peace and stability in Asia, they would have to give Japan a sense of political and economic security. To do this, Japan must be assured that other powers would not use force against it and that it could gain access to the raw materials it needed. Hornbeck had not undergone a change of heart, just a change of tactics. He still believed Japan was dominated by military leaders who respected only force and he intended to apply the stick along with the carrot; in addition to giving Japan assurances of political and economic security the powers must show they were willing to obstruct Japan's resorting to force.[44]

Noninterventionists in the State Department were immediately suspicious of the proposal, first because it came from Hornbeck and second because it rested on the assumption that war in Asia warranted American involvement to bring it to a close. If, as was likely, the "constructive" proposal failed, a momentum would have been established for an assertive Asian policy and it would be almost impossible to return to the passive policy Hull had so carefully crafted. The Far Eastern Division realized this and endorsed economic concessions to Japan but rejected restrictive measures other than symbolic acts of American "moral disapprobation."[45] At one time this disagreement would have been thrashed out in Hull's office. But in October the president had demonstrated his interest in the course of American foreign policy, so the question was taken to the White House.

Roosevelt wanted action. He agreed with the activists that Japan had to be stopped before its expansion made war with the United States inevitable. But as usual, the president's plan of action was "sketchy." He wanted the Brussels Conference to begin in a mood of peace and goodwill, emphasizing constructive measures. (He called Hornbeck's "constructive" proposal "very good.") If that approach failed to bring peace to Asia, he warned, "we must then consider taking further steps." Though he had not determined precisely what those steps would be, he did refer to aiding China and "ostracizing" Japan, a term that remained undefined.[46] Thus, when Norman Davis left for Brussels on October 20 he took with him no specific proposals, only a very clear understanding that he and the president agreed that the time for action had come.

A different mood prevailed within the State Department. There the advocates of a moderate foreign policy, including Hull, Wilson, and Under Secretary Sumner Welles, opposed not only sanctions but any diplomatic confrontation with Japan. They worried that the conference created "the temptation to do something in circumstances where there is nothing efficacious to be done."[47]

Dominated by this attitude, State's officers applied themselves to ending the conference as soon as possible. Even before the opening session, when it became clear Japan would not attend, they advised the American delegation that the conferees should appoint Britain, Germany, and the United States a committee to keep in touch with the situation and adjourn for a prolonged period. This proposal stunned Davis, Hornbeck, and Moffat, who had come to Brussels understanding that the president expected more from the conference than a rapid adjournment. "The Department's mind was obviously running along different lines from that of the President," Moffat concluded. "Either the latter had changed his mind, which seemed unlikely, or else the Department and the President were working at cross purposes."[48]

Roosevelt had not changed his mind about the Brussels Conference, and it is inconceivable that Hull and Welles were unaware of the president's desire for an assertive foreign policy. Roosevelt had been remarkably consistent in insisting that the nation needed to act, and Hull had been present when he told Davis that if mediation failed "we must consider taking further steps." It is probable that Hull, realizing that Roosevelt had not thought through the consequences of his new policy, felt a responsibility to avoid the pitfalls that lay in the president's path. It was not mutiny. Roosevelt had expressed an attitude but had not given any specific orders. In that situation it was easy for department officers to rationalize their actions not as disobedience but simply as the assertion of their professional responsibility.

If Hull and Welles were to be successful in directing American policy back to its less aggressive posture, they had to control Norman Davis. An old warhorse at such conferences, Ambassador-at-Large Davis was a fervent Anglophile and had favored firm action to stop

Japan prior to Roosevelt's speech.[49] Given enough freedom, Davis was sure to push for action. Hornbeck would not argue for moderation and Moffat did not have the authority to restrain Davis. It was up to Hull and Welles to see that Davis did not take the bit in his teeth and drag the nation farther than they wanted it to go. The tight rein they intended to keep on Davis was soon apparent, for while the delegation had drafted its own opening remarks, so had State, which insisted that its version be used. The differences were not great, but it was apparent that Hull and company intended the delegation to be nothing more than a cipher for policy determined in the State Department.[50]

Norman Davis had no intention of being restricted by a State Department he derided as following a "do nothing" policy. He promptly took the offensive, suggesting to the British a program of far-reaching Anglo-American embargoes on the sale of arms to Japan, refusal to recognize Japan's gains, refusal to lend money to Japan for the development of conquered territories, and a joint boycott of Japanese goods. Davis assured the British that Roosevelt was anxious to take some action in this conflict and he (Davis) hoped the president would ask Congress to suspend the Neutrality Act as it applied to the Sino-Japanese War. It was Roosevelt's belief, Davis asserted, that some attempt had to be made to put a stop to the increasingly menacing challenge of totalitarian states.[51]

Knowing Hull would never tolerate anything along those lines, Davis did not tell the secretary what he had suggested. Instead, he cabled Roosevelt and Hull that the time had come for the conference to act. While economic sanctions were impractical at the conference, a "halfway course" was not. The nations present would avoid any economic or political actions harmful to China, deny Japan funds it needed to develop conquered territories, and give no military assistance to Japan should it attack one of the conferees. Davis noted that such a policy would require repeal of the Neutrality Act and urged the president to recommend such to Congress. Though Davis termed his suggestions "halfway" and "middle," Hull saw them as extreme and dismissed them without serious consideration.[52]

The State Department only discovered the full extent of Davis's machinations from the British, who were suspicious of the "woolyheaded" Mr. Davis and asked State for confirmation of what Davis was proposing. Welles was shocked. He warned the British that "Mr. Norman Davis had had it made clear to him that this Government was not favorably disposed to consider participation in such agreements and that Mr. Davis had been requested to submit any proposals of this character which might come up to Washington for decision before making any commitments whatever with regard thereto."[53]

Hull's confidence in Davis was at a low point when the ambassador sent one more appeal for action, on the morning of November 15. He addressed his cable to both Roosevelt and Hull in the hope that, at this eleventh hour, the president would intervene to endorse a "progressive" policy. But Roosevelt never responded. Perhaps he was never as committed to concerted action as Davis thought he was. Certainly, by mid-November, a public sympathy to a "quarantine" policy had not been aroused the way Roosevelt had hoped. Instead, press reports indicated that Congress was hostile to the idea of action at Brussels. Moreover, a bold policy required the president to overrule Cordell Hull, a confrontation Roosevelt undoubtedly wished to avoid. Lacking public support and opposed by his secretary of state, Roosevelt abandoned Norman Davis, his hand-picked delegate. Hull promptly rejected Davis's proposal and on November 17 Davis capitulated, cabling the department that he bowed to its wisdom.[54]

The Brussels Conference has been viewed as a monument to American isolationism, and so it may be. But it is also a monument to the influence of the Department of State in general and Cordell Hull in particular. The Quarantine Speech and the resulting Brussels Conference experiences indicate how Roosevelt was unable to alter the course of American foreign policy. Hornbeck described the whole episode: "The course which a country is following is not unlike the course of some large and heavy physical body in motion; somebody may give the rudder or the wheel a terrific jerk, but the craft, having its momentum, comes about only slowly and on a wide arc; and, more often than not, after the jerk, the chap or chaps at the wheel have a tendency to swing the wheel back on itself and right the craft on its general course."[55]

Roosevelt had given the wheel a hard jerk, but it was Hull who had steered the ship of state back to its original cautious course in Asia. The experience of the Brussels Conference illustrated how effective a foreign policy manager Hull was and how determined he was to prevent Washington "hotheads" from provoking a confrontation with Japan that could lead to war.

However, there was another dimension to Hull's policy that did not bode well for long-range peace between the two nations. It became apparent just as the Brussels Conference was ending and Japanese diplomats in Tokyo, Washington, and Paris hinted at their government's willingness to moderate its peace terms and accept American mediation. Hull was suspicious and asked for a more definitive statement of Japanese intentions. The official Foreign Office response was that the only form of good offices Japan would accept "would be an effort to persuade the Chinese government to enter into negotiations for peace." Grew interpreted this for Hull, explaining that moderate elements within Japan wanted a compromise peace but lived in fear of assassination by extremists if they spoke publicly. Consequently, while the formal Japanese statements were not encouraging, the actual terms Japan might offer in peace negotiations could be consistent with the principles espoused in the Nine Power Treaty. Hull never reacted to Grew's analysis, and allowed the "peace initiative" to die.[56]

Hull's failure to explore Grew's interpretation is partly due to his fear that once involved in mediation, the British would try to maneuver the United States into a position where, if the peace talks failed, the United States would be left confronting Japan in order to protect British interests in China. Hull would have none of that. Yet there was a more telling explanation for his behavior.

Like almost all policy managers in Washington, the secretary put the worst possible interpretation on Japanese statements. Where Grew had seen a desire by moderates to wean Japan away from extremist control, Hull used the same facts to demonstrate that the moderates were so weak that they need not be listened to.[57] The moderates were indeed weak, but Hull ignored Grew's advice that careful nurturing of those moderates might increase their strength until someday they would be stronger than the military. Grew repeated this message for another four years and not until 1941 would Hull give it serious consideration. By then it was too late.

An assessment of Hull's performance during the first five months of the Sino-Japanese War must give him high marks for implementing a policy based upon real American interests and adjusting the ends of American policy to the means available. He also showed himself to be a tenacious and gifted manipulator of power within the Washington foreign policy establishment. Yet his skill at establishing and implementing a foreign policy was accompanied by an insensitivity to the intricacies of Japanese politics and a proclivity to demand clear-cut and decisive positions from a government that could not provide them. This flaw, widely shared in Washington, would prove fatal to Japanese-American peace.

CHAPTER TWO

THE FORTUNES OF WAR

Hull had been in Washington politics for thirty years; he understood how the game was played. The first requirement was to keep control of foreign policy. He had done that by knowing when to confront the opposition and when to ignore it. Moreover, he established a record of action that would diffuse criticism, whether it came from internationalists or isolationists. But all these precautions could not protect Hull from the fortunes of war. The secretary had justified his cautious Asian policy by claiming that it was not provocative of Japan and that time worked to the advantage of the United States. Events of December 1937 shattered those assumptions.

By December, China appeared to be collapsing militarily. With Chinese armies in retreat, its air force destroyed, and supplies dwindling, Ambassador Johnson had lost hope. When the Japanese took Beiping, Johnson had moved the American Embassy to Nanjing. Now, with the Japanese moving into Nanjing, he transported the embassy to Hankou. Clearly depressed, Johnson cabled Washington that China was losing the war and would soon capitulate.[1]

State Department analysts were far removed from the strains and carnage of the war zone and their analyses tended to be more dispassionate than Johnson's, but their conclusions were the same; Japan would win and would dictate severe peace terms. If China rejected them, Japan would set up its own puppet government in northern China and treat the government at Hankou as a bandit group. Northern China would fall under Japanese control just as Manchuria had in 1932.[2]

The Japanese conquest of Nanjing not only shook American confidence in China's ability to continue the war, it endangered American lives. As Japanese troops approached the city in November, Johnson closed down the embassy and urged all Americans to evacuate. Inevitably, some refused to leave, and the United States government was loath to abandon them. Standing by to help them evacuate at the eleventh hour was the U.S.S. *Panay*, one of a handful of overaged gunboats that made up the colorful Yangzi Patrol of the Asiatic Fleet. With little fire power, isolated deep in China, they posed no military threat to Japanese armed forces. But their very presence served notice on Japan that the United States would not abandon American rights in China and accept Japanese hegemony over the land.

On December 12 the *Panay* stood twenty seven miles above Nanjing, waiting for the military situation to improve so it could return to Nanjing and succor American nationals. Its mission paralleled Hull's East Asian policy: avoid confrontation with the Japanese, do not abandon the area, wait for the situation to improve. The situation did not improve. Instead, Japanese naval aircraft attacked the *Panay*, killing two American sailors and wounding fifty other Americans, twelve seriously. In the opinion of the diplomatic and military personnel on board, it was a deliberate attack.[3]

Hull's policy had resulted in America's loss of a gunboat and in China's losing the war. Perhaps it was time for a change.

Navy Department officers, understandably upset by the loss of the *Panay*, called for a naval demonstration to warn Japan to behave. But Navy's opposition to Hull's passive Asian policy did not originate with the *Panay* incident. The two departments had been at odds over the proper Asian posture almost from the start of the war.

Since World War I, American naval officers had believed that their mission was to protect American interests from the Japanese threat.[4] So when Hull developed a response to Japanese aggression that did not include a vigorous defense of American interests in China, the Navy Department found itself in conflict with the "striped pants boys" of State. Where Hull sought not to be a disservice to China, Navy wanted to help it. Hull distrusted the British and kept them at a distance; Navy favored cooperation with the British fleet. Hull insisted upon avoiding any risk of confrontation; Navy refused to retreat even if that increased the risk of conflict. In short, Hull wanted to wait and Navy wanted to act. Nowhere was this difference more apparent than in the conflict between the State Department and the outspoken commander of the Asiatic Fleet, Admiral Harry E. Yarnell.

As one would expect of a professional naval officer, Yarnell was an avowed internationalist who insisted the United States must not withdraw from Asia, an area with half the world's population where the United States had been involved for over 150 years. "The time has passed when a great nation can increase her safety by such a method," he declared. "The world has shrunk too much." This was conventional naval wisdom. But Yarnell's examination of Asian developments led him to a more fundamental conclusion: a stable China was the rock on which an Asian peace must stand and the present government in China was the key to that stability. Japan saw that, Yarnell believed, and went to war to defeat China before it could unify itself.[5] Thus, if Asia was to be stabilized, the Western powers would have to help China. That might require challenging Japanese "warlords," and it was certainly important for the United States to avoid any retreat in the face of Japanese expansion.[6]

In August, Yarnell sought reinforcements to help him in his mission. He asked for additional troops to garrison the international settlements of China and cruisers to bolster his weak naval force. Hull readily approved sending twelve hundred marines to Shanghai in order to control the hordes of refugees pouring into the city and to facilitate evacuation of Americans should it become necessary. But he opposed dispatching four cruisers to the Asiatic Fleet. He worried that such an open challenge to the Japanese navy could arouse American isolationists and provoke Japan. It was precisely because a naval buildup threatened Japan that Yarnell favored it and Hull opposed it. Chief of Naval Operations William D. Leahy supported Yarnell's request for ships, taking it all the way to the White House. But Roosevelt stood by his secretary of state and the cruisers remained in home waters.[7]

Though Hull's influence prevailed in Washington, it did not extend to the Asiatic Fleet, where the secretary and the admiral repeatedly clashed over how to deal with the Japanese. For example, in September Yarnell ordered his officers to station their ships at those ports where American nationals were concentrated and remain there as long as they were needed. In an eloquent statement that he released to the press, Yarnell declared that he would not be pushed out of China:

> Most American citizens now in China are engaged in businesses or professions which are their only means of livelihood. These persons are unwilling to leave until their businesses have been destroyed or they are forced to leave due to actual physical danger. Until such time comes our naval forces can not be withdrawn without failure in our duty and without bringing great discredit on the United States Navy. In giving assistance and protection our naval forces may at times be exposed to dangers which will in most cases be slight but in any case these risks must be accepted.[8]

Yarnell's public declaration was inappropriate in content and disastrous in timing, appearing as it did in the middle of the domestic debate over application of the Neutrality Act. Roosevelt and Hull had assured the nation that American ships in China were not in danger; Yarnell said there was danger. The State Department had requested American nationals to leave China and Roosevelt had warned American shippers that they continued in the China trade at their own risk; Yarnell assured American nationals that as long as they remained in China they would be protected by American naval forces.

Much as he disliked what Yarnell said, Hull could not publicly contradict the admiral lest he appear to be abandoning China and Americans in China. What he tried to do was arrange with Navy to play down the incident and to muzzle the admiral.[9] But Navy was not easily controlled.

Chief of Naval Operations (CNO) Leahy, like most naval officers, was "extremely proud" of Yarnell and believed he "saved much American face at a time when the State Department had just about lost it." Even the secretary of the navy was reportedly "highly pleased both with the contents and the timeliness" of Yarnell's statement. Leahy had no intention of muzzling Yarnell and only belatedly asked him to clear future statements with the secretary of the navy, who after all liked the original statement. Moreover, it was an officer close to the CNO who encouraged the Washington press corps to keep the story alive.[10]

Had Hull known what the Navy Department was doing, he might have been able to restrain it. But the secretary was unaware of Navy's machinations. What he did know came from Stanley Hornbeck, State's liaison with the Navy Department, who reported that Leahy felt "some concern" regarding Yarnell's actions. At the same time

Hornbeck seems to have been assuring naval officers that the lower echelons in the State Department thought Yarnell was "doing a better job than their own Department."[11]

Hull's protest to Leahy would have been only partially effective under the best of circumstances; filtered through Hornbeck, it had no impact. Leahy continued to support Yarnell and Yarnell continued to churn up Asian waters with his public statements. At the start of October Yarnell declared to the world that he intended to stand and protect American nationals. Hull protested (through Hornbeck) and Leahy did nothing. At the end of October Yarnell released another salvo, announcing that he had ordered his ships to defend themselves by firing upon any attacking aircraft. When Hull complained, Leahy retorted that Yarnell was very busy and the CNO would not bother the admiral with any instructions about avoiding adverse publicity. But Hull insisted and went to Roosevelt for support. Only then did Leahy yield and cable Yarnell to exercise more caution.[12]

Thus, when the *Panay* was sunk, State-Navy relations were already tense. The *Panay* incident convinced Leahy that it was "time now to get the fleet ready for sea, to make an agreement with the British Navy for joint action, and to inform the Japanese that we expect to protect our nationals." The CNO wanted to protect American interests in China and he had given up on a State Department he derided as interested only in protecting itself from domestic critics.[13]

There was an element of truth in Leahy's snide comment. Hull *was* concerned about the domestic reaction to the *Panay* sinking. But Hull and company worried less about criticism than about the possibility that the American public might push the nation into an unwise stance. Public opinion continued to harden against Japan as newspapers and newsreels brought eyewitness accounts of the attack to the United States. The international and domestic situation was delicate, State Department officers believed, and any provocative American action would be the first step toward an unwise involvement in the Sino-Japanese War. Leahy did not share this concern and favored making the fleet ready for the kind of forceful demonstration that he thought was necessary to teach Japan a lesson.[14]

Roosevelt too was ready to act. Dissatisfied with Hull's constant warnings that strong action would provoke a confrontation with Japan, he wanted something that went beyond Hull's futile diplomatic protests yet stopped short of war.[15] It was this frustration that in October had led Roosevelt to speak of a quarantine. Now, in December, he considered trade restrictions established within the United States and a long-range naval blockade. Roosevelt refused to label his ideas economic warfare or even sanctions, though that is what they amounted to, using such euphemisms as "quarantine" or "pressure" even in discussions with his closest foreign policy advisers. The president just wanted to pay back Japan for what it had done to the United States and to deter it from doing any more. There must be a way to do that short of war, he was convinced. Two days after the *Panay* went down, Roosevelt began to explore what might be done.

He began by asking Secretary of the Treasury Henry Morgenthau, Jr. whether a president had authority to confiscate Japanese property in retaliation for Japanese destruction of American property in China. Morgenthau was prepared for this question. He had had his department studying how economic pressure could be applied against Japan. It had been no mere theoretical research project but a matter of utmost importance to Treasury officers, who believed that "the peace of the world is tied up with China's ability to win or to prolong its resistance."[16] By the December 17 cabinet meeting, Morgenthau had reported to Roosevelt and the president had said he wanted the treasury secretary to take the lead. In the first blush of this newfound support for a "positive" policy, Morgenthau phoned his counterpart in the British government and asked whether the British would cooperate to restrict foreign exchange made available to Japan. The British were startled by such an unconventional action. Put it in writing, they suggested.[17]

Morgenthau represented the activist wing of the Roosevelt administration and was ready to stand up to anyone who still preached caution, including his own assistant secretary, George Taylor. "I think it's time to call a halt," Morgenthau admonished Taylor,

> when a United States battleship has been sunk and three of our people have been killed. For us to let them put their sword into our insides and sit there and take it and like it, and not do anything about it, I think is un-American, and I think that we've got to begin to inch in on those boys, and that's what the President is doing. Now, if you'll let me see three steps—one, two, three—I don't know what it will lead to, but if it should lead— I mean there is such a thing as exposing both cheeks and one's behind in this thing, and one's human life—there's a limit to what you can do. . . . Now, how long are you going to sit there and let these fellows kill American soldiers and sailors and sink our battleships?

Secretary of the Treasury Henry Morgenthau, Jr. disagreed with Hull's policy and tried to change it. (File 208-PU-104D-2, NA. Courtesy of Associated Press/Wide World Photos).

To which Taylor replied, "A hell of a while."[18]

It was indeed "a hell of a while" before the United States imposed economic sanctions against Japan. This failure to carry through on such a bold program was a result of Japan's response to the *Panay* incident and Roosevelt's lack of commitment to economic sanctions as a means of stopping Japan. Even Morgenthau had understood that sanctions were being considered as only one possible action against Japan if the Japanese failed to respond satisfactorily to American protests.[19] But Japan responded about as well as the United States could have hoped. Roosevelt had insisted on a Japanese apology, indemnities, and measures to prevent a recurrence. By Christmas Eve, Japan had done all that as well as disciplined eleven naval officers involved in the incident and recalled the commanding admiral in disgrace. The State Department concluded that the matter was closed. Thus, the issue of economic sanctions lost its urgency. Besides, the cautious British had declined to participate in sanctions, Hull opposed them, and Roosevelt ultimately was more intrigued by naval pressure than economic warfare.[20]

In his heart, Roosevelt was a navy man. He had been assistant secretary of the navy from 1913–1920 and still kept personal contact with the fleet officers. When Roosevelt thought in terms of a "quarantine" he pictured naval action more than commercial pressure. As early as March 1936 he had encouraged Britain to employ a blockade to force Hitler's armies from the demilitarized Rhineland. Shortly after the Sino-Japanese War began, Roosevelt considered the possibility of a naval blockade to bring Japan to terms.[21] Though his experience with the Quarantine Speech indicated that the country was not then ready for anything as bold as a naval blockade, the commander-in-chief had not abandoned the idea, and he raised it again following the *Panay* incident.

Roosevelt envisioned a string of American warships from the Aleutian Islands to the Philippines and then British warships to Singapore. These cruisers, sitting thousands of miles from Japan's home waters, would cut off Japan's supply of raw materials and bring the island empire to its knees within a year to eighteen months. So enthusiastic was Roosevelt about his idea of a naval blockade that he explained his plan to the British ambassador and dispatched Captain Royal Ingersoll, director of Navy's War Plans Division, to London for naval staff talks.[22]

Though the British had sought greater American involvement in containing Japan, at the moment Roosevelt suffered from a credibility gap.[23] The president sounded sincere when he spoke privately to the British about a naval blockade. He had also sounded sincere in October, when he spoke of aggression as a disease that needed to be quarantined. Those sincere public comments had led to the Brussels Conference, where Norman Davis assured the British that the president was determined to act. But Roosevelt did not act, and the British left Brussels skeptical of his reliability. It was on New Year's Day, 1938, less than six weeks later, that Ingersoll arrived in London. The British soon noted that Ingersoll's mission was to draft contingency plans for Anglo-American cooperation and not to discuss immediate naval action.[24]

If Roosevelt was sincere, he had a chance to show his determination almost immediately. Japanese soldiers had beaten two British police officers in the Shanghai international settlement and the British were considering a forceful response that would include making ready their fleet, just short of full mobilization. If they did that, the British asked, what would Roosevelt do?

The president was not prepared to do very much. After conferring with Hull, Welles, and Leahy on January 10, 1938, he approved preparing the fleet for sea and advancing naval maneuvers already scheduled for March in Hawaiian waters. As a symbol of solidarity with Britain, Roosevelt would have some American cruisers already on a voyage in the South Pacific pay a courtesy call to the British naval base at Singapore. While that matched British actions, it was a far cry from the blustering Roosevelt who, just a few weeks earlier, had spoken with gusto about an Anglo-American blockade of Japan. Now the president favored a world conference to resolve such fundamental international questions as reduction of armaments, rules of warfare, and equal access to raw materials. In London, policy managers concluded that the United States could not be counted on to stop Japan, and the British promptly notified Washington that rather than activate its fleet, it would send a stiff note of protest to Japan.[25]

By the end of January 1938, the *Panay* crisis had come and gone without any change in American policy. Roosevelt's grand ideas of economic sanctions, a naval blockade, and a world conference had all come to naught. His tough talk in cabinet meetings reflected his dissatisfaction with the traditional tools of diplomacy, but as had been the case in the past, when it came time to act Roosevelt's actions failed to keep pace with his rhetoric. American policy toward Japan was guided by Hull's caution rather than Roosevelt's pugnacity.[26]

Sometimes things change even when they seem to stay the same. The *Panay* incident brought about no change in American policy; no sanctions were applied, no naval demonstrations prepared. But it did change the way policymakers looked at Japan. Traditionally they saw two Japans. One was militaristic, seeking an empire by conquest; the other was moderate and repelled by the excesses of the militarists. Although it was the "hotheads" among the militarists who had been responsible for sinking the *Panay,* all the Japanese militarists were cruel, barbaric, and influenced only by power. It had been the moderates who had apologized for the "accidental" sinking of the *Panay* and had demonstrated that the government of Japan did not want war with the United States. But while the moderates could apologize for the military, they could not control it. The *Panay* incident reinforced the idea that diplomacy with the moderates was becoming increasingly irrelevant because it was the military that held power. And the Japanese military, American officials believed, sought the total exclusion from Asia of Western influence.[27]

From Tokyo, Ambassador Joseph Grew tried to provide his government with a more balanced view of Japan. He stressed that all Japanese, moderates and extremists alike, "are thoroughly convinced that the present China Incident is no mere military excursion but rather a movement in which the safety of the Empire itself is at stake." Believing that Britain and the United States threatened them, they sought to carve out an economic sphere in which to operate should the Western world deny them access to raw materials and markets.[28]

Asian specialists in the State Department did not want to hear this viewpoint. They discounted Grew's analysis and chided him for being too concerned for Japan and not enough for the United States. How fear of Western powers and of communism, inequitable distribution of raw materials, and population pressures affected Japan were considerations scarcely mentioned in Washington. Insensitive to Japanese fears, State Department analysts simply concluded that Japan was expanding because it wanted an Asian empire and had been trying to conquer one throughout the century.[29] The only thing on which Grew and State Department officials could agree was that whatever the motive, Japan's immediate goal was to squeeze out Western merchants from northern China and turn it into an economic colony, just as it had done to Manchuria in 1932.[30]

Many in the State Department saw Japan as not only a regional threat but part of a global movement of aggressor nations. Though the Axis Alliance would not be formalized until the signing of the Tripartite Pact in September 1940, by early 1938 State Department officers saw Japan, Germany, and Italy linked in an unholy crusade that threatened not only the foreign interests of the United States but quite possibly its very existence. Guided by fanatical militarist leaders, bent upon making Asia into its own empire, Japan would surely cooperate with the Fascist forces of Europe. Even the usually complacent Grew was alarmed by the German annexation of Austria in March 1938. "With fascistic control firmly established in Europe and in East Asia," he wrote Hornbeck, "what price the Western hemisphere—first South and eventually North America? Is not the moment likely to come when we shall have to fight in self defense . . . against the danger of world fascism? And can we allow these movements to get to a point where the danger would no longer be merely potential but actual?"[31]

One might suspect that with such fear and distrust of Japan dominating Washington, American policy would have noticeably stiffened during the spring of 1938. That was not the case. Cordell Hull held tenaciously to his established Asia policy. As we have already seen, Hull and many of his associates did not believe there was anything in China that justified fighting Japan. So even if China was about to fall, the secretary would have opposed American intervention. But by the spring of 1938, the situation in China had not deteriorated. In some respects it had actually improved.

Though Nanjing had fallen, an American gunboat had been sunk, the Chinese countryside ravaged by war, and American interests in China hurt by Japanese restrictions on commerce and travel, the fact remained that China held on; and as long as it did, Japanese hopes of an Asian empire and dreams of world Axis domination could not be realized. The doomsayers of December had been proven wrong. China had not collapsed.

Moreover, it appeared that Japan was overextended and did not have the human, material, or financial resources to conquer China, much less develop it. State's Asian officers had always believed that any Japanese success in China would come not from Japanese abilities but from the Chinese "traditional instinct for resort to compromise." Thus, when they saw that China would fight on, they concluded that Japan could lose the war, but never win it. With guerrilla resistance continuing to exact a high price and with British and American armaments increasing, "it would become evident to Japan that she cannot both have her way in China and keep up in an armament race—if either—and that, because of relative changes in strength and of other developments in the general situation, her self-interest will be best served by her showing reasonable regard for the rights, the interests and the opinions of . . . concerned powers."[32]

Military and naval attachés in China came to this conclusion much more slowly, hampered as they were by firsthand knowledge of the incompetence of the Chinese officer corps. But when they became convinced that the resiliance of the Chinese soldiers was more important than the incompetence of their ranking officers, the attachés became more optimistic. By March, Colonel Joseph W. Stilwell could report to Washington: "Since Japan cannot pull out and China refuses to quit, the prospect of a long-drawn-out struggle increases. It is possible for China to win."[33]

This shift in the fortunes of war greatly enhanced the American diplomatic position. Japanese leaders, aware they risked becoming bogged down in an endless China war, sought to involve the United States in mediation efforts. But Hull was not eager to help Japan extricate itself from the China mess. The longer Japan fought a futile war in China the more precarious would become the position of the Japanese military at home. As one FE officer put it: "Should the reports of a succession of brilliant victories be proved untrue and faith in the invincibility of Japanese arms be destroyed, Japanese leadership would be likely to encounter new problems at home."[34]

When Grew told the Japanese foreign minister that "the Japanese could have peace immediately if they really wanted it, and without mediation of any kind," the foreign minister merely muttered something about "saving face." It was just such a face-saving settlement that Hull wanted to avoid. From the secretary's perspective, it was better to keep Japan mired in the Chinese tar pit until the Japanese people had become disillusioned and the influence of the military was broken. Only when Japan was prepared to give up its plan of military expansion would Hull cooperate in negotiating a peace.[35]

Meanwhile, Hull's policy of "non-interference and non-cooperation economically or politically, with either Japan or China" would perpetuate a long period of anarchy and incomplete pacification of China, which would bring suffering to the Chinese people and hardship to American economic and cultural interests there.[36] But it was a price Hull and Roosevelt were prepared to pay. They could have ended the fighting by fashioning a compromise settlement, but they saw no future in that. It was better to let the fighting continue to its inevitable conclusion, a military debacle that would drag down the Japanese militarists. The possibility that, before giving up, the Japanese military might lash out at the United States as the source of its problems was not given serious consideration in Washington. Had it been, many voices would have been raised in favor of reaching an understanding with Japan now rather than risking war later.

While Hull waited for Japan to collapse, American diplomacy fell into a routine. Grew would protest Japanese actions, Japan would appear conciliatory but do nothing, and after an appropriate delay the United States would issue another protest. Japan understood that the United States did not like what it was doing, but it also knew the United States had no intention of doing anything about it.[37]

Some people in the State Department chafed at such a do-nothing policy, but they had little chance to urge stronger action. Once in March 1938 the question briefly arose whether State should consider whether the United States should threaten Japan. Even *talk of talking* about action went beyond Hull's cautious policy and was promptly dropped.[38] On another occasion FE and the division of Trade Agreements examined the 1930 Trade Agreements Act to see if the president could retaliate against Japan for discriminating against American commerce in China. They concluded he could not, since Japan was discriminating against American commerce in favor of Japanese commerce, not that of a third power. The telling commentary, however, was that since Japan would interpret any retaliation as politically motivated, nothing should be done. Some officers grumbled at their department's inability to find a justification for action, but their grumbling changed nothing. More serious was the growing tension between the hard-liners and the soft-liners within the department. On one occasion, so angry did hard-liner Herbert Feis become that he denounced FE for selling out China.[39]

Dissatisfaction with Hull's Asian policy was also growing through the nation. A boycott of Japanese goods sputtered but talk of embargoing exports of war materials to Japan grew. The embargo idea appealed to both isolationists, who saw it as consistent with the meaning of the Neutrality Act, and internationalists, who were dismayed to see American supplies fueling Japan's war machine. Without the American "blood trade" in oil, cotton, scrap iron, or machine tools, they believed, Japan could not continue its aggression against China.[40]

This anger over American complicity in Japanese aggression reached its peak in May 1938 when Japan loosed its modern war machine against Guangshou (Canton). The American people were horrified by newspaper and newsreel accounts of Japanese bombers waging war against Chinese civilians with devastating consequences. Outraged, former secretary of state Henry L. Stimson wrote Hull: "I am so impressed by the barbarities of the Japanese bombings as well as by the future danger that the unchallenged continuance of such barbarity means to the world and us that I am pretty soon going to explode again. I cannot believe that the opinion of this country would not back up still further expressions and non-military action against Japanese conduct."[41] So great was the public outcry that Hull could no longer denounce Japanese bombings of civilians while simultaneously doing nothing to stop American firms from selling Japan the planes used in those bombings.

The decision to act was good news to those within the State Department who had been unsuccessfully prodding Hull into a more aggressive policy. Now that public indignation had moved Hull to act, they tried to make that action as assertive as possible.

As usual, Stanley Hornbeck was a leader in this group. Unlike Hull, who thought Japan would eventually crack, Hornbeck believed Japan could continue the war almost indefinitely, causing great suffering and destroying the cultural and economic progress China had made. Hornbeck believed the United States would have to intervene to stop that and hoped continued Japanese depredations would educate the American people to the folly of remaining aloof. Far from fearing an aroused public, Hornbeck welcomed it, because he saw Japan as a paper tiger that would collapse before a strong American effort.[42]

Since it was a foregone conclusion that the United States would have to block the sale of aircraft to Japan, when Hull gathered his staff in his office on June 10 the debate was over what form the embargo should take. Hard-liners urged a public announcement explaining why Japan was being denied American-built aircraft. Moderates thought an embargo without the name calling would be wiser. As was his style, Hull allowed both sides to thrash out the issues at great length. But when the secretary went to Roosevelt the next day, he guided the president in approving a discreetly phrased moral embargo.[43] The State Department would write aircraft manufacturers that the department "would with great regret issue any licenses authorizing exportation . . . of any aircraft . . . to countries the armed forces of which are making use of airplanes for attack upon civilian populations." Japan was never mentioned by name in this extralegal action, but by the end of the year, only one manufacturer had applied for a license to export aircraft to Japan.[44]

The moral embargo accomplished its primary goal—it calmed the American public. Hull gave the American people just enough action to satisfy most of them without doing anything that would provoke Japan. Though the Japanese were not pleased with the embargo, it hurt little more than their pride; Japan could no longer buy planes from the United States, but it could and did continue to buy the machine tools to make them, spare parts to repair them, gasoline to power them, and scrap iron to make the bombs they dropped.

If the moral embargo mollified the American public, it did not satisfy the hard-liners within the State Department. Worried that Japan could gain a victory unless the United States applied economic pressure against it, they favored the abrogation of the 1911 Japanese-American commercial treaty in order to free the United States to impose economic sanctions whenever the Roosevelt administration wished.[45] Hull listened to these arguments and even called one lengthy memorandum "excellent." But he would not budge from his policy of avoiding any action that might conceivably result in a confrontation with Japan. Though some rank-and-file officers disagreed with Hull, the disagreement was kept "in house" and the practical implementation of policy conformed to Hull's wishes.[46] The secretary did not receive the same treatment from Navy.

During the first half of 1938, Admiral Yarnell had shown only slightly more restraint than he had in 1937. In June, the problem with Navy involved the U.S.S. *Monocacy*, a gunboat stationed at Jiujiang, a city on the Yangzi River about 250 miles above Nanjing, where the *Panay* had been sunk six months earlier. One hundred miles further upriver was Hankou, which the Japanese were in the process of capturing. Since Jiujiang was likely to become a war zone, the Japanese requested American gunboats leave the area, a request Hull considered reasonable. Neither Yarnell nor his superiors thought it reasonable, and they refused to comply.

Hull "manifested more perturbation" and expressed more impatience on the *Monocacy* issue than any other Hornbeck could recall. The secretary was painfully aware that a reckless Navy decision could ruin his entire Asian policy. For a year Hull had been building public support for his middle-course policy of avoiding both involvement in the Sino-Japanese conflict and abandonment of Asia. He had

Chief of Naval Operations William D. Leahy believed American prestige in Asia had to be preserved. (File 80-G-47436, NA.)

made some progress. Though most Americans did not actively support maintenance of American gunboats and troops in China, they were willing to let them remain; in effect, to ignore the matter. If another gunboat should be attacked, Hull feared a "horseback" decision to pull out of China. Such a retreat would demoralize China and could well lead to a Japanese victory, with far-reaching consequences for Asia. The secretary did not object to American gunboats remaining at certain points to help American nationals, but he strongly believed it was just as important that those vessels be withdrawn before hostilities began. He wanted the *Monocacy* out of the area.[47]

In China, Ambassador Johnson thought Hull was yielding too much. Precautions had been taken to protect the *Monocacy*, Johnson reported; the boat had been moved to the safest point on the river and the Japanese had been notified of her position. Unless Japan deliberately sought to attack the gunboat, she would be safe. "We have to take certain risks," he wrote Hull. "I have never believed that it was characteristic of the American to scuttle and run when his rights and interests are involved." Once she was withdrawn, the Japanese would do everything in their power to keep the *Monocacy* from returning. "Japanese activities and attitudes are deliberately calculated to make conditions so unbearable for foreigners here in China as to drive them from the country and I see no reason why we should make the aim any easier of accomplishment than is absolutely necessary."[48]

Many in the State Department shared the ambassador's viewpoint. Hornbeck reassured him that Hull had been very much worried about the question of naval vessels, but the Asian specialists were not; they were confident that Johnson and the naval officers on the scene would handle the situation properly.[49]

Either because Hull sensed that his staff did not totally share his concern or because he considered the *Monocacy* case so important, he took personal charge of the effort to get the gunboat moved. When Leahy offered no assurances to Hornbeck, Hull met personally with the CNO to express his concern about another *Panay* type of incident and the importance of withdrawing the *Monocacy* to a safer position. Leahy brushed off Hull's comments. "I informed the Secretary of State," he recorded smugly in his diary, "that the navy will comply exactly with any orders issued by the President but that in the absence of orders to withdraw from danger areas the Navy will remain for as long a time as appears necessary for the protection or rescue of Americans."[50]

Leahy probably never sensed how angry Hull was becoming. The secretary was a mild-mannered, soft-spoken gentlemen who was always scrupulously polite. But he had a temper and a vocabulary to match, and it is probable that he volunteered a few choice expletives after Leahy had left. Hull's frustration and anger with Leahy boiled over in unusually strong language when he cabled Johnson the next day. "I cannot too emphatically express my hope that no unfortunate incident will occur," he wrote. "There is much more involved and at stake than what is involved in any local situation." He urged Johnson to give "intensive thought" to the question of avoiding risks; to refuse to comply with any Chinese or Japanese request and to couch all replies in conciliatory tones. "I have neither authority nor desire to give commands regarding naval operations, especially at long range," Hull declared, "but I am responsible in regard to the conducting of the foreign relations of the United States as a whole, and I am extremely solicitous that important efforts in other connections be not jeopardized by possible occurrence of unfortunate incidents in the local situation."[51]

The cable may have made Hull feel better, but it did not get the *Monocacy* moved. Still, nothing happened to the gunboat where she was, and in late August Yarnell ordered her to proceed downriver to Shanghai for refueling. But that raised an even more alarming prospect, for the Japanese had mined the Yangzi and denied the *Monocacy* permission to proceed through the mine field. Leahy was determined to take a stand. In his view, Japan was simply trying to injure American prestige in Asia, and the United States must meet that challenge. Convinced that the spineless State Department would do nothing diplomatically, Leahy resolved to force the issue by sending the *Monocacy* to Shanghai with or without Japanese permission. "Sending the ship down river might result in its loss by accident or design," Leahy proclaimed, "but some strong stand by this Government is, in my opinion, necessary to preserve what little prestige America now has in the Orient." Admiral Yarnell, it should be added, was decidedly less enthusiastic about sending one of his antiquated gunboats through a mine field. Even Leahy realized he was going to lose on this issue, noting in his diary that the question was one of "grand international politics" and as such was beyond "the cognizance of the Navy Department." To make sure that the

Monocacy stayed where she was, Hull went to Roosevelt for presidential approval and obtained Leahy's acknowledgment.[52]

Hull won that battle, and avoided an incident that could have wrecked his Asian policy. But it seemed that he was expending as much time and energy trying to control portions of his own government as he was dealing with Japan. More important, these conflicts raised a question about the real nature of American policy. Was it what Hull said it was, or was policy what the people on the scene—Yarnell, for example—were prepared to do? And what was a policy worth when both Army and Navy disagreed with Hull and with each other?

Asia was about the last place in the world American army officers wanted to fight a war. Yet Army officers were saddled with a war plan that expected them to engage in a "prompt strategic offensive against ORANGE [the code name for Japan] across seven thousand miles of sea, via the Mandate Islands." Such an offensive would strain "to the utmost the resources of the United States" and "would be justified only if our vital interests are at stake." These officers did not see any vital interests in Asia. America's only commitment was the Philippines, and they were scheduled for independence in 1946. So unimportant were the Philippines that, in Army's opinion, since 1906 the United States had consciously "written off the books the practical possibility" of defending them. "Even at this late day, if we were seriously intending to defend the Philippines, we could do much to retrieve the steps of the past by sending now the Fleet to Manila Bay. Why is it not there? To ask the question is to reveal the obvious answer—even in peace the defense of the Philippines is not worth the risk to the Fleet in that exposed position, and not worth the risk of provoking retaliation by Japan."[53]

Not only did the Army General Staff oppose any reinforcement of the American position in Asia, it favored a withdrawal from Asia to a more defensible position in the eastern Pacific. So adamant was Army that Hornbeck complained it was actually infringing on a foreign policy question by "endeavoring to propagate and bring about adoption of a particular course of action . . . namely, a general withdrawal of American interests, American armed forces, and American influence, from the Far East."[54] Navy, of course, also strenuously disagreed with the War Department claiming that to withdraw would be more dangerous than to stand firm. It was a running battle, which Army and Navy continued through 1938 and 1939.[55]

This split between those who created policy and those who were expected to implement it posed a serious problem for the conduct of American foreign relations. It was a problem that Hull never faced. Being a veteran of much Washington combat, he may have thought better of trying to force the War and Navy departments to accept his perspective so long as their dissent was not translated into action. The secretary could block the type of withdrawal the army sought, and if the Japanese army would show even modest restraint, there would be no conflict with American naval units in Chinese waters. It seemed best to wait for Japan to grow tired. But Japan did not grow tired. As Hitler expanded in Europe, so did Japan in Asia.

CHAPTER THREE

NEW ORDER: CHALLENGE AND RESPONSE

I n September 1938 the world held its breath as Germany, Britain, and France moved inexorably toward war. The immediate question was whether Britain and France would fight Germany to save Czechoslovakia or would try to appease Hitler. They chose appeasement, and at the Munich Conference assented to the dismemberment of Czechoslovakia. Europe had avoided war, but only for the moment. With war still pending in Europe the British continued their retreat from Asia.[1]

Back in Washington, officials were uneasy that British retreat would encourage Japan to expand its influence beyond China, and that the British might seek to salvage some of their Asian investment by appeasing Japan just as they sought to appease Germany.[2] It was apparent that the United States could no longer count on Britain to preserve the Asian status quo. If Japan was to be restrained, the United States would have to fill the power vacuum Britain was creating.

Hull's concept of filling a vacuum was to put a little more force in his diplomatic language. In early October he had Ambassador Grew warn Japan that there was a "great and growing disparity" between the treatment received by American interests in China and Japanese interests in the United States. It was hardly a saber-rattling declaration, but the implication was clear: Unless Japan discontinued its restrictions on American interests in China, the United States might impose its own discriminatory measures against Japanese commerce. Though not an ultimatum, it was an important departure from earlier American policy.[3] Just the previous spring Hull had excluded any hint of retaliation from American protests. Now European events had pushed the secretary of state farther than he had ever gone.

If Hull believed his tougher language would restrain Japan, he was totally mistaken. Rather than moderate its war, Japan expanded it to the area around Xianggang (Hong Kong), and on November 3, 1938, Prime Minister Konoye Fumimaro delivered a radio address in which he blamed foreign power imperialism for disrupting peace in Asia. Japan, he said, intended to establish a "new peace fabric in [the] Far East on the basis of justice. . . . If the Powers understand the real intentions of Japan and devise a policy in accordance with the new situation in the Far East, Japan does not grudge to cooperate with them for peace in the Far East."[4] No one in Washington was surprised by the message, but the tone was troubling. Formerly, the Japanese had said, "Have patience and all will be well." Now they were saying, "You can do this but you cannot do that, and that means permanently." Such language forced Hull to make some difficult decisions. Was Japan in China a menace to the United States? If so, what line of action should the State Department follow in order to "limit or neutralize that meance?"[5]

The hard-liners in the State Department considered Japan's declaration of a New Order a turning point and urged the abrogation of the 1911 Japanese-American commercial treaty preparatory to economic sanctions. But Hull had no intention of confronting Japan by commercial or any other form of sanctions and there was strong opposition within the department to making abrogation part of a concerted program of commercial retaliation against Japan. So when Hull gathered his staff on November 5 the debate focused on whether the current policy should be continued or a mild program of commercial pressure instituted, designed to annoy Japan and make its war effort a little more difficult while avoiding crippling sanctions. Even such mild commercial pressures went beyond what Hull was prepared to do. The meeting in his office on that Saturday afternoon produced not the slightest deviation from the established policy.[6]

If Hull was unwilling to apply commercial pressure against Japan, would he consent to giving aid to China? Secretary of the Treasury

Morgenthau had a plan to give China $25 million, to be repaid by ten years of tung oil exports to the United States. Since tung oil was used widely in the paint and varnish industry the credit would appear to be a normal business transaction, even though its real purpose was to keep China fighting. Morgenthau began work on the credit deal in the spring of 1938 because he thought China needed help and was convinced Hull would not provide it.[7] An adept operator in the Washington scene, Morgenthau gained the support of the Export-Import Bank, President Roosevelt, and even State's cautious Pierrepont Moffat, who agreed that a loan would do wonders for Chinese morale. The one endorsement he had not obtained was the only one that counted—Cordell Hull was keeping his own counsel.[8]

While Hull hesitated, Morgenthau tried to persuade Roosevelt to ignore his secretary of state, arguing that a large loan to China would do more for peace in Asia than building a battleship. He even thought he had Roosevelt convinced. "Well, if there's war in Europe we'll give them the credit," the president told Morgenthau, adding after a reflective pause, "and if there isn't maybe we'll do it anyway." But nothing happened. By mid-October Morgenthau was beside himself with worry. He had his staff prepare an impassioned plea to the president.

> I am taking the liberty of pleading China's cause so earnestly because you have three times told me to proceed with the proposals for assistance to China. All my efforts have proved of no avail against Secretary Hull's adamant policy of doing nothing which could possibly be objected to by an aggressor nation. I need not tell you I respect Secretary Hull's integrity and sincerity of belief and that his course is the right one, but the issues at stake go beyond any one of us and do not permit me to remain silent. It is the future peace and present honor of the United States that are in question. It is the future of democracy, the future of civilization that are at stake.

Yet Roosevelt remained cautious. Guangzhou had fallen to Japanese troops and the president worried that a loan might be followed by a Chinese surrender. He needed assurances from Generalissimo Jiang Jieshi (Chiang Kai-shek) that China would fight on. Morgenthau quickly obtained the necessary assurances and pressed Roosevelt for implementation, asking him to obtain Hull's acquiescence in the proposal.[9]

It was now November 13. Japan's intransigent New Order was apparent and Hull had already rejected any form of commercial retaliation. Would he modify his policy to include aid to China? Not one to make a snap decision, Hull asked Hornbeck and Far Eastern Affairs Division Chief Maxwell Hamilton to present position papers. Hornbeck argued in favor of the loan, Hamilton against it. "It is my view," Hamilton wrote, "that to adopt a course of assistance to China now, after Japan has almost completed its positional warfare, would be of no decisive aid to China and would be a profitless irritant to Japan, unless the United States is prepared to give really substantial and long-continued assistance to China. And if that decision be made, it should be made with realization that that course may lead to armed conflict with Japan."[10]

Hornbeck's argument was equally familiar: "Unless the Japanese march is halted by the Chinese or by some other nation, the time will come when Japan and the United States will be face to face and definitely opposed to each other in the international political arena." The commodity credit by itself would not be enough, he warned. What was needed was a "diplomatic 'war plan' " that included aid to China, economic pressure against Japan, and naval demonstrations as part of a concerted effort to stop Japan's "predatory advance." The United States must be prepared to use armed force if it proved necessary, Hornbeck declared.[11]

Predictably, Hull favored Hamilton's caution over Hornbeck's assertiveness. When he went to the White House the next day he argued strongly that Japan would view the credit as a hostile act and would in all probability retaliate against the United States. If that led to repeated incidents in China Hull feared the United States might be drawn into a war with Japan. France and England were preoccupied in Europe; China was not about to crumble; there was time to wait for further developments.[12]

Hull would not agree to Morgenthau's tung oil credit and Roosevelt would not overrule him. As a result the credit proposal remained on the president's desk, unsigned. Then, on Friday, November 25, Hull left Washington to attend a conference of American states in Lima. In his absence, Under Secretary Sumner Welles became acting secretary of state.

Welles was not one of Hull's trusted associates. In temperament Hull was cautious, Welles mercurial. Hull liked to work with his staff searching out every aspect of a problem; Welles tended to act more impulsively and do more work on his own. Roosevelt selected Hull as secretary of state because he could not fail to reward Hull's political influence among southern Democrats. He selected Welles as under secretary because he liked him. Hull had not wanted Welles as his number two man, but he realized that Roosevelt wanted Welles and remained silent.[13]

Ambitious and energetic, Welles expanded his power as under secretary. He eagerly accepted new responsibilities and rarely gave up old ones. All along he had the ear of the president. Hull resented that. While he did not exclude his under secretary from important department business, Welles had little involvement with Japanese-American relations, which Hull personally controlled. Now Hull was out of the country and Welles was in charge.

On Monday morning, November 28, Welles phoned Morgenthau seeking the secretary's support on a matter pertaining to Cuba. After assuring Welles that he could help him, Morgenthau raised the question of the commodity credit to China. Roosevelt had given his word, Morgenthau explained, but Hull had blocked the deal. Welles was accommodating, promising to speak with the president. By the end of the day Welles phoned Morgenthau to say that Roosevelt had given his "go ahead" for the deal.[14]

By basing his case on the issue of the presidential word rather than the desirability of the credit, Morgenthau provided a useful, perhaps essential, justification for disregarding Hull's strong opposition. But it was more than just the issue of the presidential word that motivated Welles—he believed it was time to put more pressure on Japan. Consequently he set the State Department to work exploring the question of economic retaliation. The Trade Agreements, Economic Affairs, and Far East divisions hurriedly reviewed the various ways pressure could be applied against Japan, including ending gold purchases, forbidding credit sales, blacklisting Japanese firms, terminating the 1911 commercial treaty, embargoing exports to Japan, instituting exchange control, and imposing discriminatory duties on Japanese ships. Welles intended to fashion a program of economic pressure against Japan and make the China loan part of that program. Morgenthau was pleased.[15]

Welles had misjudged the level of support for sanctions; rather than endorsements he found only opposition. Grew objected. The British refused to cooperate. The task force studying the problems at Welles's behest reported that the consequences of economic retaliation generally outweighed the advantages and recommended further study before taking action. Consequently, when Roosevelt met in cabinet on December 9 the only measure he had before him was the China credit. He approved that and economic pressure against Japan remained in abeyance.[16]

Meanwhile, unaware of Welles's attempted coup, Hull had been concentrating on uniting the American republics against the German menace. The secretary only knew what Welles told him, and that was not much.

On December 2, Welles cabled his chief: "The President has informed me . . . that he desires to go ahead with the tung oil project." It was a truthful but inaccurate report that never mentioned that Welles had approached Roosevelt and obtained the presidential approval for the loan. Instead, Welles assured Hull that he had arranged to have implementation of the credit held in abeyance until Roosevelt returned to Washington. Though Welles was using that delay to prepare a program of economic pressure against Japan, he gave Hull quite a different impression:

> I propose to call to [the president's] attention again the view which you expressed in your memorandum of November 14 and to raise for his consideration the question of general policy and procedure in reference to the Far Eastern situation and the question whether he desires to continue for the time being the policy and procedure which this Government has heretofore followed and to proceed with the tung oil project as an isolated act.

Welles never revealed how far consideration of "punitive pressure" had gone, nor did he explain his own role in those activities. Had he done so Hull would have been alarmed. Instead, the acting secretary assured the secretary that he and those in the Treasury Department leaned toward treating the China credit, "if consummated, as an independent and self contained commercial transaction."[17]

Ultimately, Hull lost the fight over the loan to China. But even in defeat he demonstrated his great power. He blocked the credit as long as he was in Washington, and even when he had left the country and was preoccupied with a major conference his enemies dared not confront him openly. Instead they based their case on the irrevocability of Roosevelt's "positive commitment" to Jiang. When Welles and Morgenthau planned more far-reaching economic pressure, they felt compelled to keep Hull uninformed.

If the hard-liners could count a victory in the tung oil credit, it was only a small one, a deviation from Hull's policy of avoiding provocative action. The $25 million credit was little more than a morale boost for China; the British called it "eyewash." It did not herald the new, tougher East Asian policy Hornbeck had sought. He had said it was time to stand up to Japan even at the risk of eventual war. Yet Morgenthau and Welles had defended the credit proposal on the ground that the president's word was at stake and that the whole thing was safe and involved no risk of war. The program of significant pressure that Hornbeck advocated and Welles and Morgenthau initially sought was not adopted. Rather than a shift in national policy, the tung oil credit to China merely represented a momentary shift of power in the Washington bureaucracy.

This was depressingly clear to Hornbeck, who lamented that the country lacked the will to bring to bear on Japan "material pressures of such weight that the Japanese would very substantially modify the program to which they have recently and openly declared themselves committed."[18]

Whether or not it was from lack of will, State Department officers prepared a toothless response to Japan's early November reference to the New Order in East Asia. As finally presented to Japan on December 30, the note branded Japanese actions "arbitrary, unjust, and unwarranted" and served notice that the American people would never "assent" to Japan's New Order in China. It also exhorted Japan to abandon its attempt to carve out a sphere of influence in East Asia. It would be in Japan's own interest to respect equality of opportunity because, to paraphrase the State Department's language, respect for that basic principle leads to economic and political stability which, in turn, nurtures mutually beneficial and peaceful relationships among nations and promotes access to the raw materials and manufactured goods of the community of nations.

Though a clear expression of the ideology of a stable, liberal commercial world order, the entire note was innocuous. While the language of the note was the strongest the government had ever employed against Japan, it could not conceal what was actually a retreat from the position the United States had taken three months earlier.[19] In October Hull had warned Japan that its continued expansion might result in American commercial retaliation. Japan had responded by declaring a New Order in East Asia. Now, at the end of December, State dropped any reference to commercial or economic retaliation. Instead, it declared that the American people would not "assent" to Japan's New Order. By implication, they would "acquiesce" in its reality. Such was the tested policy Hull had been following since the war began. Before that, it was the United States' response to Japanese conquest of Manchuria in 1932 and Japanese demands on China in 1915.[20]

A week after the December 30 note Maxwell Hamilton, chief of FE, summarized this policy to the officers in the Army War College.

"The sanctity of treaties, equality of commercial opportunity, and respect for the sovereignty of countries are concepts basic to American foreign policy. To abandon them in the Pacific would be to compromise the principles of our entire foreign relations," he explained, then hastened to add that defense of those principles did not require American involvement in the Sino-Japanese War. Even action short of war could be justified only if it could be shown that it would stop Japanese aggression that actually menaced important American interests. Hamilton did not address the first point but he did indicate that Japan was so bogged down in China that it could not expand elsewhere. Clearly, policy managers in the State Department had concluded that China was not important enough to warrant confronting Japan.[21]

There were those in the State Department, however, who were less confident that Japan was bogged down in China. One of these was John Carter Vincent, a young FE officer. Vincent had been deeply impressed by political columnist Walter Lippman's view that the Japanese army was of little interest to the United States, confined as it was to the Asian land mass, while the Japanese navy could extend Japan's influence over the vital raw materials and communication lines of Southeast Asia. Vincent believed that the best way to contain Japan in China was to give aid to China and apply economic pressure against Japan. He sought not to liberate China but to "prevent Japan from consolidating her position in China and drawing sufficient strength therefrom to allow for further aggressive action in other fields which would seriously menace our interests and probably lead us to war."[22]

Vincent's call for action was seconded by another of the State Department's China officers, Walter Adams. Adams viewed Japan more as a global threat, "what, coupled with German and Italian action, amounts to international gangsterism that must sometime be checked unless all 'order under law' is to be destroyed." If Japan went unchecked, it would not only mean the loss of important Asian territory (which was Vincent's argument) but would encourage the aggressor states of Europe. The solution, Adams believed, was to cripple the Japanese economy by restricting its exports to the United States. Like Vincent, Adams thought first about Japanese expansion beyond China. But unlike Vincent, Adams was particularly interested in recovering the China market. Though trade with China was not, by itself, important enough to warrant a strong anti-

Japanese policy, once such a policy had been established it should seek expulsion of Japan and restoration of the China market. To achieve that end, Adams admitted, might require war with Japan, a consequence from which he did not shrink.[23]

Hornbeck jumped into this debate, bridling at Vincent's willingness to abandon China. The United States had a commitment to China, Hornbeck asserted, and to the Open Door there. Moreover, if the United States did not act promptly to save China, someday Japan may be "claiming everything west of the 180th meridian." As he had been doing for months, Hornbeck urged abandoning a policy of diplomatic protests in favor of an active policy designed to keep Japan off balance in East Asia.[24]

Though they had their differences, these three men were in accord that one way or another, Japan menaced important American interests, and should be stopped by a well-orchestrated program of economic sanctions.

Such arguments from the China specialists did not impress the Japan specialists, who warned that economic sanctions were more likely to provoke Japan to turn on the United States than to persuade it to give up its Asian ambitions. Do not depend on statistics in judging Japanese vulnerability, Grew warned, because they do not reflect the Japanese willingness to submit to any deprivation rather than see their nation humbled by Western powers. Thus, something of a split was developing even among the Asian specialists. The China officers advocated stronger action while the Japan specialists urged moderation.[25]

In the midst of this gentlemanly debate Japan began to act just as Vincent and Adams had warned it would. The more ardent nationalists proclaimed the need for closer ties with the Rome-Berlin Axis as well as further military expansion.[26] Words gave way to action in February 1939, when Japanese troops occupied Hainan Island, and again at the end of March, when Japan claimed sovereignty over the Spratly Islands.

Hainan Island, lying off the coast of southern China, was a strategically important base from which Japanese ships could interdict supplies bound for China. It was also important to any Japanese drive into Southeast Asia, because it dominated the coast of Indochina and the northern portion of the South China Sea and thus limited the effectiveness of the giant British naval base at Singapore. The Spratly Islands, seven hundred miles south of Hainan and seven hundred miles northeast of Singapore, were irrelevant to the war in

State's chief Asian specialist, Stanley Hornbeck (above) called for action while Chief of the Far Eastern Division, Maxwell Hamilton (right), urged caution. (Files 208-N-37062-PHE and 208-PU-6699-1, NA.)

China, but could be useful if Japan sought to expand anywhere in Southeast Asia. The problem of Japan in Southeast Asia was no longer theoretical.

Such unchecked aggression, Roosevelt declared in an April press conference, would choke off free trade in the world and thus overburden the economies of the democratic states. As the authoritarian states entered into barter deals with each other, "the nations of the world that pay better wages and work shorter hours are immediately faced, because of the barter system of the aggressor nations, with a loss of world trade. That is obvious," the president explained, "because the aggressor nations can and do work their people much longer hours and for much lower pay."[27]

Roosevelt was warning that while the United States opposed all aggression it could not tolerate authoritarian states dominating too great a portion of the world market. The important question was what constituted such a portion. In Europe, German conquest of the Continent with the fall of France in 1940 would be the turning point. In Asia the line was not so clear. There was a point beyond which Japan could not go without provoking a strong American response. But in Washington there was no consensus where that point was and what, if anything, should be done to keep Japan from reaching it.[28]

Disagreement over what should be done to stop Japan prevailed just when public and congressional opinion made the application of sanctions against Japan politically feasible. Pro-China groups maintained that Japan could not wage its war in China without drawing freely on the supplies available from the United States. The most influential of these groups was the American Committee for Non-Participation in Japanese Aggression. Its awkward name revealed its goal, the embargo of iron, steel, cotton, and gasoline exports to Japan. Simply by refusing to sell these goods to Japan, the committee argued, Japan's aggression could be halted. "Japan furnishes the pilot," one of its pamphlets declared; "America furnishes the airplane, gasoline, oil and bombs for the ravaging of undefended Chinese cities." Walter Judd, a leading critic of American Asian policy, returned from his medical missionary work in China and denounced this "blood trade" to a nationwide radio audience.

> The airplanes bombed and machine-gunned us day after day, but it never made me feel any happier about it to know, all through that first year of the war, how many of the planes were from my country. One-third of all the stuff they drop down to kill, maim, and destroy

comes from the scrap-iron yards and steel mills of my country. I have worked hours on end, night after night, removing these things from the bodies and brains of Chinese men and women and children. I never could say it was none of our business when we were supplying almost everything except the pilot.

Such impassioned appeals, combined with press reports of Japanese atrocities in China, served to turn American opinion against continued trade with Japan. By June 1939, Gallup polls showed that 72 percent of the American people favored an embargo on war materials shipped to Japan.[29] In spite of this growing anti-Japanese feeling, the pro-embargo forces in the country had not been able to get an embargo bill before Congress. In April 1939 that changed, because of developments in Europe.

The likelihood of war erupting in Europe moved Roosevelt to seek a revised neutrality law that would permit belligerent powers (Britain and France for example) to buy supplies with cash and carry them away in their own ships.[30] That maneuver would help Britain and France but would hurt China, which lacked both cash and ships, while favoring Japan, which had both. Though Hull was not interested in becoming involved in the Sino-Japanese War, he also wished to avoid doing a disservice to China—and a cash-and-carry law would be just that.[31]

At this point, Henry L. Stimson (Hoover's secretary of state, currently honorary chairman of the American Committee and vehemently anti-Japanese) suggested to Senator Key Pittman, chairman of the Senate Foreign Relations Committee, that cash and carry could also single out Japan for embargoes. Encouraged by Stimson, Pittman proposed that the next neutrality act empower the president to embargo sale of war materials to any nation that violated the Nine Power Treaty—in other words, Japan.[32]

Here was another made-to-order opportunity for the Roosevelt administration to "tighten the screws" on Japan. Japan had proclaimed its New Order in East Asia in direct violation of basic American principles and rights, had moved closer to Nazi Germany, and had clearly shown its intention of expanding into Southeast Asia. Britain and France were looking to the United States for leadership, public opinion would support an embargo by a 3 to 1 margin (probably more if Roosevelt had endorsed it,) and now congressional support for an embargo was apparent. Yet nothing came of it. There was no embargo; not even a threat of an embargo was made. The strongest language came from Ambassador Grew, who suggested that Japan be reminded that its ultimate welfare was tied to the United States and Great Britain, "without whose liberal trade policies and abundant natural resources, and important markets Japan's rapid economic and industrial development would not have been possible." Hull approved the language but urged Grew to stress the mutual benefit that came from friendly relations rather than the vulnerability of Japan's economy.[33]

So much did Hull want to avoid confronting Japan at that time that he abandoned a perfectly innocent plan to revise the 1911 Japanese-American commercial treaty. Treaty revision would give the United States an opportunity to restrict Japanese textile imports, and Hull was persuaded to accept a combined program of abrogation and renegotiation of a new treaty. When Senator Pittman introduced his embargo resolution, however, there was no chance that Japan would view abrogation and renegotiation as simply the commercially motivated act it was. Though officers in the State Department's Trade Agreements Division insisted that the terms of the commercial treaty acted unilaterally against the United States and needed to be revised, FE officials were adamant; abrogation at that time would have serious diplomatic consequences and should not be undertaken. Diplomatic considerations easily overrode the commercial arguments and the proposal was set aside.[34]

What Hull was willing to do was discourage business from helping Japan or hurting China. State Department officers quietly dissuaded American firms from granting credit to Japan, blocked a Reconstruction Finance Corporation loan to an American business in occupied China, and urged American bankers to avoid "courses of action which would increase the difficulties of the Chinese and be helpful to the Japanese." At the same time, Hull was cooperative in helping China economically. While no new loans were forthcoming, the State Department allowed China to use its existing credit to buy aircraft, even though the terms of the credit prohibited the purchase of any military equipment. An equally sympathetic attitude governed State's response to China's decision to suspend payment of its foreign obligations.[35] All that was in keeping with Hull's policy of not doing a disservice to China and was pale in comparison to even the mildest form of an embargo advocated by the anti-Japanese groups.

Refusal to act in response to Japan's closing the door in China was the natural result of Hull's conclusion that China held no vital American interests, while refusal to act in response to Japan's looking toward Southeast Asia and the South Seas was partly the result of uncertainty (foreign policy managers were not clear how far or how fast Japan intended to move south) and partly the consequence of spending so much time and energy thinking about Europe. In fact, European events so dominated Washington's attention during the spring that Asian questions began to be defined in terms of their impact on Europe.

Since the Czechoslovakian crisis of September 1938, the Roosevelt administration had been uneasy about the European situation. British prime minister Neville Chamberlain had labeled the Munich accord "peace in our time," but few Americans believed him. Their skepticism was justified on March 15, when German armies occupied the remainder of Czechoslovakia. Once again the world held its breath while Europe teetered on the edge of war. This time, like the last, Britain and France did not want to fight and the war scare passed, though the international situation remained precarious. Nothing in Asia could compete with the drama of these European events and Asian analysts quickly learned to couch their arguments in terms of Europe. Vincent shifted his justification for action against Japan from the need to protect the vital regions of Southeast Asia to the need to help Britain and France fend off the Axis. An isolationist public prohibited any involvement in Europe, he pointed out, but the United States could forestall Japanese expansion in Asia and thus "contribute toward strengthening the Anglo-French front against Hitler."[36] It was just this desire to help Britain and France that finally moved the United States into a more aggressive posture toward Japan.

Though his hands were effectively tied by the strong isolationist feeling across the land, Roosevelt wanted to do something to restrain Germany and bolster Anglo-French resistance. So in mid-April the president sent Hitler a letter seeking the Führer's assurances that Germany would not attack any other European nations. Such an expression of American interest could have no influence if it was coupled with a weakening of British resolve, and Britain was preparing to transfer part of its fleet from the Mediterranean to Singapore. Roosevelt could not send the United States Fleet into the Mediterranean in order to restore the original balance of power there, but he could publicly and dramatically transfer the fleet from the Atlantic (where it was about to pay a courtesy call on the New York World's Fair) to the Pacific, its traditional base. That would satisfy the Australians and allow the British to retain their full naval strength in the Atlantic and Mediterranean. So that neither Germany nor Japan would misunderstand the intent of the action, the White House announced the fleet transfer and the Roosevelt letter to Hitler within a half-hour of each other, on April 15, 1939.[37]

This entire episode was a microcosm of what was to come. It was not through a careful review of national policy or the stakes involved in Asia that the United States would place itself in the path of Japanese expansion, but incrementally, without long-range planning, and as often as not as a stopgap measure necessitated, or so planners thought, by the events in Europe. To a remarkable extent, the reasons for American confrontation of Japan in 1941 are to be found in Europe rather than Asia.

Asian specialists in the State Department did not care what caused the fleet transfer, they were just pleased that Roosevelt had ordered it. As they saw the situation, a war in Europe would disrupt the Asian power balance and encourage Japanese expansion into Southeast Asia, something that would eventually bring Japan and the United States into conflict. The concerted Roosevelt action might help to prevent a war in Europe and in any case would work to deter Japanese expansion beyond China and thus preserve peace between the United States and Japan.[38] The problem with this analysis was that it assumed the United States could persist in its policy of discreet help for China without risking any Japanese retaliation. Grew had disagreed. Americans might be content to let Japan wage its futile war in China, he warned, but the Japanese would become increasingly frustrated and would blame the Western powers for their failure in China. The longer the war dragged on the greater the likelihood that frustrated Japanese leaders might confront one of the Western powers, including the United States. This is precisely what happened.

The Japanese army focused its discontent on the self-governing international settlements operating in China's important port cities. Within these settlements, Chinese law did not apply. Instead, the merchants and bankers who paid the taxes (the rate payers) controlled a municipal council, which administered the settlement. Some of these settlements were small and commercially insignificant, such as Gulangsu, an island within gunshot of the port of Xiamen (Amoy). Others, such as Tianjin, were large and important centers of commerce. The largest was Shanghai, the commercial nerve center of China. Because these settlements were operated by the nationals of the great powers and were outside Chinese jurisdiction, they were treated as neutral territory that Chinese and Japanese armies usually avoided. But it was hard to maintain neutrality when a great war raged all around. Sometimes Chinese guerrillas used the settlements as bases of operation. This was particularly true of Shanghai, where Chinese newspapers in the British and American sectors freely published anti-Japanese reports and terrorist organizations sought shelter. Just as important, large amounts of Chinese wealth took refuge in the Shanghai and Tianjin settlements, where influential Chinese used it to bolster Chinese currency and hinder Japan's attempt to exploit the occupied areas of China. For all these reasons, the international settlements were prime targets against which the Japanese military could vent their frustration.

The challenge came in February and March 1939, when Japanese authorities used the issue of Chinese terrorist activities to demand concessions from the Shanghai Municipal Council. That would give Japanese control of the settlement.[39] Consul General Clarence Gauss believed that Japan was motivated by two factors. One was the need for a victory; unable to defeat the Chinese in the field, Japanese military leaders sought a victory over the Western powers in Shanghai. The other factor was the need to remove Shanghai and the other international settlements as a sanctuary for Chinese-controlled wealth that the Japanese believed prevented them from exploiting occupied China. While the United States could have some influence in deterring a Japanese attempt to seize the settlement, Gauss warned, "the matter is so vital to the Japanese that they will not long be deterred from carrying it out." By May the crisis had reached a peak, when rumors indicated that Japanese troops on the scene were preparing to occupy the settlement.[40]

It was an alarming situation, and Hull applied pressure everywhere to avoid the confrontation. In strong language he warned the Japanese government that the United States would regard "as unlawful and unwarranted and as a deliberate impairment of rights and interests of the United States" any Japanese takeover of the Shanghai settlement. Then he urged the Chinese to understand that the Municipal Council was faced with an "extremely difficult situation" and the Chinese should not do anything that would "tend to prejudice the position of the Settlement and of the Settlement authorities." Finally, turning to the Municipal Council itself, he instructed Gauss to discreetly use his influence "toward encouraging exercise of self-restraint." Hull would not give the Japanese an excuse for intervention.[41]

The British were less discreet. Through a remarkable demonstration of diplomatic ineptitude the Foreign Office managed to stumble into a confrontation with Japan that threatened to wreck Hull's entire Asian policy.

The nominal issue was the disposition of four Chinese terrorists whom the British held in their sector of the Tianjin settlement. When the British refused to surrender them to the local Japanese army commander, he retaliated by forcing all who entered the British sector to undergo an exhaustive, time-consuming, and frequently embarrassing search that made commerce almost impossible.[42] Far more than simply a conflict over a local issue, this was a test of strength between Japan's New Order and the old order epitomized by Britain, the largest concession holder in China, an outspoken critic of Japanese aggression, and a nation that was currently negotiating a nonaggression pact with Japan's traditional enemy, the Soviet Union. Moreover, it was a struggle between Japan whose power was ascending and Britain whose power had been sapped by the crisis in Europe. When the British realized how helpless they were in Tianjin and tried to negotiate their way out they found that the Japanese government, pressured by the army, was demanding a high price. Bear in mind, Foreign Minister Arita Hachiro told British Ambassador Sir Robert Craigie in Tokyo, that it is the unanimous Japanese belief that the "China affair could have been brought to an end long before this but for the continued assistance given by your country to Jiang Jieshi," and that it was the Japanese wish that Britain would, in due course, abandon assistance to Jiang and bring its China policy into line with that of Japan.[43]

Some within the State Department thought it a crisis of great importance that required immediate American action. Sumner Welles exclaimed, "I can't emphasize too strongly my own feeling that if the Japanese get away with this particular matter, the next move will be Shanghai. I don't think the United States Government ought to back down." But Hull, not Welles, was in charge of American Asian policy, and from the secretary's perspective it was not time to confront Japan. By harboring terrorists the British had selected a poor issue on which to make their stand. Moreover, neutrality legislation was coming to a vote in Congress and the administration did not want to do anything to jeopardize its passage. Most important, to challenge Japan over Tianjin might provoke a confrontation at Shanghai, a confrontation the United States would lose. As ever, Hull preferred to wait.[44]

The mood in Washington changed when it became apparent that

Britain was going to make sweeping concessions to Japan bordering on crass appeasement. Hull considered warning Japan that the United States government viewed Japan's desire to establish complete control over all of China with "serious concern," but hesitated because he was uncertain whether the note would do any good. From Tokyo, Chargé Eugene Dooman (Grew was on vacation in the United States) cabled that the protest would accomplish nothing because the military extremists who were in charge of the affair would not be swayed by anything the Americans said to Japanese diplomats.[45]

But Dooman's note conflicted with the strong advice Hull was receiving from his Far Eastern Division. "Surrender by the British in the present situation at Tianjin," an FE memo concluded, "will be an important step forward toward the ultimate disappearance of foreign power interests and rights in China." Hull reluctantly yielded to this advice and approved the drafting of a strong warning to Japan. As approved by the president on July 1, the note reiterated the ideology of liberal commercialism, and stated: "Civilized life would deteriorate steadily if conquest and forceful domination would become a rule in international relations." If this continued, it added ominously, "a situation would be created where other nations would have no course but to take under consideration measures necessary for the protection of their own civilization and security."[46]

Not convinced it was time to use such blunt language against Japan, Hull turned to Dooman for corroboration. This time, the chargé's response was clear and unequivocal: the note would have an immediate adverse impact upon Japanese-American relations with the probable result that the Japanese military would begin treating American interests very much as it was treating British interests. By now, Hull had decided to withhold the note. But since it had strong support in the State Department and the president had approved it, Hull turned to Grew for the ambassador's predictable response. From his vacation retreat in New Hampshire, Grew urged that the warning not be delivered. If the secretary wanted to be certain that Japan understood American concern he could ask Dooman to present the substance of the memo through informal representations to the foreign minister.[47] Discretion, and Hull, triumphed and the United States stood by while the British caved in to Japanese demands and signed the Craigie-Arita agreement of July 24.

It was a stunning blow against everything for which the United States stood in Asia. Britain recognized that as long as there were

large-scale hostilties in China, Japanese forces enjoyed "special requirements" to protect themselves in occupied areas, including suppressing or removing anything that would obstruct Japan or benefit
China. The British agreed to do nothing to hinder Japan in its
fulfillment of its "special requirements."[48] In practice, Hull had been
following this policy for some time. He had acquiesced in the demands of the Japanese military concerned with maintaining security
in occupied China. But he had never assented to the Japanese position and had always asserted American rights. By acting in that way
Hull had avoided confronting Japan while neither betraying American principles nor undercutting Chinese morale. In the Craigie-Arita
agreement, the British had not only acquiesced in Japanese infringe-
ment of Western rights, they had assented to it. In one blow Britain
had belittled Hull's principles of right conduct and leveled a stinging
slap at Chinese morale.

The timing of the Craigie-Arita agreement was particularly disturbing, coming as it did just a few weeks after Congress rejected
Roosevelt's revised neutrality bill. Japanese extremists could now
argue that neither Britain nor the United States was prepared to act in
Asia. It was true, neither power *was* prepared to act in Asia; but Hull
did not want the Japanese to be so confident in that assessment. Thus
it was obvious the United States would have to do something to fill
the power vacuum left by the British capitulation. The precise form
of the American response, however, was determined by developments in Congress.

While Tokyo and London were negotiating the terms of the British
retreat, the Senate Foreign Relations Committee contemplated the
Pittman resolution, which called for embargoing nations in violation
of the Nine Power Treaty. In addition, Republican Senator Arthur A.
Vandenberg had introduced his own resolution calling for the
abrogation of the 1911 Japanese-American commercial treaty while
remaining silent on the question of a subsequent embargo. Hull
found himself in a delicate diplomatic and political situation. He
opposed passage of the Pittman resolution because it would mean
confrontation with Japan; yet he feared that defeat of the resolution
would convince Japan that isolationism reigned supreme in the
United States. The Vandenberg resolution was more palatable, but
the Democrats would probably attack the plan. If it failed, and
whether the Pittman resolution passed *or* failed, Hull's Asian policy
would suffer. Even debate on the resolutions would probably provoke language that could only strain Japanese-American relations.

Roosevelt and Hull decided they could avoid these dangers only by preempting the legislation, and on July 26 Roosevelt served Japan the required six months' notice for abrogation of the 1911 commercial treaty.[49]

Abrogation was a powerful act not because it did anything at the moment but because it permitted far-reaching action as of January 26, 1940. The press interpreted abrogation as "clearing the decks for action" and the public gave it overwhelming support.[50] To many people, perhaps most, this was the turning point, the place where the United States said, "Enough! We will not be pushed farther." But many earlier events had been hailed as turning points only to be seen later as powerless actions. The Quarantine Speech in October 1937, the moral embargo of June 1938, the stiff note of October 1938, the tung oil credit the following December, the fleet transfer in April 1939—none of these had brought a new American foreign policy. Whether abrogation was part of a new policy or was just another in a series of actions that were more show than substance remained to be seen.

Whatever the abrogation turned out to be, the fact remained that, almost imperceptibly, American involvement in the Pacific had been increasing. Whether because of the machinations of the "hawks" within the Roosevelt administration or reflex actions to fill a power vacuum created by war scares in Europe, the United States was moving toward a confrontation with Japan. This was not a calculated or even recognizable shift, and American policy was the same in the summer of 1939 as it had been two years earlier: do not confront Japan, do no disservice to China, and wait. Yet to some, like Ambassador Grew, the course of American policy was alarmingly apparent. Unless something was done about it, the United States would find itself at war with Japan before anyone realized it was approaching.

CHAPTER FOUR

DOWNHILL TOWARD WAR

J oseph Grew came home during the summer of 1939 to rest and to gauge the mood of the nation. What he saw alarmed him. Japan and the United States were drifting toward war, yet no one in the United States or in Japan seemed to be aware of it. Public opinion was hardening, and the Roosevelt administration was saying it would not be crowded out of China. Unless Japan moderated its behavior, Grew concluded, the United States would embargo exports of essential materials to Japan even though the ultimate consequence of such action was war.[1]

Grew had laid bare an important aspect of American foreign policy. Though national leaders did not want war with Japan, their policy was moving the United States along a path that could, and Grew believed would, eventually result in war. At some point American or Japanese leaders would awake to see that the two nations were on the brink of war, but by then it might be too late. Grew resolved to undertake a personal diplomatic effort in order to change the course of Japanese-American relations. It was a noble task, but it failed, and in the process, it made war more likely.

It is easy to see why Grew was so alarmed. The impact of popular hatred of Japan was greater on Grew, who had been isolated from American public opinion, than on American officials in Washington who were used to the lobbying campaigns, speeches, and articles of the anti-Japanese groups. As he traveled among the American people, Grew delivered the same message he had often cabled to the State Department: there were two Japans, one moderate and the other extremist. He urged Americans to understand the legitimate aims of the moderate Japanese just as they rejected the goals of the extremists. This message had no more impact on the American people than it had had on policymakers in Washington. The public was not interested in Japan's legitimate complaints; it was outraged by Japan's actions in China, and was prepared to embargo exports to Japan.[2] Grew understood that Congress remained divided over the issue of an embargo, but he also knew the pro-embargo forces across the land were growing.

In Washington, Grew noted, distrust of Japan was so great that a diplomatic solution was hardly considered. Grew's approach of trying to see both sides of the question simply did not exist in the capital. The policymakers' image of Japan was clear. First, Japan was intent upon driving all Western influence out of Asia; that was the meaning of the New Order and that was precisely what Japan had been trying to do for the past two years. At the moment the British were feeling the brunt of Japanese pressure, but once they were removed the Japanese would turn against the Americans. Second, in achieving this goal, Japan would make minor concessions and yield on insignificant points. Such concessions were simply tactical, to be followed by still greater attacks upon American rights in Asia. Third, any attempt to reach agreement with Japan on principles was useless because Japan could not be trusted to apply principles to specific situations. Though the word *liar* was never used, the word *untrustworthy* was. If any power reached an agreement with Japan in principle it would be written in such vague and unclear terms that it would cloak Japan's real intentions. This was not just a Japanese tactic but part of the "Oriental character" or the "Oriental tendency to give adherence to principles in the abstract without any intention to observe them in practice."[3]

This attitude placed a virtually insurmountable obstacle in the way of any diplomatic settlement. Japanese hints at mediation were dismissed almost out of hand as insincere. Even if Japan should go some way toward compromise, the conventional wisdom in Washington was that Japan sought a settlement only as a means of escape from the China entanglement. With its prestige preserved, the military would still hold power in Japan and pursue its policy of expansion. Since the only way to bring peace in Asia was for the Japanese to abandon expansion, and that could only happen when

the military was discredited, the best policy was to avoid any diplomatic efforts to end the fighting short of a total and humiliating
retreat by the Japanese military.[4] State Department officers spent
their time devising a foreign policy that would perpetuate the strain
on the Japanese economy, negotiating a diplomatic solution to the
Sino-Japanese War. Grew feared that time would wear down American patience and result in some action by the United States that
would provoke a confrontation with Japan. As far as Grew was
concerned, there was ample evidence for this view.

In late August and early September 1939 the Japanese pressed for
British and French withdrawal from Shanghai. Grew was present as
the State Department formulated its response to these Japanese
demands and received the distinct impression that the Roosevelt
administration had no intention of "being crowded out of China."
On September 7, as Grew's stay in Washington neared its end, Hull
lectured the Japanese ambassador: "Shanghai is international. For
several other powers to be forced out would mean to the United
States that all powers are being forced out. The American government cannot and does not admit any right on the part of any power to
force it out." In a thinly veiled threat, the secretary added, "How does
your Government expect us to prevent the Congress and the country,
if we should attempt to do so, from taking up the question of our
monetary and financial and trade relations with your country and
dealing with it in a way that you can well imagine in light of all the
circumstances?"[5]

The last thing Grew heard before he returned to Tokyo was an
equally strong warning from Hornbeck. There could be no peace in
Asia until the Japanese military machine ceased to dominate Japan,
Hornbeck maintained. It might be discredited through military defeat in China or by action of other elements in Japan, "but, so long as
Japanese diplomats and businessmen are able to keep open sources
of and channels for a continuous flow of supplies to the Japanese
military machine, other elements in the Japanese state are not likely
to take the Japanese Army in hand."[6]

Even Roosevelt seemed to be caught up in what Grew considered a
"marked disinclination to allow American interests to be crowded
out of China." In two conferences with the president, June 13 and
September 12, Grew clearly put forward his view that "if we once
start sanctions against Japan we must see them through to the end,
and the end may conceivably be war." In one of those conferences,
probably September 12, Grew was struck by the equanimity with

which Roosevelt considered the consequences of sanctions. "If we cut off Japan's supply of oil and if Japan then finds that she cannot obtain sufficient oil from other commercial sources to ensure her national security," Grew told the president, "she will in all probability send her fleet down to take the Dutch East Indies." Grew recorded in his diary that the "President replied significantly: 'Then we could easily intercept her fleet.' "[7]

Shocked by such statements, Grew realized that if he had been so out of touch with the mood of his government, then surely the moderates in Japan had to be even less aware of what was developing in the United States. So long as those moderates operated under the misconception that the United States would not confront Japan over its New Order in Asia, they had no incentive to challenge the militarists who guided Japanese foreign policy. "Hitherto we in the Embassy have aimed to follow, so far as reasonable, a policy of avoiding words or action which might tend to irritate the military," he recorded in his diary. It was time to speak out and disabuse Japanese leaders of their belief that in the final analysis the United States would back down. Grew selected as his forum a luncheon address at the American Japan Society upon his return to Tokyo. He began drafting his speech while still on leave, receiving help from officers in the State Department and finished it after his return to Japan. What emerged, therefore, was more than a diplomatic statement; it was a candid explanation of the United States perception of the Sino-Japanese War stripped of superficial issues and dealing directly and clearly with the fundamental questions.[8]

Grew said as much to the influential Japanese gathered at the luncheon on October 19. "I know whereof I speak," he told his listeners, and promised them a message that came "straight from the horse's mouth." He avoided a "bill of particulars" and avoided branding Japan an aggressor. Instead, he sought to explain that Japanese-American relations had reached such a low point because Japanese foreign policy had challenged the basic principle underlying all of American foreign policy:

> Nations are now increasingly dependent on others both for commodities they do not produce themselves and for the disposal of the things which they produce in excess. . . . It is this system of exchange which has not only raised the standard of living everywhere but has made it possible for two or even three persons to live in comfort where but one had lived in discomfort under a simple self-contained economy. Not only the benefits of our advanced civilization but the very existence of

most of us depends on maintaining in equilibrium a delicately balanced and complex world economy . . . postulated upon the ability of
nations to buy and sell where they please under conditions of free
competition—conditions which cannot exist in areas where preemptive rights are claimed and asserted on behalf of nationals of one
particular country. The American people . . . have good reason to
believe that an effort is being made to establish control, in Japan's own
interest, of large areas on the continent of Asia and to impose upon
those areas a system of closed economy. It is this thought, added to the
effect of the bombings, the indignities, the manifold interference with
American rights that accounts for the attitude of the American people
toward Japan today.[9]

By deemphasizing Japan's flagrant violation of treaties, its shame-
ful bombing of Chinese civilians, and the insults it had heaped upon
American nationals in China, Grew acknowledged that these factors
were not responsible for bringing Japanese-American relations to
such a critical state. While such depredations upset and angered the
American people, Grew recognized that they would not by themselves cause the economic sanctions that would lead to war. The
important factor, the factor that would transform dislike for Japan
into action against Japan, was the Japanese assault on the liberal
commercial world order. The Roosevelt administration was not
overly concerned that Japan denied some American merchants access to certain markets in China, but was greatly agitated when the
New Order attacked the delicate international economic equilibrium
responsible for the material progress and advancement of civilization
the world had witnessed in the past century.

The United States had prospered under that liberal commercial
system and consequently Americans had elevated it to the preemi-
nent position in their perception of how the world should function.
Cordell Hull's emphasis on the sanctity of treaties and international
law was part of this American view of the proper world order. In his
speech Grew had not ignored Hull's stress on international law; he
had simply cut to the heart of the matter. Treaties and international
law were not ends in themselves but ways of assuring an orderly
world in which nations could compete freely in trade and investment.

Grew's judgment that the United States would not confront Japan
over the violation of human rights in China or its disregard of a treaty
or two was correct. He was also correct when he concluded that the
Roosevelt administration would not stand by and watch whole
sections of the world be monopolized by conquest. Roosevelt had

explained that to reporters in a news conference the preceding April. The importance of an open-door world economy had also been emphasized in a draft note to Japan that the president had approved on July 1.[10]

The important question was at what point the Roosevelt administration would decide that Japan had gone too far and actively resist further Japanese expansion. Grew concluded that Japan had already reached the limit of American tolerance. Not only could Japan go no farther in its expansion, it had to change its present policy. Unless that happened, Grew earnestly believed, the United States would respond with an embargo against Japan that would lead to war.

Grew hid none of this from the new Japanese foreign minister, Nomura Kichisaburo. Someday Japan and the United States would have to settle their fundamental differences, Grew explained early in November, but now Japan had to act to stop the public outcry for an embargo. Grew suggested two actions. First, "Stop the bombings, indignities and more flagrant interferences with American rights in China." Second, provide "concrete evidence" that Japan intended to improve relations with the United States. Specifically, Grew mentioned reopening the Yangzi River to American commercial traffic. He understood the difficulty of what he was asking. Assassination of unpopular government officials was not alien to Japanese politics and the type of concession Grew sought risked more than just the political lives of the moderates in Tokyo.

This was a bold effort by the ambassador because it was made mostly on his own initiative. Certainly the proposal concerning opening the Yangzi River exceeded his diplomatic instructions. He knew Washington would not have approved his suggestion, and the summary of the Nomura conversation he cabled Washington contained no reference to the Yangzi. That idea was confined to the longer memorandum the ambassador dispatched by the more leisurely diplomatic pouch.[11] The delay would give him all the time he needed.

Grew's plan went like this. First he would convince the Japanese they must make a concession—opening the Yangzi River. Then he would convince his own government that a perpetuation of the current policy was fraught with danger. When the Japanese offered to open the Yangzi the United States would respond with its own concession, and the cycling toward war would be reversed. It would not be easy, because Washington foreign policy managers believed that Japan could not sustain a protracted war and were in no hurry to negotiate a settlement. Moreover, their deep suspicion of Japan prompted them to brush aside Japanese concessions as insincere or inconsequential.[12] If his plan was going to work, Grew knew he had to change those attitudes.

Washington had to face facts, Grew cabled bluntly. Japan was not going to crumble and give up its New Order even if the United States applied tremendous economic pressure. The Japanese army was too intertwined with Japanese society to collapse or be rejected by the Japanese people. The New Order in Asia meant, at the very least, Japanese domination of northern China. If the United States followed a policy of complete intransigence, Grew warned, it would push Japanese-American relations rapidly downhill. The alternative, was for Washington to respond positively to any "concrete evidence" of Japan's willingness to respect American interests in Asia. He suggested a temporary agreement and an offer to negotiate a new trade treaty.[13]

Grew's arguments did not impress Washington policy managers, who continued to believe that the army controlled Japan and that the most the moderates could do was reduce the number of flagrant incidents. They acknowledged that Japan was trying to prevent personal insults to American nationals, decrease bombings of American property in China, and settle a few outstanding claims against the Japanese government. But such Japanese moderation only "touched the fringe of the problem." Japan had shown no serious disposition to enter into a settlement based on the "fundamentals of American rights and interests in the Far East." In Washington's view, Japan only wanted a victor's peace.[14]

Thus, official Washington viewed with a skeptical eye the Japanese offer to open the Yangzi to general navigation as far as Nanjing and under military supervision "in about two months." In return, Japan expected a temporary agreement to preserve normal commercial relations while the United States and Japan negotiated a new commercial treaty. Grew urged his government to respond constructively. "Please permit me very respectfully to express to you the following views," he began his report to Hull. "The simple fact is that we are here dealing not with a unified Japan but with a Japanese Government which is endeavoring courageously, even with only gradual success, to fight against a recalcitrant Japanese army, a battle which happens to be our own battle. We 'obviously' cannot count on the Yangzi being opened until it actually happens," he conceded, "but it will come sooner if we respond positively to this offer than if we rebuff it, offer a temporary agreement on trade, and hold off negotiation of a new trade treaty until we see that Japan lives up to its pledge. Whatever the reply is," he pleaded, "I earnestly recommend that it not close the door" but that it encourage further efforts by the Japanese government. If this offer is rebuffed, he warned, it may well bring down the Japanese cabinet and provide the Japanese army with powerful arguments to use in its own behalf.[15]

This was Grew's moment of truth. Months of effort had gone into obtaining a Japanese offer and in this moment of extreme stress he was certain that this was not just another diplomatic opportunity but the diplomatic turning point. "I am convinced that at this juncture we are in a position either to direct American-Japanese relations into a progressively healthy channel or to accelerate their movement straight down hill."[16] For Grew it was a simple either/or proposition. Either the State Department would recognize the "simple fact" involved and accept Grew's recommendation or it would rebuff the Japanese offer and push Japanese-American relations "straight down hill" to war.

This eloquent and somewhat desperate plea did not move Hull. The secretary and his associates considered Grew's appeal and even took it to Roosevelt, but they remained too suspicious of Japan to put any credence in Grew's views. Hull would do no more than allow Grew to continue his talks with Nomura while continuing normal trade with Japan on a day-to-day basis.[17]

In one respect, State was correct. What Nomura offered was not a renunciation of Japan's New Order but only a small concession designed to get the United States to negotiate a new trade treaty. But the department was wrong when it considered this small concession of "no particular significance." Small as it was, the promise to open the Yangzi represented an important victory by Japanese moderates, who believed their country's future was tied to the United States. When Hull rebuffed their overture, they were discredited, and as their influence fell, that of the pro-Axis group rose. To this other group, the United States was an implacable enemy and Japan's future was better served by moving closer to Nazi Germany.

Grew had understood the danger involved but was prepared to take the risk because of the critical state of Japanese-American relations. Unfortunately, the crisis existed only in Grew's mind. American officials saw the alternative to an agreement to be the continuation of the status quo, not an embargo or war. Hornbeck explained to Grew bluntly: "You overestimate the degree to which and the brevity of the time within which the tension between the United States and Japan will become acute."[18]

There were two reasons why Hull and company did not believe their present policy would lead to either embargo or war. One was that the situation in China would not deteriorate to a point where American military or economic pressure would be required to prevent a Japanese victory. A million-man Japanese army had not been able to conquer China and could hold on to parts of it only with great effort. Japan did not have the financial resources, the industrial potential, or the administrative personnel to develop an empire in China. With just a touch of racism showing, State Department officers smugly concluded that the Japanese could not do in China what the British had done in India. Instead, Japan would be worn down and eventually would have to withdraw, though this might take a long time.[19]

The second reason was that the threatened loss of China could not justify a war with Japan. Grew was correct when he told the Japanese that the United States believed in a world governed by an open door to trade, but he was wrong in assuming that China itself was a significant enough part of that world to warrant American action. The United States had never considered China important enough to justify a fight (except possibly against the Chinese.) Hull had scrupulously avoided a confrontation with Japan during the first two years of the war and he would continue to avoid one during the next two.

There was ample evidence of Hull's conservative policy. What makes this entire episode tragic is that if Grew had paid less attention to what American policy managers *said* and more to what they were *doing*, he would not have seen a crisis approaching. To understand this we must go back to the events of 1939 and look at the Roosevelt administration's response to Japanese restrictions against the international settlements at Gulangsu, Tianjin, and Shanghai.

At Gulangsu, the test of will began in May when Japan landed a small party of marines to search for anti-Japanese terrorists and the United States, Britain, and France each landed a like number. The Westerners at Gulangsu were convinced Japan intended to take control of the settlement by gaining control of the local police and expelling all Westerners. The Americans at Gulangsu refused to yield control of the police and their obstinacy brought on a Japanese blockade of food and fuel into the settlement. The local American consul, Karl MacVitty, persuaded that it was only the presence of the

Ambassador Joseph C. Grew feared the officials in Washington were leading the United States to war and worked to alter the course of events (File 208-N-3783, NA.)

Western troops that gave the Municipal Council any chance to negotiate with the Japanese, urged that Washington support the Americans at Gulangsu.[20]

Officers in the State Department were reluctant to become embroiled at Gulangsu; it seemed to be the wrong place to take a stand against Japanese expansion. The decision to land marines in the first place had been taken by local naval and diplomatic personnel without consulting Washington, and State officials had never been happy about that decision. Unwilling to simply retreat in the face of this Japanese challenge, the State Department was prepared to "meet the Japanese more than half-way" in order to defuse the crisis. In practice, that meant State would accept Japanese control of the police at Gulangsu.[21] But the Americans there proved stubborn and steadfastly resisted the Japanese demands. Not until September, when the British and French withdrew their troops following the outbreak of war in Europe, was the impasse broken. It was obvious that with the British and French gone, American marines would soon follow. By the fifteenth, MacVitty cabled Washington that the Municipal Council was prepared to "capitulate" to Japanese demands. MacVitty's use of the word *capitulate* irritated some State Department officials, but it was accurate. The withdrawal of British and French forces "left the Americans holding a baby which they hastened, if not to drop, to put down rather hurriedly."[22] Much the same attitude governed American policy when Japan challenged the powers in the larger, more important settlement of Tianjin.

The issue at Tianjin was Chinese silver in British banks. The United States could have bought the silver or had it transferred to American-owned banks, but Hull refused to allow the United States to become involved, even when the British looked to Washington for help.[23] But Tianjin and Gulangsu were insignificant compared to Shanghai, which contained more foreign nationals and banks than any other Chinese city. If the United States was going to resist Japanese pressure anywhere in China, it would have to be Shanghai, which was the symbol of Western rights in China.

By mid-August 1939 the Shanghai situation had become precarious, when Japanese-controlled Chinese police clashed with a British patrol. The Japanese army then landed six thousand soldiers to blockade the settlement. At that critical moment, Germany, Japan's ally in the Anti-Commintern Pact, announced its alliance with the Soviet Union—Japan's traditional enemy, with which it had just fought a brief but bloody war. Startled by this dramatic shift in diplomatic alignments, Japan postponed the blockade while it reassessed its international position. While Japan hesitated, the British decided to withdraw.[24]

Roosevelt and Hull were understandably unhappy with Britain's decision and tried to stiffen British resolve. It was in this situation that Hull summoned the Japanese ambassador and lectured him about Western rights in China. In his conversation with the ambassador on September 7, Hull denounced the Japanese attempt to force out a Western power and threatened Japan with a congressionally mandated embargo. It was this conversation, mentioned earlier, that so impressed Grew and convinced him that an embargo against Japan was likely. But Hull's language was aimed more at the British than the Japanese. In an obvious attempt to forestall their withdrawal from China, he promptly cabled the substance of this conversation to the British and French governments. (When Hull spoke again to the Japanese ambassador a week later, he used much less forceful language, and did not cable the substance of that conversation to London or Paris.) Roosevelt tried his hand at stiffening the British spine on September 17, by declaring to the British ambassador that the United States would retain its troops and ships in East Asia and the British should do the same. There was a difference between Tianjin and Shanghai, Roosevelt said; Shanghai was the vital place. In addition, "reliable sources" in Shanghai informed London that the United States intended to resist these Japanese encroachments on Western rights and perhaps cooperate with British troops in defense of the international settlement.[25]

Though still skeptical, the British and French could not ignore the possibility of a joint Anglo-French-American stand in Shanghai. On September 19 and 20 they notified Washington that vague promises and empty words would no longer do—the United States would have to commit itself to stand with its friends in Shanghai or they would withdraw. Hull did not like the choice. He opposed withdrawal but was not prepared to stand and confront Japan. The American reply was evasive, and the British and French governments served notice that they would withdraw all gunboats and troops from all areas of China, including Shanghai.[26]

Hull's strong words to the Japanese ambassador and Roosevelt's encouragement to the British ambassador had misled the British just as they had misled Grew. The Roosevelt administration was not prepared to confront Japan in China, even over Shanghai. The same day Roosevelt assured the British ambassador that the United States would not be crowded out of China, Hull was cabling the American consul general in Shanghai that the United States had only two choices: protest Japanese actions or negotiate an accommodation. Hull favored a negotiated settlement and urged convening a multi-power conference to resolve the disputes over the international settlement. But Consul General Clarence Gauss and Chargê Eugene Dooman in Tokyo strongly advised against that tactic, pointing out that the crisis had been provoked by the army, which would not allow the matter to be handled by the diplomats. If a conference were held, they explained, the Japanese army would demand that a variety of issues be opened for negotiation and this would not serve American interests. Hull reluctantly agreed and settled for another "for the record" protest lodged with the Japanese government. It was a safe policy that risked little and promised to accomplish nothing.[27]

Caution was the watchword in Washington during the fall of 1939. Foreign policy managers would not even consider naval action and economic pressure was approached with great caution. Moderates like Hugh Wilson warned against an embargo as useful only if effective and if effective leading to war. Hornbeck admitted that any discussion of economic pressure would have to be characterized by "constant alertness, unremitting effort, and delicacy of procedure." Even the nonpolicymaking Legal Affairs Division warned that any use of the economic weapon was an extremely important question deserving the "most careful consideration."[28] It soon became apparent that a sweeping economic embargo against Japan was not one of the options the Roosevelt administration considered. As early as October 1939 Hornbeck acknowledged that. Even the pro-embargo forces in Congress had given up trying to achieve anything immediately. Senator Pittman conceded that any legislation Congress passed would have to give the president discretionary powers and be nonbinding.[29] His prediction was correct; embargo legislation did not pass Congress until July 1940 and then it was enabling legislation designed to permit the stockpiling of materials necessary for the developing American war machine. The embargo Grew feared and the anti-Japanese forces sought did not come until July 1941, two years after the decision to abrogate the commercial treaty was made and in a world setting radically different from that of 1939.

Of course, there was more than one way to apply commercial pressure on Japan. If the "meat-ax" approach of the embargo was too radical there was the more sophisticated method of applying discriminatory duties authorized by the 1930 Tariff Act. Because

Japanese silk, wool, and cotton received preferential treatment in occupied China the United States could place punitive duties on Japanese silk, wool, and cotton imported into the United States. Since those commodities comprised 74 percent of Japan's exports to the United States, any reduction in their sales would further strain an already struggling Japanese economy. More important to a State Department intent upon not provoking Japan, the discriminatory duties avoided most of the dangers inherent in a total embargo: the authority already existed in law and would not require any congressional involvement, the duties could be applied quietly under the guise of commercial necessity, and they could be nominal at first. Japan would get the message without suffering a loss of face, and thus would not be provoked to retaliation.

If there was any desire to increase commercial pressure against Japan, this law gave the Roosevelt administration a ready tool. But there was little interest in such action. In August 1939 FE raised the possibility of applying the Tariff Act in August, but not until October did the Legal Affairs Division get around to rendering a judgment that such discriminatory duties would be perfectly legitimate.[30] When the solicitor general said it was legal, Hornbeck urged action, but the mood within the State Department was to wait and see how Japan responded to the abrogation of the trade treaty. As it developed, the Tariff Act of 1930 was never applied against Japan.[31]

An even easier way to apply commercial pressure against Japan was simply to do nothing. Existing American law required a discriminatory duty against cargoes and ships from countries that did not have a trade treaty with the United States. When the 1911 treaty expired in January 1940, the United States would automatically impose an additional 10 percent ad valorum duty on Japanese cargoes, while tonnage duties on Japanese ships would jump from five cents per ton to $1.35 per ton. (Thus, for example, tonnage duties on a 10,000-ton Japanese tanker would rise from $500 per visit to $13,500 per visit.)

In order to waive these duties, Roosevelt had to publicly proclaim that Japan did not discriminate against American ships in Japanese ports. Even though this was true, Roosevelt could not say so without misleading Japan into believing that its current behavior was acceptable and that the United States contemplated no action against Japan when the treaty expired. That was not the message Hull wanted the Japanese to receive. The solution lay in a bit of creative research. In 1872, President Ulysses S. Grant had proclaimed that Japan did not discriminate against American shipping; and since no president since had rescinded that proclamation, it remained in force and Hull was able to inform the Japanese simply that the discriminatory duties would not be applied when the treaty ended.[32]

Roosevelt accepted Hull's recommendation against application of the discriminatory duties but stressed that the Japanese government be clearly informed that this decision to suspend tonnage and import duties was only "temporary" and if a settlement was not reached the duties would be applied with thirty days' advance notice. Hull did not fully carry out the president's instructions. In briefing Grew and in talking to the Japanese ambassador, Hull did not mention the temporary nature of the suspension. Instead, he told the Japanese that the duties would not be collected "unless and until further instructions are issued." Hull's "whole attitude," Morgenthau complained, "was that he didn't want to do something which would at this time arouse the Japanese." Hull did not think it desirable to remind Japan of its commercial vulnerability.[33]

Meanwhile, the moral embargo program continued, with State Department officers discouraging loans or credit sales to Japan. On one occasion Hull personally phoned an official of the Chase Bank to express the department's opposition to credit deals with Japan.[34] Hull's strategy was not to cripple Japan but to harass it slightly and keep it economically dependent upon the Western powers.[35] In practice that meant State Department pressure to prohibit export of plans and processes for the manufacture of aviation gasoline, while permitting the free export of the gasoline itself. When the Japanese protested this "moral embargo" Hull would talk tough, enumerating Japanese acts against American commerce. But if his words were harsh, his actions were not. Even the moral embargo on plans for manufacture of gasoline was limited to high-octane, aviation gasoline. When an American corporation announced that it intended to sell plans and equipment for the installation of an ordinary refining plant in Manchukuo, Hull expressed no objection.[36] There were those in the Roosevelt administration who opposed such deals and even sought the total embargo of oil sales to Japan (Secretary of the Treasury Morgenthau and Secretary of the Interior Harold Ickes were the two most outspoken proponents of that tactic) but such restriction was so provocative that it was not even considered in the State Department. The president recognized this, commenting that it was perhaps just as well that the United States was sending oil to Japan "because otherwise Japan might raid the Dutch East Indies."[37]

(This was the same man who, a few months earlier, had horrified Grew by casually suggesting that if Japan did try to raid the Indies the United States could intercept it. Grew made a mistake in hanging on every remark of any individual in such a complicated situation, especially one as indecisive as Roosevelt.)

Not surprisingly, when the treaty died on January 26, 1940 nothing happened. No embargo was applied, no showdown took place over Shanghai, Japan was given no assurances about the future. Trade continued on a twenty-four-hour basis and Japan was kept in a high state of uncertainty. The policy was explained in a letter to Grew that Hornbeck drafted for Roosevelt's signature: "We feel that we have been patient and cautious, and we intend to continue trying to be so." Meanwhile, the United States would not follow Grew's suggestion and negotiate a new trade treaty. "I feel that it will be a good thing to have this Government's hands free, and that the uncertainties which may prevail may cause the Japanese to think more deeply and more liberally." In this summary description of U.S. East Asian policy the termination of the treaty was described as not being a major turning point. "The views and the efforts of Japan and the United States have been in conflict for a long time since and will continue to be so into the indefinite future." The United States would be patient but firm while the war in China dragged on, wearing down Japan until it tired of the price of war and withdrew. "Congenitally," Hornbeck's draft said, the Japanese lacked the qualities and capacities that would allow them to bring about peace, order, stability, and security in China. They would lose in China because of their own ineptitude and because of the constant resistance shown by the Chinese and other nations of the world.[38] Hornbeck believed that, and so did just about everyone else in Washington.

Long before this letter arrived in Tokyo, Grew had recognized the moderation that characterized his nation's policy. He was pleased that State had heeded "the essence if not the letter" of his recommendations and he praised his government for a policy that had "maneuvered Japan into a position where she will be kept constantly guessing whether and when the sword of Damocles will fall," while permitting trade to continue.[39] But Grew was putting the best face on a bad situation. He was hopelessly out of step with his government. His analysis of what was happening in East Asia and how it should be dealt with was fundamentally different from that of policymakers in Washington.

Grew believed in Japan and the Japanese. He saw that island

empire as a have-not nation plagued by its lack of raw materials, dependence on overseas markets, and excess population. There could be no "permanent contentment and peace until some reasonable and practical balance is found between" the have powers and the have-not powers, Grew maintained. "Japan in China has a good case and a strong case if she knew how to present it, but her stupidity in publicity and propaganda is only exceeded by her stupidity in methods."[40] A policy that encouraged the moderates could produce wonders, Grew earnestly believed.

All of this was totally alien to the foreign policy managers in Washington. They did not believe that the moderates could restrain the military; they did not believe that Japan had any case in China, or that Japan was a have-not nation with legitimate grievances. They saw Japan simply as a bandit nation bent upon conquest. Unwilling either to appease Japan or to fight it, they fashioned an East Asian policy strong enough to deny Japan victory but restrained enough to avoid war.

It was a policy that assumed the Japanese people would eventually tire of war and turn against their military rulers, allowing the moderates to regain power and lead Japan back to its proper place in the world. It was a long-term policy; some British observers concluded that the United States was prepared to maintain it for ten or twenty years.[41] Meanwhile, the United States would continue pressure on Japan through a program of mild economic action characterized by the moral embargo, modest economic aid to China (in March 1940 there was a second commodity loan of $20 million), and a general posture of uncertainty concerning future American actions. There was some danger that such a drawn-out program risked loss of American patience and might precipitate American action that could lead to war, but the American policy managers thought such an eventuality remote.[42]

Hull understood the meaning of power. He would tell his associates of a story from his rural Tennessee days about a man who went to talk with a highwayman and left his guns at home. "I leave it to you," he told his staff, "how that conversation ended." When the secretary argued with the Japanese he was careful to leave the American guns of military and economic sanctions at home. That meant the United States would lose the argument in the short run, but there would be no war, and in the long run an overextended Japan would fail.[43]

Hull felt confident that if he acquiesced in superior Japanese power as he had done in respect to the *Monocacy*, Gulangsu, Tianjin, Shanghai, and the various restrictions Japan had imposed on the movement of American nationals throughout China, there would be no war. State Department officers believed that Japan held a healthy respect for American power and would avoid starting a war over the type of incident that might arise in China. And they were right.

The more dangerous possibility was that Japan might respond to its frustration in China and the uncertainty of the United States as a source of raw materials by expanding into Southeast Asia. It had already shown some interest in that region, occupying Hainan Island and laying claim to the Spratly Islands. The Roosevelt administration had demonstrated that it would not confront Japan over China, but how would it respond to Japanese expansion beyond China? In the winter of 1940 that was a hypothetical question, and Hull did not spend time on hypothetical questions. By the spring, however, it was no longer hypothetical.

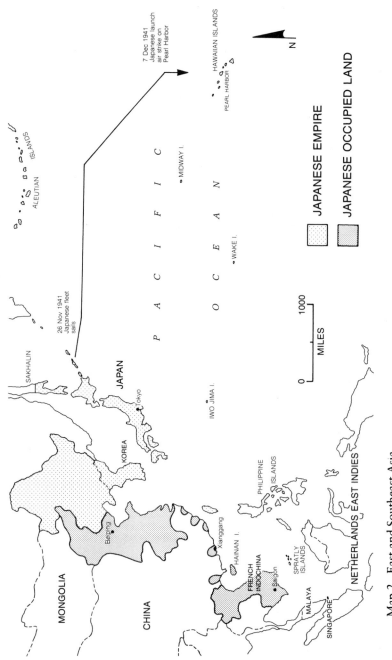

Map 2. East and Southeast Asia

CHAPTER FIVE

NEW CHALLENGES AT HOME AND ABROAD

During the spring and summer of 1940, the tenor of policymaking toward Asia changed in two important ways. First, sweeping German military victories in Europe upset the precarious balance of power in Asia and created the likelihood of imminent Japanese expansion into Southeast Asia. That prospect required a more dynamic response from Washington than had Japanese expansion into China. Second, the collapse of allied forces in Europe prompted the Roosevelt administration to undertake a preparedness program that brought new agencies and administrators to Washington. Frequently unfamiliar with the history or intricacies of Japanese-American relations, these newcomers threatened to tip the balance of bureaucratic power in Washington in favor of the hard-liners. Cordell Hull found he had to cope with a rapidly shifting world and bureaucratic situation, both of which challenged his traditional policy.

To a great extent, the fate of Asia rested on the fortunes of war in Europe. If the German spring offensive, which began on April 9 with attacks on Norway and Denmark, was successful, Britain and France would pull out of Asia, leaving the United States the only power to confront Japan. But even if German armies faltered, there would be little difficulty in their overrunning the Netherlands and making the oil-rich Netherlands East Indies an orphan in search of a guardian, a role Japan was eager to adopt.

It was in this tense situation that, on April 15, Foreign Minister Hachiro Arita declared Japan's special interest in seeing that nothing interrupted the flow of oil from the Indies. On its face, the Arita statement was a call for all nations to respect the status quo of the Indies, but Hull and his staff suspected more devious motives and assumed that Arita was laying the groundwork for stronger action once Germany had conquered the Netherlands. Hull intended to deny Japan that diplomatic high ground.[1]

In two marathon sessions with his staff, Hull reviewed his options, excluded anything that would provoke a confrontation with Japan, such as a naval demonstration, and settled on a strongly worded public declaration that the United States also had economic interests in the Indies and could not ignore any challenge to the independence of that territory. Avoiding the rhetoric of law and treaty, Hull employed pragmatic language, direct and forceful. Whether it did any good or not, Grew noted from Tokyo, it put the United States "squarely on record in this important issue."[2]

European developments soon made Hull's recourse to strong words inadequate. On April 18 the British dispatched an expeditionary force to help Norway. The undertaking was disastrous, and by May 2 the British had been forced to withdraw. Roosevelt and Hull feared that these British reverses would embolden Japan to move into Southeast Asia, and they wanted to prevent that. Note writing was not enough and sending the fleet to Singapore too much. Instead, they decided to transfer the United States Fleet from its base in southern California to Pearl Harbor. Since the fleet was already on its annual maneuvers in the vicinity of the Hawaiian Islands, it was only necessary to keep it there for an indefinite time under the pretext of further fleet maneuvers. Thus, without public fanfare, the bulk of the United States Navy was moved two thousand miles closer to Japan, an act the Japanese were certain to note.[3]

The dramatic Japanese attack on Pearl Harbor nineteen months later has given this decision to transfer the fleet more importance than it warrants. It did not represent a decision for war, or even a willingness to fight Japan. Roosevelt had not ordered a mobilization of the fleet, so it remained understaffed and lacking the necessary supply train of ships for any offensive operation across the Pacific. Fleet commander J. O. Richardson complained that the Japanese knew the fleet was not ready to fight and would not be impressed by its location. But Roosevelt and Hull, convinced that the display of American concern involved in the fleet transfer was having a salutary diplomatic effect on the Japanese, held off mobilization for a later day.[4] Nevertheless, these actions in April and May 1940 were the most assertive the Roosevelt administration had taken during the Sino-Japanese War, and point up how much more important Southeast Asia was to the United States than China.

Some people in the Washington foreign policy establishment worried that Japanese expansion into Southeast Asia jeopardized American access to important raw materials. With the exception of tung oil, China provided nothing the United States could not obtain elsewhere. The East Indies, on the other hand, supplied 90 percent of United States rubber and tin, according to an army-navy study in February 1940. It became commonplace to call Southeast Asia the "arsenal of strategic raw materials for the democracies," producing 37 percent of the world's rubber, 17 percent of its tin, 90 percent of its quinine, and 28 percent of its palm oil products. Hull had emphasized this point when he warned Arita on April 17 that the United States and many other nations had just as great an economic interest in the Indies as Japan did.[5]

Yet when Roosevelt and Hull looked at the Asian situation they took a larger view of the problem. While admitting that the area held important sources of raw materials, the president was quick to note that the United States could survive without those sources. He told members of the Business Advisory Council that the United States could produce the more expensive synthetic rubber, acquire tin from Bolivia, and increase the production of manganese within the United States. Following his boss's lead, Welles echoed these sentiments a few days later in a policy planning meeting within the Department of State.[6]

What really worried Roosevelt and Hull was the loss of whole sections of the world to an autarchic economic system controlled by Germany or Japan. This was a question not of a few supplies, but of the preservation of a world order that had brought unparalleled prosperity for the industrial nations in general and the United States in particular.

Roosevelt had warned of the threat to this system a year earlier, when he lectured reporters that unchecked German or Japanese expansion would adversely affect world trade. Working their laborers long hours for little pay and bartering their products among themselves, the autarchic states would drive the products of free labor from the market. Grew recognized how central this argument was to Roosevelt and Hull's view of Japanese expansion and made it the focus of his "horse's mouth" speech in October. Now, in the spring of 1940, three days after Arita's speech and the day after Hull had sent off a sharp warning to the foreign minister, the president described the nature of the threat as he spoke to the American Society of Newspaper Editors. "Every man, woman and child ought to ask themselves the question: 'What is going to happen to the United States if dictatorship wins in Europe and the Far East?' " he declared. After discussing the danger of Germany dominating the European economy he turned to Asia. "Suppose the Yangzi remains permanently closed to American products, the China treaty ports, Cochin China, Xianggang, Siam, the Straits Settlements, the Dutch Indies?" Roosevelt's message was clear. It was not just the loss of a few raw materials that was at stake, but the destruction of a world economic system that had permitted free commercial opportunity for private enterprise. The specter that hung over a German victory in Europe and a Japanese victory in Asia was the establishment of systems of "economic autarchy" around the world and eventually closing in on the Western Hemisphere.[7]

From this perspective, the challenge of the dictators was neither passing nor superficial but one that struck at the fundamental values of the American people. Maxwell Hamilton tried to explain it to a Japanese diplomat he had known for many years. The American resistance to Japan's New Order was not the result of some policy decision that could be changed, he pointed out—it was based in the most fundamental beliefs of the American people. Americans had come to North America to be free of the political rivalries and oppressions in Europe and for greater economic opportunities. These people believed strongly in equality of opportunity and in the worth of the individual. Those same values were held by present-day Americans, who saw Japan's New Order denying them. American opposition was both fundamental and unalterable.[8]

The connection between human progress and the liberal commercial world order was explicity stated by Will Clayton, a millionaire cotton exporter who had joined the Roosevelt team and was taking the message to the business community. Speaking early in 1941, Clayton put the present crisis in its historical perspective. The world had made tremendous progress in the last century and a half because of the industrial revolution. That revolution established the principle of the division of labor on an international scale and brought about the interdependence of nations. "It was not mere coincidence that democracy commenced to take widespread form at the same time that man's inventive genius enormously speeded up the production and distribution of goods," Clayton reminded his audience. Painting a picture of the economic interdependence of the world, he denounced nationalism, autarchy, isolationism for being "man's stupid attempt to circumvent the law of the machine," a law that demanded "production and more production and the free movement thereof throughout the world." If the dictators won the war, Clayton warned, the tentacles of their control would reach into the vitals of much of the Western Hemisphere as the industrial areas of Europe, working with slave labor, bartering their products for the cotton and other raw materials of South America, Africa, and Asia, destroyed the foreign trade of the United States. "Standing alone in a hostile world, with our foreign trade destroyed, with the colossal readjustments this would entail, and with the enormous sacrifice imposed by total defense, the strain on our traditional way of life would probably be too great."[9]

This liberal commercial perspective on the world did not easily translate into precise policy. Granted that the loss of East and Southeast Asia was too much to be tolerated, at precisely what point did Japanese expansion become intolerable? Should Japanese control of French Indochina trigger a harsh American response, or would it have to wait until Burma, Thailand, and British Malaya had fallen? One reason American policy managers were unable to identify the precise point of no return was that Asian problems had to be related to a rapidly changing situation in Europe. German armies needed only a three-week offensive to drive the British off the Continent. Three weeks more and they had overrun France. With France and the Netherlands conquered and Britain preparing for a German invasion, Japan had its greatest opportunity to extend its New Order throughout Asia. It was impossible for Washington to be fully concerned about Asia when the fate of Europe was so precarious.

At the end of May Roosevelt asked Congress for and received a $1.3 billion military appropriation. In June he ordered the War Department to give Britain more than $43 million worth of surplus military stocks. On June 20 he established what would become his war cabinet with the addition of two Republicans: Henry L. Stimson as secretary of war and Frank Knox as secretary of the navy. Both men were internationalists. Stimson had publicly called for a harder line against Japan, and Knox had concluded that American entry into the war in Europe was inevitable, so the sooner the better.[10]

Hull could no longer maintain the appearance of harmony. Europeanists insisted it was past time for the United States to cut its losses in Asia and concentrate national energies on Europe. Hornbeck scornfully denounced those people as ill informed and lashed out at the entire department, charging that not since 1930 had the United States had a secretariat interested in Asian affairs. Today, he lamented, the Asian specialists within the department were in agreement but the others, a conglomeration of European and Latin American specialists who knew nothing about Asia, wanted it abandoned in favor of Europe.[11]

Hugh Wilson personified every view Hornbeck decried. Since returning to the State Department as an assistant secretary after a stint as ambassador to Germany, Wilson continued his argument that Asia held no important American national interests. Though opposed to using American power to impose a new order in either Europe or Asia, Wilson was more adamant when it came to Asia. An Asian equilibrium would have to come from Japan and China working out—or fighting out—their differences; it could not come from the United States or other Western powers.[12] At the end of May, when the State Department debated the importance of Southeast Asia, Wilson warned his colleagues that the United States could not replace Britain in remote parts of the world. "We are not confronting a period of the nineteenth century but are living in a century where industry and war-like power are growing in various portions of the world, thus making infinitely more difficult the maintenance of a far-flung empire."[13]

A symbol of the split between the Asian and European factions in Washington was the location of the United States Fleet. At the moment it was at Pearl Harbor but many people thought most or all of it should be moved to the Atlantic, where if it was needed it would be needed in a hurry.[14] In the Navy Department, which was most concerned with this question, a dramatic transformation took place in only a few weeks.

Traditionally, Navy had seen Japan as its primary enemy. Britain would secure the Atlantic and help out in the Pacific while the United States would range across the Pacific to do battle with Japan. However, growing German power forced naval officers to divide its attention with the Atlantic. Then, when the European war began,

Roosevelt ordered Navy to undertake aggressive "neutrality patrols" in hemispheric waters, patrols that strained Navy's resources. Still, naval planners concentrated on the Pacific and planned for a war with Japan. As late as the middle of May 1940 R. S. Crenshaw, Naval War Plans Division director, recommended dispatching cruisers to the Netherlands East Indies on a "courtesy call" to impress Japan. But a week later, following German victories, Crenshaw was preparing contingency plans in case the British navy should surrender. By the middle of June talk of confronting Japan had given way to talk of transferring fully one-quarter of the fleet to the Atlantic.[15]

Navy Department officials were not alone in these views. Army officers had never liked the idea of fighting in Asia and had consistently rejected efforts to build up American forces in the Philippines. Any war with Japan, Army believed, would have to be one of attrition, fought with cruisers and submarines, not one of massive confrontation. Transferring battleships and aircraft carriers to the Atlantic was in keeping with this attitude, and Army endorsed it.[16]

From his post in Tokyo, Ambassador Grew sensed that the department was interested in reaching a diplomatic accord with Japan.[17] The ambassador had never given up his belief that the moderates in Japan, if properly encouraged by the United States, could regain control of the Japanese government and guide that nation onto an acceptable course. It was an old story, heard for years: just beneath the surface there existed an important body of moderates who only needed a little encouragement from abroad to wrest control from the military reactionaries. "But now there is something in it," Grew declared. The moderates were hindered by a strong Japanese suspicion that the United States was not interested in reestablishing the old economic ties that had once bound the two nations, he explained. The failure of Grew's effort with Nomura in December 1939 had strengthened this suspicion. What was needed was American assurances that if Japan moved in the direction of peace Washington would respond sympathetically with a restoration of the old relationship. Hull would not have to give any specific promises, just a general assurance that any concrete Japanese offer would not be spurned.[18]

Europe-firsters within the department such as Assistant Secretary Adolf A. Berle, pounced on Grew's suggestion as a reasonable way to withdraw from Asia. It seemed logical to draw Japan away from its aggression by offering "whole-hearted cooperation in commercial and economic development" as soon as Japan demonstrated its good intentions, Berle argued. This would not be appeasement, he hastened to add, but a realistic appraisal of Asian factors.[19]

Six months earlier, the secretary had responded to a similar Grew request with an almost contemptuous assertion that Japan had not shown the proper attitude to justify talks. But the intervening months had brought an increase in the pro-Axis forces in Japan, a disastrous weakening of British power in Asia, and clear signals that Japan intended to expand its New Order into Southeast Asia and the South Seas. In this delicate situation, Hull was quite willing to follow Grew's lead. But this time, Hull made sure Grew only said what he wanted him to say, instructing his ambassador to stress basic issues and make it clear to Japan that just because the United States was talking did not mean Washington had lost its determination to protect American rights in Asia.[20]

At first this diplomatic effort went very well. Foreign Minister Arita showed a particularly cordial demeanor, but within a few days, as he listed specific Japanese interests, the talks ran into a snag. It was apparent that Japan intended to dominate China when the war was over. Meanwhile, if the United States wanted a reapproachement with Japan, the Americans would have to stop giving aid to Jiang, promise to help Japan finance the reconstruction of China, and reestablish normal Japanese-American trade relations.[21]

If Arita's positive demeanor reflected the mood of the moderates, his list of specifics reflected the mood of the militants. As if to emphasize just which group was dominant, the Japanese army and navy proclaimed a new set of orders in China that prohibited every type of anti-Japanese activity, both physical and intellectual, even when practiced by "nationals of third powers." So sweeping were these orders that the American consul remarked that they must be seen as a message to "occidentals, Chinese puppet regimes, Japanese politicians and perhaps even to the Japanese Government itself exactly where the real authority in occupied China lies."[22]

In spite of these setbacks, Hull did not give up on the talks. Instead, he offered Japanese moderates some assurances of future cooperation. To Hull's mind, each nation had a right to protect itself, but that did not give it a right to intervene in the internal affairs of another state or to set up special economic privileges there. Since both the United States and Japan were interested in Asia's trade, neither would accept the subversion of that trade. If Japan was willing to accept peace and free trade in Asia, Hull assured, the United States would look with favor upon economic cooperation with Japan.[23]

Undoubtedly, Hull's offer seemed reasonable to him, as it would to nearly all Americans. He asked only for fair play; Japan and the United States would compete in the world economic arena, neither seeking any special advantage. Such a doctrine of liberal commercialism had served the United States well and Japan had embraced it during the 1920s. But the worldwide depression of the 1930s saw many nations move away from open to closed economic systems. No longer able to rely upon a liberal commercial world order to provide the markets and supplies Japan needed, the Japanese government sought to establish its own sphere of influence throughout eastern Asia, an autarchic system to replace a liberal one.

Foreign Minister Arita did not hide this ambition. "Japan has always advocated free movement of both men and commodities," he told Grew in late June. But this principle "has been frequently violated and Japan has been obliged to undergo bitter experiences. Immigration is restricted, and markets are opened or closed to suit the convenience of the importing countries while the importation of the necessities into Japan is prohibited or limited at will by the exporting countries." Under the best of circumstances, Arita protested, Japan would find such actions intolerable. With the war in China, Japan was compelled to preserve certain special trade relationships with neighboring countries and regions. This was the meaning of Japan's New Order, and Arita reiterated it the next day in a public address calling for a Japanese-controlled "co-prosperity" sphere among peoples related geographically, culturally, racially, and economically. It was a statement that seemed to include Southeast Asia within the New Order.[24]

Hull was not impressed by Arita's complaints of commercial discrimination. He granted that Japan needed access to markets and resources but emphasized that in the long run, the only productive way to assure that access was through the liberal commercial world order, not militarily imposed autarchic systems. Japan's New Order was shortsighted, Hull was convinced. If Japan sought to exploit Asia through conquest it would quickly impoverish the region, and suffer the consequences. But if it sought a peaceful, cooperative economic expansion all of the Asian states would prosper indefinitely.[25] Both the foreign minister and the secretary of state were sincere and neither converted the other.

Hornbeck did not like this whole episode. He did not think Hull should have allowed Grew to engage in such talks and was furious that European specialists were dominating Asian policy. People who did not understand Asia or know Japan believed that somehow two strokes of a pen by two diplomats would, overnight, change a "predatory nation into a contented, peace-loving and peace-supporting power." It was not going to happen, he argued. In fact, Hornbeck held no hope for Japan reforming itself. In a candid memo to Sumner Welles, Hornbeck admitted that he did not believe there could ever be cordial relations between the United States and Japan. Even if the Americans yielded everything in Asia, Japanese fanatical leaders would continue to expand until they were no longer able to do so. What would make Japan abandon its path of aggression? Only when their leaders were convinced they had more to lose than gain by aggression would they change, Hornbeck argued: "They will yield not to persuasion but to fear." He brushed aside Grew's analysis, saying that the ambassador was too influenced by a few aged Japanese who wanted good relations with the United States but who had no influence in Japan.[26]

Though often overbearing, and almost pathologically anti-Japanese, Hornbeck understood what was happening in Washington and adjusted his actions accordingly. If policy managers were interested only in Europe, he would relate the situation in Asia to Europe. "There is an essential unity of aggression on the one side, and whatever is done or can be done against any one of the aggressors is action against the aggressor group," he argued. Unless Japan was stopped it would take the Netherlands East Indies and "sooner or later . . . Australia, New Zealand, Singapore, Burma, India, et cetera; in other words, a Japanese dominated littoral of Asia." The result would be a serious blow to Britain's power in Europe, since it would not be able to draw upon the human and material resources of Asia. The important question, he told Hull, was not what would "Hitler do in regard to the Western Hemisphere after he has made himself supreme in Europe, it is what will Germany *and Japan* do, if and after Germany has become supreme in Europe *and* Japan has become supreme in the Western Pacific and Eastern Asia."[27]

Hornbeck's appeal for aid to Britain in Asia was coordinated with a direct British appeal. Hopelessly overextended in Asia and with the Japanese demanding that they close the Burma frontier to China and withdraw from Shanghai, the British came to Hull with something of their own ultimatum: stop Japan either by transferring the American Fleet to Singapore or applying economic sanctions against Japan, or be prepared for Britain to reach an agreement with Japan.[28]

It was a time of extremes. The Europeanists in the State Department insisted that Hull abandon Asia in favor of Europe, while Hornbeck and the Asianists argued that firm opposition of Japan was more important than ever. The army and navy favored fleet transfer to the Atlantic, while the British threatened to strike a deal with Japan unless the fleet was sent deeper into the Pacific. It was Cordell Hull who charted a course that avoided these extremes.

To the British he responded with one of his patented lectures. Japan had violated many rights. "We all have had to acquiesce in various of them. Acquiescence may be a matter of necessity. Giving of assent is, however, quite another matter." If the British wanted to know what the United States was going to do, Hull declared, they need only look at what the United States had done over the past year.[29] That meant he would avoid extremes of action. Sending the fleet to Singapore was so provocative Hull would not give it serious consideration. Nor would he yield to those who wanted the fleet sent to reinforce the Atlantic, lest Japan misinterpret it as an American retreat from Asia.[30]

While Hull held to his cautious policy of avoiding confrontation, the rest of Washington was alive with activity. Shocked by German victories, the Roosevelt administration began to prepare for war. Ships, tanks, trucks, and planes had to be built. Armaments had to be developed. Massive amounts of raw materials and basic goods had to be stockpiled. All that required planning to assure that the raw materials, tools, and labor were available when and where they were needed. But there had been no planning. In January 1940 the Army-Navy Munitions Board identified twenty-nine strategic or critical materials, items vital to the American defense establishment. Yet as late as May the government had no legal authority to purchase vast quantities of those materials or prevent their export to any nation with the money to buy them, be that nation friend or foe. The only tool at hand was the moral embargo, a clumsy system of questionable legality that relied upon government arm twisting rather than lawful authority to achieve its purpose. What was needed was the power to embargo export of badly needed items and some agency or agencies to advise just what those materials were.[31]

Fearing the consequences of an embargo, Hull had kept the embargo bills bottled up in committee. But toward the end of April the secretary saw the need for legislation to build domestic stockpiles and informed the American Committee for Non-Participation in Japanese Aggression that he would support passage of an embargo

German military triumphs in Europe turned attention away from Asia. Among those who looked to Europe first were William Bullit (Ambassador to France and then Germany), Under Secretary Sumner Welles, Hugh Wilson (Ambassador to Germany and Assistant Secretary of State), and William Phillips (Ambassador to Italy). (File 306NT-127047, NA.)

bill if he was not expected to apply it against Japan. Though far less than they wanted, the committee's leaders recognized that Hull had the power to block any embargo bill he did not like, so they agreed to support the legislation he wanted.[32] With the political alliance formed and with continued bad news pouring in from Europe, the bill worked its way through Congress and Roosevelt signed it on July 2, 1940.

This National Defense Act gave the president authority to declare certain items vital to the national defense and thus eligible for export only under license. Within a year there would be 259 items under license, with exports of most of them limited to "friendly nations." Though drafted for the purpose of helping the preparedness program, the law could be used to wage economic warfare against Japan if the Roosevelt administration wanted to do so.[33]

To oversee the preparedness program, Roosevelt activated the National Defense Advisory Commission (NDAC), appointing some of the best corporate leaders in the nation to head its various divisions. They were to examine the state of preparedness, determine what needed to be done, and tell the president the best ways to achieve those goals. There were seven divisions, each operating independent of the others and enjoying, theoretically at least, equal standing. But in practice, four were the most important: the Industrial Materials Division, run by Edward R. Stettinius, Jr., chairman of the board of U.S. Steel; the Industrial Production Division, under William S. Knudsen, who came from the presidency of General Motors; the Labor Division, directed by "Clear it with Sidney" Hillman, president of the Amalgamated Clothing Workers of America since 1915 and a major power in organized labor; and the Price Stabilization Division, under Leon Henderson, an economist with long service in new Deal agencies. To handle the daily routine of license paperwork, Roosevelt established the Export Control Office, under Lieutenant Colonel Russell L. Maxwell.[34]

The new embargo law, the creation of Export Control, and the establishment of the NDAC were all essential if the nation was going to be prepared to defend itself. But their existence altered the execution of American foreign policy, because these people and agencies were not adequately integrated into the foreign policy establishment. They constituted a gray area not under Hull's control yet still affecting the implementation of national policy. This shift in the bureaucratic power structure within Washington soon made itself felt through a gasoline embargo.

Buried in the third level of the NDAC bureaucracy was Robert E. Wilson. Formerly vice-president for research and development for Standard Oil of Indiana and currently president of Pan American Petroleum and Transport Company, Wilson now served as the executive director of the petroleum group under the Chemical Products Division of Stettinius's Industrial Materials section of the NDAC. While it was hardly a prominent position, he did direct a staff of ten men recruited from the ranks of oil company junior executives, lobbyists, academicians, and scientific researchers. Wilson's job was to find the best way to assure adequate supplies of petroleum. His immediate concern was aviation gasoline.

Wilson's initial examination revealed a serious problem. While there was more than enough aviation gasoline being produced in order to fuel the existent meager air force, to fuel the fifty thousand planes Roosevelt intended to build required a tenfold increase in production. Further study revealed that American refineries could produce enough aviation gasoline if what they produced could be stored. But stockpiling would be impossible as long as Japan continued buying such large amounts of aviation gasoline. It would be necessary, Wilson concluded, to embargo the export of all 100-octane gasoline.[35]

The report sailed through the NDAC with praise from various chiefs, particularly Knudsen and Hillman, who urged prompt action. Stettinius took the study to Roosevelt, who encouraged establishing a program to store vast amounts of aviation gasoline. Thus, by the start of July 1940, Robert Wilson had firmly planted in the president's mind as well as the NDAC and the War and Navy departments that the aircraft building program required the embargo and subsequent stockpiling of aviation gasoline.[36]

Ironically, on the same day that the NDAC had its embargo plan ready to go, Stanley Hornbeck suggested the same thing in the State Department, where the proposal languished. Because officials at State and the NDAC never talked to each other, neither was aware of what the other was doing. NDAC officials did not realize how sensitive an issue the State Department considered a gasoline embargo, and State had no idea of what the NDAC was proposing.[37] Had Hull known what the NDAC was up to, he probably could not have objected, since the legitimate needs of the preparedness program demanded action along those lines. But what began as a legitimate domestic act soon became a major struggle for control of American foreign policy as Secretary of the Treasury Henry Morgenthau, Jr. sprang into action.

Morgenthau was convinced that the German and Japanese aggressor states could be put in their place through economic action. He had never been able to put his beliefs to the test, however, because Roosevelt refused to overrule Hull, who would hear nothing of such talk. But by July the balance of power in the cabinet had changed. The addition of Frank Knox as secretary of the navy and Henry Stimson as secretary of war added two influential voices that would support Morgenthau's anti-Japanese policy. The time had passed for pinpricks and warnings, Morgenthau asserted—it was time for strong economic blows. The pending NDAC plan to embargo aviation gasoline provided the perfect opportunity.

On the night of July 18, Morgenthau outlined his plan to British ambassador Lord Lindsay, Stimson, and Knox. It was a global plan. The British and Americans would embargo exports of petroleum to the aggressor states. The British would destroy the oil fields in the Netherlands East Indies, rendering them useless to the Japanese. Then the British and Americans would combine to purchase all the other petroleum for sale in the world (primarily from Latin America), and the British would bomb the German synthetic fuel plants. While the Germans might get a little oil from the Balkans, Morgenthau believed it would not be enough to permit them to carry on a war. Lord Lindsay was enthusiastic about the plan. Stimson and Knox, less mercurial than Morgenthau, were probably more reserved, but they still encouraged him. He decided to present his plan in cabinet the following afternoon without giving the president or the State Department any prior warning.[38]

The last time Morgenthau had tried to push something by Hull he had waited until the secretary left Washington, then persuaded Sumner Welles to gain the president's approval for the tung oil credit to China in November 1938. This time Hull was again out of the country at an international conference, and Welles represented the State Department at the cabinet meeting on July 19. But Morgenthau found no ally in Welles, who was prepared to accept an aviation gasoline embargo in order to build domestic stockpiles but not Morgenthau's plan, which could very easily provoke a war with Japan. The debate dragged on for two hours. Morgenthau insisted that the democracies had to deny occupied Europe oil. Welles agreed to action vis-à-vis Europe but he pleaded for exempting Asia.[39]

Intrigued as Roosevelt was with the idea of economic warfare (it was not unlike his old quarantine idea), he showed no inclination to approve Morgenthau's plan. By the time the freewheeling discussion ended, Morgenthau was no closer to getting his embargo than he had been when the session began. But neither had Roosevelt vetoed the idea; that was not the president's style. Besides, he was about to begin his campaign for a third term (the nomination was only days away) and Morgenthau's ideas had the support of Stimson, Knox, and eventually Ickes. To flatly overrule four such prominent members of the cabinet would not be prudent. So the issue remained unresolved. Welles could rest easy that the president had heeded his advice, but Morgenthau came away from the cabinet meeting determined to carry on his effort for an embargo.

The situation came to a head the following Monday, July 22. Roosevelt was in Hyde Park when Morgenthau learned from the War Department that Japan was buying all the aviation gasoline and tetraethyl lead it could find on the West Coast. He asked Stimson to send that information to the president while Morgenthau dispatched a written version of his plan to Hyde Park. It made no difference, however, because Roosevelt had already decided to act. Advised by the NDAC of the need for aviation motor fuel and aware of Japanese buying in the West, Roosevelt instructed Welles on Monday, July 22, to place aviation gasoline under embargo "with the least possible delay." The instructions were specific and State Department officials drafted an order for an embargo on aviation motor fuel, tetraethyl lead, and aviation lubricating oils, promptly sending it off to Colonel Maxwell at Export Control.[40]

Up to this point Morgenthau, while very much in evidence, had not influenced the action taken. He had sought a total embargo on petroleum exports but Roosevelt had ordered only an aviation gasoline embargo. But when Morgenthau learned that oil sold to Spain had been transferred to German submarines right on the Spanish docks, he was furious. Convinced that the president liked his plan but was held back by the "appeasers" in the State Department, Morgenthau decided to act on his own. He phoned Colonel Maxwell and told him to change the wording of the draft proclamation State had prepared on Monday, July 22, replacing references to aviation motor fuel with "petroleum products." For good measure, Morgenthau added scrap iron and steel to the list. It was this altered proclamation that went to the president for his signature. Unaware of the small coup Morgenthau had undertaken, Roosevelt signed the document late on Thursday, and sent it to State for the pro forma countersignature and affixing of the seal. Meanwhile it was announced that a gasoline and scrap embargo was being imposed.[41]

Welles learned of Morgenthau's sleight of hand only when he saw the document he was supposed to countersign, and raised a storm of protest. Roosevelt quickly tried to limit the damage done, announcing in a press conference Friday morning that reports of an oil and scrap embargo were incorrect, that it was a matter of licensing certain types of petroleum products and scrap, and that its purpose was to make sure that the nation had an adequate supply of aviation gasoline on hand. Thus, when the cabinet met that afternoon, July 26, Roosevelt had already taken his stand. Morgenthau was going to lose the contest.[42]

At the cabinet meeting there should have been a debate on the merits of economic sanctions against Japan. Instead, there was a dull and tedious debate over what was the most efficient procedure for restricting trade, a topic that bored Roosevelt, who threw up his hands and told Morgenthau and Welles to lock themselves in a room somewhere to fashion a modification. When they emerged, Welles was victorious. The petroleum embargo had been reduced to aviation gasoline and lubricating oil, the original intention of the order Roosevelt had issued four days earlier. Morgenthau's only consolation was that scrap iron remained on the list, albeit reduced to number one heavy melting scrap, which accounted for only one-fifth of the scrap exports to Japan. Given the emotional public debate over American sales of scrap to Japan, it was simply not possible to totally rescind the scrap embargo, and Welles made it as inoffensive to Japan as he dared.[43]

It had been a frantic week, during which the supremacy of the Department of State in foreign affairs had been challenged and nearly toppled. But by the close of business on Friday, July 26, Hull, who had just returned to Washington, could feel confident that those who would force a confrontation through the medium of economic warfare had lost the battle. But it was far from the last battle in this war within the bureaucracy. Even as Welles forced Morgenthau to retreat, individuals buried deep in the bowels of the Washington bureaucracy were establishing a nearly total oil embargo against Japan.

Robert Wilson met with a representative from the Aeronautics Board and one from the Army-Navy Munitions Board to draft a definition of aviation gasoline. They produced two definitions, one "confined to Aviation Motor Fuel and blending stock and the second broadened to embrace these commodities and practically any form of petroleum from which they could be derived." In great haste on the next day, July 27, "the result of our considerations was required," Wilson later recalled. Both definitions were presented and their effect explained. The broader one was chosen and written into the regulations. Though there is no firm evidence who made the selection of definitions, circumstantial evidence indicates that it was someone from the War or Treasury Department.[44]

It took less than a week for Stettinius to discover what had happened and begin revising the definition of aviation gasoline along the lines of the original presidential intention. In doing so he assured Roosevelt that "we regard our responsibility as limited to our domestic economy and anything getting into the territory of international relations is something over which we have no control. We assume that conditions were involved in this decision which are none of our business." Roosevelt agreed and the faithful administrator, in cooperation with officers from the State Department, narrowed the definition of aviation gasoline to include only gasoline of 87 or higher octane.[45]

Setting the octane level at 87 was significant. Since American aircraft burned 100-octane gasoline, the embargo would assure ample supplies of the type of aviation gasoline American aircraft needed. But Japanese aircraft, with less powerful engines, could run on the 86-octane gasoline that remained unrestricted. Thus, Japan was able to buy 550 percent more 86-octane "aviation" fuel during the five months following the embargo than during the five months preceeding it.

Still, Hull regretted even this slight inconvenience to Japan because he worried that it would give Japan "a vestige of excuse for its own actions in the Far East."[46] Hull was thinking about Japan's southern expansion. By late summer, Japan had paused, awaiting the outcome of the Battle of Britain. If Germany won, Japan would be able to run wild over Asia. If Germany failed to beat down Britain, Hull believed combined Anglo-American pressure might restrain Japan. While the outcome of the battle was in doubt, Hull wanted to avoid anything that might provoke Japanese extremists.[47]

This was also the wrong time to disrupt the flow of oil to Japan, because Japan and the Netherlands East Indies were in sensitive negotiations over how much Indies oil Japan would be permitted to buy. Originally Tokyo had sought one million metric tons annually, but as the threat of an American oil embargo increased, Japan raised its demands to three million metric tons. When it was obvious the United States could not be counted on to supply aviation gasoline indefinitely, Japan sought to have 20 percent of the crude oil imported from the Indies treated with enough tetraethyl lead to yield adequate octane aviation gasoline once refined. It was just this sort of deal that Hull sought to avoid.[48]

All of this—the Japanese negotiations with the Indies, the influence of the Battle of Britain on Japan's actions, the whole idea of postponing a conflict in Asia until the situation in Europe had stabilized—was foreign to the people who connived or acquiesced in the imposing of an oil embargo against Japan. With no awareness of the consequences of their actions they nearly succeeded in declaring economic warfare against Japan. Such conflict and maneuvering were not new to the Washington foreign policy scene. Hull had spent many exasperated months trying to control an overly aggressive navy during the first two years of the Sino-Japanese War, and on more than one occasion he had to deal with Morgenthau's machinations. More recently he had seen deep divisions in his own department. But this situation was different. It was becoming increasingly difficult to assure continuity between the policy Hull and Roosevelt established and the actions taken by the proliferating band of preparedness bureaucrats. This time, the policy managers had triumphed. But what would happen next time?

CHAPTER SIX

AN ADMINISTRATION DIVIDED
AGAINST ITSELF

T he second half of 1940 witnessed a major fight for control of foreign policy. On one side was Cordell Hull and his cautious policy of strong words and discreet force to deter Japan from any further expansion. This would buy the time necessary for the European situation to improve and the Asian imbalance of power to right itself. On the other side was a growing number of cabinet members, State Department officers, and preparedness bureaucrats who had decided that the time had come for the United States to show some muscle to Japan.

Hull won most of these battles and thus kept American policy on its traditional course. But the Roosevelt administration remained a government divided against itself. Not only were Hull and his many critics at odds, but the Navy Department developed its own plan of action that had nothing in common with either the moderate policy of Hull or the aggressive policy of the hard-liners. The problem, by the end of 1940, was not the absence of a foreign policy, but too many policies within one administration.

A new government took over in Japan during July 1940. Its prime minister was Prince Konoye Fumimaro, who had held that post when Japan began its war against China in 1937. As foreign minister was Matsuoka Yasuko, who was pro-Axis and critical of the United

States. No sooner had Matsuoka taken office than he warned the United States that while Japan sought world peace, that peace would not be possible if the United States and other Western powers insisted upon the status quo.[1]

Surveying the situation, the recently appointed commander-in-chief of the Asiatic Fleet, Admiral Thomas B. Hart, lamented that "the status of the white man in China has deteriorated since the allied defeat in Europe." Even the usually optimistic Grew had to admit that the teetering process had ended by Japan's moving into the totalitarian camp. Dismayed by the tone of this new government, the ambassador reluctantly concluded that the time had come for stronger American action and gave Washington the "green light."[2]

Amidst all this, Hull held tenaciously to his chosen path, avoiding anything that might bring on a confrontation in Southeast Asia. Hull was soon put to the test when the Japanese decided in July 1940 to expel Western powers from China, forcibly if necessary.[3] The showdown would be in Shanghai.

The weak link in the Western defense of Shanghai was Britain. Preoccupied by its own troubles in Europe, the British government yielded to Japanese pressure and agreed to close the supply road into China from Burma, the famous Burma Road, and to withdraw its last remaining troops from Shanghai. Of the two actions, Admiral Hart considered the withdrawal from Shanghai the more serious, because it would allow the Japanese to control seven blocks in the heart of the Shanghai financial district that housed financial influence that was "a vital factor all over the East" and represented "the last open chink in the 'open' door in China. . . . Further Japanese encroachment into the international Settlement, which would still more imperil its political and economic integrity, is just something which must not happen."[4]

The immediate solution was to have American marines in Shanghai replace the British, a substitution the State Department assumed would be made in consultation with the Japanese. But when the marine commandant in Shanghai announced the American intention to patrol the British sector, the Japanese threatened to send in their own troops to stop the Americans. Unwilling to have American and Japanese troops confront each other, Acting Secretary Welles kept the marines out of the disputed sector and allowed the Japanese-controlled Shanghai Volunteer Corps to dominate the area.[5]

Hull knew that the only responsible way to dispute Japanese control of China was with words. Thus, as he avoided a confrontation of troops in Shanghai he warned Foreign Minister Matsuoka that if Japan did not stop its pressure on American rights in Shanghai, he would unleash American public opinion, which could mean the United States would treat Japanese commerce the way Japan treated American commerce and nationals in China. Though the United States sought friendly relations with Japan, the secretary explained, sometimes "a country thus disposed is forced by the acts of another country into a position in which some sort of positive action in defense of legitimate interests becomes inevitable."[6]

Take these strong statements in conjunction with the gasoline and scrap embargoes of late July and it is easy to conclude that the United States government had been pushed about as far as it would go. A program of economic sanctions was imminent, if it had not already begun. But that conclusion would be incorrect. Hull had not abandoned his opposition to economic sanctions and he still had the power to stop those who favored this newly discovered weapon.[7]

Continually frustrated by Hull's refusal to act and the department's preoccupation with Europe, Hull's capitulation at Shanghai prompted Hornbeck to write a stinging rebuke of departmental policy:

> For 35 years I have been confidently affirming, and during the most recent 8 years I have consistently contended, and I still affirm and am prepared to contend that the United States has a Far Eastern policy. Also I have assumed, I have affirmed, and I have contended that the Government of the United States has a Far Eastern Policy.
>
> I am still convinced that the United States has a Far Eastern policy. I have, however, during the past 8 years been driven toward, and I have during the past 48 hours been forced to the conclusion that the Government has not since 1933 had and that it does not today have a Far Eastern policy.[8]

Hornbeck was mistaken—Hull did have a policy, and it was to avoid war with Japan. But it is easy to see why the hard-liners in the Roosevelt administration thought Hull was allowing the nation to drift. Ickes too was disgusted with Hull. Rather than embargo exports to Japan months earlier when he should have, Ickes complained, Hull continued to pull petals off the daisy. Morgenthau had never given up on strangling Japan and blindly believed the United States could do anything to Japan without risk of retaliation. His simplistic solution was to persuade Indies officials to blow up their oil wells at the first sign of a Japanese invasion. Since that would make the Indies useless, the Japanese would not invade. But would Indies officials really blow the oil wells when they had relatives held hostage in German-occupied Holland? Morgenthau ignored the question. The important thing to remember, he insisted, was that Japan would do what it was going to do and neither conciliation nor sanctions by the United States would affect Japan's actions. Therefore the United States should do what was necessary to deny Japan the resources that fueled its war machine. Was that not right, he asked Hornbeck? He quickly received confirmation.[9]

With Ickes and Morgenthau in the lead and Stimson and Knox offering encouragement, the stage was set for a cabinet-level showdown with Hull. It came in September, when Japan occupied northern French Indochina. The hawks responded by demanding powerful economic sanctions against Japan. Hull would agree only to a new loan for China and to a total scrap embargo (the present embargo was limited only to number one heavy melting scrap.) On the surface it seemed that Hull, though more conservative than the other foreign policy managers in the cabinet, had finally agreed to apply economic pressure on Japan. Actually, he was doing nothing of the sort—the action he proposed was already in the works.

Another loan to China had been approved since July 1940. The delay in releasing the money stemmed not from foreign policy considerations but from a disagreement over who would fund it. Morgenthau wanted Jesse Jones's Commodity Loan Fund to underwrite the loan and Jones wanted Morgenthau to use his own Monetary Stabilization Fund. Neither man was able to overrule the other, and it was not until the events of September brought Roosevelt into the debate that it was resolved in favor of Morgenthau. The China loan Hull agreed to in late September, therefore, was not a response to Japanese expansion into Indochina and would have been enacted anyway.[10]

Much the same story is behind the scrap embargo Hull agreed to in cabinet. But to understand that situation we must once again journey back into the bureaucratic world of the National Defense Advisory Commission.

In July, Morgenthau had won a hollow victory when he had number one heavy melting scrap included under the export licensing program. From July 26, when the licensing began, to September 26, when the full embargo was imposed, Japan obtained license for 563,000 tons of heavy melting scrap. Though Japan was not able to actually purchase or export that much scrap in such a short time, the figures show that the so-called "scrap embargo" of July was nothing of the sort.[11]

These substantial exports were of particular concern to the steel industry and to Leon Henderson, who directed the Price Stabilization Division of the NDAC. Henderson's job was to see that the rapid growth in defense building did not result in serious inflation. There was a real danger that rapidly increasing steel production coupled with large scrap exports could lead to higher scrap prices. Since scrap was an important part of the production of steel, steel producers would either have to raise their prices or reduce their profits. They did not want to reduce their profits and Henderson's job was to see that they did not raise their prices.

The person who kept his eye on all this was Walter S. Tower, executive secretary of the American Iron and Steel Institute and the steel specialist within Stettinius's Industrial Materials Division of the NDAC. (Tower was to steel what Robert Wilson was to petroleum in the NDAC.) Following the figures of production and export, Tower persistently warned of possible scrap shortages and urged placing all grades of scrap under license so that the government could act when a shortage developed. But the crisis was not imminent and his superiors did not approve any action until mid-August, when the scrap shortage Tower had predicted actually materialized. At that time, NDAC representatives met with Morgenthau and Charles Yost from the State Department's Division of Controls. Morgenthau wanted a total scrap embargo, while Yost said State would accept such an embargo only if it was required for reasons of domestic defense programs.[12]

Meanwhile, the steel industry became uneasy. *Iron Age,* its leading journal, noted that the government would not permit the price of steel to rise unchecked. To fix the price of scrap, however, would require fixing the price of pig iron and effectively this would lead to fixing steel prices. The alternative approach was to restrict exports of scrap and let supply and demand keep the price down. Faced with the choice of a scrap embargo or price fixing, the steel manufacturers urged imposition of the embargo.[13]

On August 30, Leon Henderson recommended to Roosevelt that all scrap exports be embargoed. By September 4, Colonel Maxwell of Export Control had drafted the regulations. Morgenthau and Ickes pressed for the embargo but Roosevelt remained perplexed. He did not mind embargoing scrap exports to Japan but he did not want to cut off the British and Canadians too. The embargo was postponed for a week at the cabinet meeting of September 6 to give Morgenthau a chance to work out a system by which Britain and Canada would be able to buy American scrap. Hull intervened to postpone the embargo for another week. He phoned Morgenthau on September 12, the day before the next cabinet meeting, and asked him to wait.

> This whole darn thing is hanging in the balance—if the British go down, then the Japs will probably spread out over all the Pacific just like wild men. If the British hold on, why we'll be able to restrain them and put on additional impediments to them and a loan to China. . . . And now just for a very few days until we see just a little further on that British thing, my judgment is that, glad as I am to go along on this, that it would be best to let it remain just on a day-to-day basis.

Hull's day-to-day basis held through the cabinet meeting on September 13 and the one on September 19. When Japan moved into northern French Indochina, on September 23, Hull dropped his objections and the embargo was imposed. To the casual observer it appeared to be a specific response to further Japanese aggression. But to the insider, those in the iron and steel industry as well as those involved in the decision to impose the embargo, it was a domestic economic measure that had to be imposed sometime. Only its timing hinged on the international situation.[14]

The hawks in the cabinet were not fooled. They understood that neither the loan nor the scrap embargo amounted to meaningful sanctions against Japan and they were not willing to give up. Though they had lost the battle of sanctions when Japan occupied northern Indochina, they had another opportunity just a few days later, when the Tripartite Pact was announced.

The Tripartite Pact, or Axis Alliance as it was called, attracted a great deal of attention both at the time and ever since. Germany, Italy, and Japan agreed to go to war against any nation that attacked any one of them. If the United States went to war against Germany, Japan would enter the war on Germany's side. That established a clear challenge to the United States and it has been common to look at this period as a turning point in Japanese-American relations, the time when the Roosevelt administration decided to take a tougher stand against Japan.[15] Still, it is hard to find any change in American policy following the announcement of the pact.

"Hull took the general line that there was nothing new in the situation; he had assumed that the three powers were acting on parallel lines right along, and that this merely recognized a state of affairs which had existed.[16] Even Stimson, who sought a tougher policy, was not particularly concerned about the alliance, concluding that it represented only what Japan would do without a treaty. "I personally have not been much worried by it and I don't think the president has. . . . So in substance the new arrangement simply means making a bad face at us."[17]

The real importance of the pact was that it served as the basis for another cabinet-level assault on Hull's Asian policy. The first salvo came in the September 27 cabinet meeting, when Secretary of the Navy Frank Knox suggested that a real aviation gasoline embargo be established by reducing the octane limit from 86 to 67. Roosevelt seemed receptive, but Hull quickly intervened to block any serious consideration of such action. Though Hull carried the day and managed to have the question "adjourned for the present," the cabinet hawks had not given up.[18] The next time, Stimson took the lead and he came prepared.

Stimson was buoyed by an article in the August issue of *Amerasia Magazine* that examined the time in 1918 when Japan moved seventy-two thousand troops into Siberia and did not back down until the United States threatened to stop silk imports from and cotton exports to Japan. The moral was that

> Japan has historically shown that she can misinterpret a pacifistic policy of the United States for weakness. She has also historically shown that when the United States indicates by clear language and bold actions that she intends to carry out a clear and affirmative policy in the Far East, Japan will yield to that policy even though it conflicts with her own Asiatic policy and conceived interests. For the United States now to indicate either by soft words or inconsistent actions that she has no such clear and definite policy toward the Far East will only encourage Japan to bolder action.[19]

Supported by the impartial judgment of history, Stimson sent copies to Felix Frankfurter, Supreme Court justice and Roosevelt confidant, Morgenthau, Knox, Stark, and General George Strong, War Plans Division chief. He brought copies to the cabinet meeting on October 4 and gave one to the president (who Stimson said was much interested in it) and even gave one to Hull. For an hour and a half the cabinet engaged in "a red hot debate on the Far East. . . . On the whole it was one of the best debates I have heard," Stimson commented.[20]

Everyone could agree that the United States had to be firm in dealing with Japan; the real split occurred over what action constituted firmness. Predictably, the hawks wanted naval demonstrations and sanctions, while Hull opposed them and held enough power to make his veto stand. The only thing Hull would agree to was Roosevelt's suggestion that the fleet at Pearl Harbor be brought to full strength by adding a supply train of ships and calling up reserves to bring the fleet to full complement. The declaration of the scrap embargo and the reinforcement of the fleet would not cripple Japan but it would send a clear message that Japan could not continue along its present path of expansion without provoking the wrath of the United States. That was not enough to satisfy Ickes, Morgenthau, Stimson, or Knox. Knox took advantage of the call-up of reserves to hold a press conference at which he responded in kind to the truculent language Foreign Minister Matsuoka had been using in Tokyo.[21] This accomplished nothing except to make Knox feel better and to increase the tension between the two nations, which resulted in a brief but severe war scare leading to the rapid evacuation of American nationals from China.[22]

One should not interpret Hull's refusal to act as a sign of indifference. The secretary was deeply upset by Japan's actions but he did not believe sanctions or naval demonstrations were appropriate responses. How angry Hull was with the Japanese is apparent only on the few occasions he permitted himself to speak frankly. One such case was when the Japanese ambassador called on the secretary to protest the scrap embargo.

It was "really amazing" that Japan would criticize the United States for its scrap embargo, Hull said, since Japan had been violating American rights in China for some time. It was "still more amazing" that Japan would call the American scrap embargo an unfriendly act. "Apparently the theory of the Japanese Government is for all other nations to acquiesce cheerfully in all injuries inflicted upon their citizens by the Japanese policy of force and conquest, accompanied by every sort of violence, unless they are to run the risk of being guilty of an unfriendly act." Accusing Japanese leaders of not being content until all of Asia had been "Manchuria-ized," Hull insisted that Germany and Japan "are undertaking to subjugate both of their respective areas of the world, and to place them on an international order and on a social basis resembling that of 750 years ago." As he berated the Japanese ambassador, Hull once again gave voice to the American ideal that Germany and Japan, with their closed economic systems, were not just bandit nations but were returning the world to the Dark Ages.[23]

Clearly, Hull saw the Axis as the ultimate threat. What threat could be greater than setting the world back to the twelfth century? But his strong language did not portend strong action. He held to his policy of not confronting Japan and Roosevelt backed him up. The flurry of activity that followed Japan's actions in September 1940 did not reflect a change of policy. Even after Roosevelt won reelection to an unprecedented third term he remained cautious. At a cabinet meeting in November, when the Japanese embargo came up for discussion, Roosevelt "announced definitely that if we went further in our embargo there was danger that Japan would go out on her own against the Far Eastern possessions of England and Holland, particularly the latter. Apparently this is to be our policy until the Japanese, by some overt act, cause us to change."[24]

This policy was clear even to Japanese ambassador Horinouchi Kensuke, who reported from Washington that in the wake of the Tripartite Pact the United States government would continue its support for Britain and follow a "determined policy toward Japan. However, for the present, the United States will endeavor to avoid war with Japan, and in order to avoid embroilment in a long struggle, she is endeavoring to restrain Japan through strengthening the joint Anglo-American policy." Some in Congress and in the Roosevelt administration, Horinouchi accurately reported, believed that Japan was bogged down in China and that the United States could finish it off. But the majority felt that it would be best to wage the war in Europe first and then turn, with Britain, to deal with Japan. Therefore, the United States would try to avoid putting so much pressure on Japan that it would result in war. However, Horinouchi warned, American officials believed that continued Japanese expansion would lead to continued embargoes with a deteriorating situation and eventually war. The United States was rearming to prepare for this eventuality.[25]

It was this last issue that most worried the ranking officers in the army and navy. They did not shy from war; in fact, Navy was eager to take on the Germans in the Atlantic. But a war with Japan in Southeast Asia and the western Pacific was the wrong war and the war plans these officers developed excluded fighting there. That ran counter to the dominant view within the Roosevelt administration. While the cabinet wrangled over the best way to deter Japanese expansion, both hard-liners and moderates agreed that Southeast Asia and the South Pacific were vital areas that needed to be de-

Unlike his predecessor, William D. Leahy, Chief of Naval Operations Harold R. "Betty" Stark was so interested in stopping Germany that he drafted a war plan that wrote off Asia. (File 208-PU-190-J-1, NA.)

fended. One officer in the War Department's War Plans Division succinctly identified the problem: "The military policy should conform to and be capable of supporting our foreign policy in that region. Conversely, the foreign policy should be such that it can be supported by the military policy. At present, the two are inconsistent; one or the other should be changed."[26] In the fragmented, bureaucratic Washington world, the only person who could bring the diplomatic and military policies of the nation into line was the president, and Roosevelt failed to do so.

In the War Department, Secretary Stimson urged a hard line against Japan, while the General Staff favored withdrawal from the Philippines, a monument to American impotence in the Pacific. Defended by obsolete fighters, airfields too small to accommodate newer American bombers, inadequate antiaircraft guns, and too few troops to hold the beaches against any Japanese assault, the islands' only hope was that Japan would not attack. More realistic army officers recommended "that the United States forces in the Philippines and the Far East be withdrawn at the earliest practicable opportunity and our outpost line be established along the approximate line of 180th meridian."[27]

Withdrawal conflicted with American foreign policy, they knew, but they saw little alternative. To stop Japan required possession and development of extensive strategically located Asian bases, which would "mean the reversal of long established United States' policy as, for example, our refusal to provide an adequate defense of the Philippines." Moreover, to build up those defenses might prove provocative to Japan "and tend to commit us to a policy which the forces available to us will be incapable of sustaining for at least one year." Given the world situation, the War Plans Division declared itself "unalterably opposed to any action which might result in committing us to war in two oceans." Convinced of the wisdom of this policy, the General Staff allowed Philippine defenses to languish.[28] Not until the end of July 1941 would Roosevelt give the War Department explicit orders to make the Philippines impregnable, and by then it was too late.

The conflict between the ends of national policy and the means of military strategy was even more pronounced within the Navy Department, where officers were ready to fight but only in the Atlantic against Germany. Chief of Naval Operations Harold R. "Betty" Stark believed Germany had to be defeated, and that could only happen if the United States was "wholeheartedly in the war." By early October 1940, Stark had concluded that "the United States should enter the war against Germany as soon as possible even if hostilities with Japan must be accepted." If there should be a two-ocean war, Stark planned to let the British worry about the South Pacific while the United States Navy took the lead in the Atlantic.[29]

The tough talk Stark heard coming from the cabinet troubled him. Ickes, Morgenthau, Stimson, and Knox all talking about drawing a line and not letting Japan go any farther implied that the navy would be asked to stop Japan, that is, to fight in the South Pacific. Stark intended to scuttle those plans. Early one October morning he sat down and began working on a plan that would place the Atlantic first and the Pacific second. He worked until two o'clock the following morning, then spent ten days with his staff refining his plan. What emerged on November 4, 1940 was a strategy for waging a two-front war, one that would eventually become the main American war plan at the time of America's entry into World War II.[30]

Stark accepted the same assumptions that guided the civilian foreign policy managers in Washington. Preservation of the integrity of the United States required adequate armed strength, which in turn rested on "the possession of a profitable foreign trade, both in raw materials and in finished goods. Without such a trade, our economy can scarcely support heavy armaments." To achieve that type of world required an end to the autarchic threats posed by Germany and Japan and a restoration of a worldwide balance of power. That was all axiomatic—the controversy arose over the best way to achieve those goals.

The underlying assumption of Stark's strategy was that Europe was the vital theater and that the war in Europe could be won only through the active infusion of American support (he discreetly avoided a call for an American declaration of war.) Thus, a war plan that called for hemispheric defense, an active war against Japan, or even a limited war of attrition in the Pacific were all wrong because they would turn attention and supplies away from the critical theater. The only satisfactory plan was plan D, or Plan Dog, as it was termed: to stand on the defensive in the Pacific while winning the war in the Atlantic.[31]

Simply put, the admiral was saying that when Japan moved against Southeast Asia the United States should not retaliate with military pressure. Southeast Asia and the western Pacific posed such problems of distance, supply, and bases that "the prospective economic costs and losses in manpower present an inescapable total of disadvantage, such that the war aims to be achieved would have to be of extreme importance to permit the expectation of a net ultimate advantage to the United States." Better for the United States to stand aside, even though to do so would mean that American political and military influence in Asia "might largely disappear until after we had defeated Germany."[32] Such were the hard choices the men charged with waging war had to make.

But Stark's choices were not those favored by civilian policymakers in the Roosevelt administration. Both groups agreed that ultimately, Japan's New Order could not be tolerated throughout the region, but Stark argued that in the short run no harm would be done to the war effort against Germany if Southeast Asia and the South Pacific were abandoned. The civilians thought differently.

Secretary of War Stimson favored sending naval reinforcements to the Philippines as a way of supporting "that vital point of defense, Singapore." Secretary of the Navy Knox declared that the way to stop the Japanese was "to match them movement for movement." Hornbeck warned that if the British naval base at Singapore fell, Japan could isolate and subdue China, deny the United States important raw materials, and deny Britain access to the human and material resources of the region, resources Britain must have to undertake the liberation of Europe from Nazi domination. Granting that Germany was more important than Japan, Hornbeck concluded that the best way to defeat Germany was to secure southern Asia for the British war effort. This was the same argument the British made in naval staff talks during December and January.[33]

Eloquently and at great length, the British argued for a strategy of active defense of Singapore and southern Asia. To abandon it was unthinkable for moral reasons. Bound by kinship and obligation to the peoples of its commonwealth and empire, Britain could not simply turn its back on them. More pragmatically, the British admirals argued that the loss of the region would be a serious blow to their ability to continue the war. It would deny Britain food, raw materials, and troops, as well as munitions, ship-building, and aircraft plants. China would be cut off and collapse, while Russia might even join the Axis. Burma and India would be transformed from a center of resources into a liability. In the long run, if Japan dominated the region "our morale and prestige, especially among the peoples of the East, would suffer a resounding blow, and those of the Axis Power and Japan would be correspondingly enhanced, with almost incalculable consequences both during and after the war." For these reasons, the British claimed "that the loss of Singapore would be a disaster of the first magnitude, second only to the loss of the British Isles."[34]

American naval officers acknowledged that Singapore was vital to the maintenance of the British Empire and support of the commonwealth, but they refused to agree that the empire or commonwealth were important to the outcome of the war. This conflict stemmed from two different approaches toward warfare. The British, with their long history of sea power and relatively modest population, had always preferred a war of attrition in which the enemy was worn down before engaged in direct land combat. (The First World War had been an exception—the British would not make that mistake again.) The United States, with its large population and massive industrial resources, thought in terms of massing its forces and crushing the enemy in full combat. If Germany was the prime enemy then the navy should seek out that enemy and defeat it, not whittle it down.[35]

Throughout the talks, American naval officers would not deviate from Stark's Plan Dog. There would be no transfer of the fleet to Singapore, no reinforcements of the Asiatic fleet, no sprinkling of American ships around the world. If the British wanted to protect Singapore they could send their own navy to do so and the Americans would look after the Atlantic. Even as he put off the British, Stark went to Roosevelt and obtained a presidential directive that the United States Fleet would stand on the defense in the Pacific and not reinforce the Asiatic Fleet.[36]

Neither the outcome of the Anglo-American staff talks nor the Roosevelt directive endorsing the essence of the Plan Dog strategy ended the debate or brought foreign policy and military strategy into harmony. Hull continued to assume that Japanese expansion into Southeast Asia would warrant a forceful American response, while the developing war plan presumed that in case of a war there would be no attempt to defend that region. The civilians were prepared to lead the nation into war over a territory that the war plans refused to defend. This was not the result of different branches of the government not knowing what each was doing. Communication among the State, War, and Navy departments had never been better—Marshall, Stark, and Welles met regularly to exchange information. But communication did not result in coordination.[37]

The problem was jurisdictional. Roosevelt and Hull were in charge of the foreign policy of the United States. They would determine the type of world the United States would seek to establish, which nations were friends and which enemies and even, at times, what specific action should be taken. But when they moved from the diplomatic arena of grand strategy into the area of naval strategy and even tactics they ventured on a domain naval officers jealously guarded. Stark could accept the presidential policy that the Axis had to be defeated, but when civilians began claiming that the best way to defeat the Axis was to protect Singapore they were no longer talking of foreign policy but of naval tactics and strategy. Stark might have to accept that from Roosevelt, the commander-in-chief, but not from Hornbeck, Knox, or any other civilians in his administration. If the civilian-military split over Asian policy was going to be resolved, Franklin Roosevelt would have to provide the leadership.

Roosevelt was at his worst when he had to coordinate conflicting views of foreign policy. That was apparent as early as the fall of 1937, when he gave his Quarantine Speech and sent off Norman Davis to the Brussels Conference to accomplish great things, only to have Hull undercut him. Since then, the conflicts had only increased. Now Roosevelt found himself with a foreign policy that endorsed the vital importance of Southeast Asia and a military strategy that ignored the same region, and he did nothing to bring the two into balance. Issuing conflicting orders, telling different people different things, Roosevelt permitted the nation to move along in two mutually exclusive directions.

For example, Roosevelt approved the Plan Dog strategy on January 16, assuring Stark that the navy would stand on the defensive in the Pacific and there would be no naval reinforcement of the Philippines. Yet at the same time, the president authorized the commander of the Asiatic Fleet to withdraw from the Philippines at his discretion and move either east toward the United States or west to Singapore. Moving the Asiatic Fleet to Singapore was totally out of keeping with Plan Dog. And to make the matter more confusing, Roosevelt ordered the navy to consider the possibility of bombing attacks against Japanese cities, an undertaking far beyond the idea of Plan Dog, not to mention the navy's ability at that time.[38] Moreover, five days later the president sent Ambassador Grew a ringing defense of the vital nature of Singapore. Drafted by Hornbeck for Roosevelt's signature, the letter had been prompted by Grew's request of the president for some guidance. Roosevelt signed Hornbeck's letter without changing a word—perhaps without even reading it. Grew was gratified to read that his thinking and the president's were "closely in line."[39]

Eugene Dooman, counselor of the American Embassy in Tokyo, who was home on furlough at the end of 1940, also concluded that Roosevelt would not tolerate a Japanese attack on Malaya and Singapore. When he returned to Tokyo in February, Dooman tried to convey to the Japanese vice foreign minister the extent of the American commitment. The United States was determined to help Britain win the war, he explained, and was therefore increasing aid for Britain. Since Britain depended upon its lifeline to the commonwealth to continue its war effort, "it would be absurd to suppose that the American people, while pouring munitions into Britain, would look with complacency upon the cutting of communications between Britain and British dominions and colonies overseas." With a note of incredulity the vice foreign minister responded, "Do you mean to say that if Japan were to attack Singapore there would be war with the United States?" To which Dooman replied, "The logic of the situation would inevitably raise that question."[40]

As was so often the case, when it came time to act, Roosevelt was much less decisive than he had led his staff to think. The test came with dramatic suddenness on February 4. Intelligence reports reached Washington that Germany had abandoned its plan for an invasion of England and was instead trying to starve the island kingdom by cutting off its supplies. Part of this strategy involved pressuring Japan to cut the British supply line in Southeast Asia. These reports alarmed Roosevelt, who summoned Hull, Stimson, Knox, Stark, and Marshall to the White House for a two-hour discussion of world strategy.

Hull thought it important to deter a Japanese move and urged the transfer of some American ships into the western Pacific. As might be expected, Stark objected strenuously, reiterating the arguments he had put forth in his Plan Dog strategy and asserting that to move units of the fleet farther west would be a "grave strategic error."[41]

Though Stark's arguments triumphed that day, no one was certain what Roosevelt ultimately had in mind. The president supported Plan Dog, but he also sympathized with Grew when the ambassador stressed the importance of holding Singapore. The problem was that Grew did not have the solution, and neither did Roosevelt.[42] Consequently, he provided no strong leadership, vacillating between relying on diplomatic warnings and employing naval demonstrations.

Meanwhile, the diplomatic and naval branches of the government remained locked in stalemate. Hull could not overrule Stark and have the navy move further across the Pacific and Stark could not overrule Hull and have the navy withdraw to the Atlantic. On one occasion, Roosevelt and Hull suggested a cruise of some American warships through the South Pacific. Stark responded with a bolder plan, a secret "courtesy call" of American aircraft carriers to Vladivostok, announcing the cruise only when they were already north of the Japanese home islands. Roosevelt liked the idea, but Stark was not serious. He had suggested the cruise only to shock Hull and intended to cancel his cruise if Hull would cancel the southern cruise. The plan worked. Stark "had a broad inward smile when the State Department, in effect, said: 'Please Mr. President, don't let him do it.' "[43]

The failure to coordinate diplomatic ends and military means was typical of the chaos that plagued foreign policy management in Washington during 1940–41. But it was more than a bureaucratic embarrassment. A policy that declared Southeast Asia vital but was incapable of defending it could not be an effective deterrent to Japanese expansion and to war. Dangerous as this gap between the diplomatic and military branches of the government was, it paled in comparison to the dangers that sprang from the administration of economic questions. Stark's Plan Dog would not cause a war but economic sanctions could, and the number of people in Washington who thought in terms of economic pressure was growing so rapidly that Hull and Roosevelt were in danger of losing control of this critical aspect of American foreign relations.

CHAPTER SEVEN

BATTLE OF THE BUREAUCRACY

As the 1940 presidential election approached, Cordell Hull made it plain that he did not intend to continue as secretary of state in Roosevelt's third administration. He was angry at "having Morgenthau or somebody else spring a fast diversion in foreign policy over his head, and finding that the President stood by some favorite. If he could get assurance that this kind of thing would not go on, he would stay."[1] Whether or not he got those assurances, Hull did stay and so did the problem. But it was not Morgenthau who would cause Hull most of the trouble, it was a growing number of administrators scattered through the ever-expanding Washington bureaucracy. As a result, a gap developed between policy articulated at the top and actions taken at lower levels. Though official policy said there would be no confrontation with Japan, the army of administrators charged with overseeing the defense preparedness program was eager to impose the type of economic sanctions against Japan that would lead to war. These men knew nothing of the intricacies of diplomacy or of the delicacy of the situation. They were energetic, intelligent, and convinced that what they sought was in the best interest of the country. Moreover, many of them believed that the State Department was "replete with budding Chamberlains, Daladiers, and Hoares" (references to the European diplomats who had sought to appease Hitler).[2] On particularly important challenges Hull could appeal to the president, who invariably supported his secretary of state. But most of the time the issues were too small to bother Roosevelt. Hull found himself spending more and more time slapping down challenges to his policy of nonconfrontation. To understand how the battle went it is necessary to look at some specific examples—which means descending into the convoluted world of the Washington bureaucracy, vintage 1940–41.

Machine-tool exports to Japan never captured headlines as scrap and gasoline exports did. Nevertheless, machine tools were an integral part of any defense industry, and an embargo on them would hurt Japan. In July and August 1940, first the NDAC and then Export Control questioned selling Japan machine tools. In both cases the State Department reaffirmed its policy of restricting exports of machine tools to Japan only if they were needed by the American munitions program.[3] It was a policy that irritated some within the department, especially Herbert Feis, chief of the Economic Affairs Division, Joseph Green, chief of the Division of Controls, and his assistant chief, Charles Yost. Those men favored sweeping economic sanctions against Japan, but failing in that area they turned their attention to embargoing machine-tool exports.

Controls (not to be confused with the Export Control office under Colonel Maxwell, which was an independent agency) was an administrative office originally concerned with the export of munitions but now involved in the export of all types of restricted materials. As chief of the division, Green was a fifth-level State Department officer, behind the secretary, under secretary, several assistant secretaries, and advisers on political affairs (Hornbeck's rank.) Because his division was administrative rather than policymaking, Green had less influence than his fellow division chief Maxwell Hamilton, of FE. But his modest position did not stop Green from trying to move the nation in a direction he thought appropriate.[4]

He began by adding to the licensed list those machine tools used to manufacture aircraft, claiming that the decision conformed to the meaning of the moral embargo against export of aircraft to Japan. Then, with Hornbeck's support, he tried to get all machine tools embargoed. By the end of October it seemed as if he might be successful, but Hull stepped in and put an end to Green's plans. Still, Green did persuade Hull to accept an embargo on the export of certain machine tools especially useful in the armaments industry. The action could be justified by the growing need for such machine tools in the United States but it also kept Japan from becoming self-sufficient in this area. Whichever motive was foremost in Hull's thoughts, the secretary took pains to see that the directive, once approved by Roosevelt, was applied gradually "in order to dispel any thought of the action being directed at any particular country."[5]

As the machine-tool case shows, it is very difficult to determine why some items were embargoed. Clearly there were those in the Roosevelt administration who wanted to cut off the sale of machine tools to Japan because they hoped to make Japan falter in its aggression. Just as clearly, Hull had no intention of confronting Japan. Whether the hard-liners wore down Hull's resistance and gained small triumphs or whether Hull accepted trade restrictions only when justified by reasons of domestic necessity is impossible to tell with accuracy. Probably something of both factors was involved. What is clear is that lower-level officers in the Roosevelt administration and the secretary of state often worked at cross-purposes. The more agencies that were involved, the more convoluted the conflict became.

The issue of copper well illustrates the total absence of central direction within the Roosevelt administration. Copper was a vital raw material for any war effort. It was mined widely in the United States and in Chile; American economic planners looked upon both sources as secure. But if the government embargoed the export of copper produced in the United States, Japan would immediately buy all the Chilean copper, both denying that source to the United States and making Japan self-sufficient in its own copper reserves.[6] So if the United States wanted to stockpile its own copper it had to buy Chilean copper as well, and that required dealing with the Metals Reserve Company, a government corporation directed by Jesse Jones, head of the Federal Loan Agency. Jones was a hard-working administrator who had no understanding of economic warfare and no interest in it. As a result, any restriction on copper exports involved a tangle of conflicting bureaucratic pressures.

At the end of December 1940, Russell Maxwell, the administrator for export control, urged the immediate restriction of copper exports from the United States. Aware of Hull's reluctance to impose sanctions against Japan, Maxwell agreed to support licenses for the reexport to Japan of South American copper. A sense of urgency was added when the chief of naval operations related Navy's interest in keeping Japan from getting the twenty-five thousand tons of copper believed to be available in Chile.[7] Though the State Department and Export Control could reach agreement, Jesse Jones delayed the purchase by continuing to haggle over the price. Nothing State did could get Jones to act and by February 1941 Feis warned that unless Metals Reserve bought the Chilean copper "*now,*" Japan would buy up all future amounts. Feis strongly urged a program to preclude Japan's purchasing more than normal—i.e., prewar—amounts. "Japan is acting as a buying agent not only for itself but for Germany," he added ominously.[8]

Rather than acting, Jones asked people to stop using "terms such as 'preclusive buying' or 'economic warfare.' "[9] Not until late February, when Jones realized that the United States would have to buy Chilean copper in order to reach its stockpile quotas, did he begin to buy. Then he moved with a vengeance, pressuring American companies to exercise their preemptive clauses and cancel contracts for sale of copper to Japan in favor of shipment to the United States. This went too far for Hull's cautious policy and the State Department again intervened, this time trying to restrain Jesse Jones and have him defer contracts rather than cancel them. It amounted to the same thing in the long run but the style was much less belligerent, and that was important to Cordell Hull.[10]

Though the copper purchase program did preclude Japan from buying much Chilean copper, it did not amount to the aggressive program of preclusive purchasing that Feis wanted. He hoped to keep Japan from building stockpiles that would make it immune to future American economic sanctions. Hull endorsed this idea so long as it did not involve anything blatant or extreme—that is, so long as it did not risk a confrontation with Japan—but he did nothing to implement it until June 1941, and even then Jones refused to act until he had Roosevelt's written "O.K. FDR." On June 12, 1941 the first program of preclusive purchasing began—almost four years after the Sino-Japanese War commenced, nearly two years after the United States abrogated the Japanese-American commercial treaty, a year after the Roosevelt administration acquired flexible embargo powers, and nine months after the Tripartite Pact was announced. Even then it was intended only to limit Japanese purchases, not stop them altogether.[11]

One person who recognized the lethargic state of the American economic warfare program and intended to do something about it was William Y. Elliott. Professor and former head of the Department of Government at Harvard University, and an outspoken interventionist with considerable experience in Washington, Elliott was a consultant to the Industrial Materials Division of the NDAC. By the fall of 1940 he had come to the conclusion that the problem in the defense preparedness program was inadequate centralization of authority, and became an active proponent of a new cabinet-level Department of Defense Supplies, which would have full authority over priorities and allocations, licensing of industries and export control, price controls, procurement of military supplies, negotiated contracts, and labor policies.[12]

Elliott urged establishment of a formal program of preclusive purchasing to keep Japan from buying cobalt from Canada, mercury from Mexico, chromium from the Philippines, and carbon black from the United States. He readily admitted that the United States had those items in abundance and that his program was intended to keep Japan weak. Preventing Japan from stockpiling cobalt, he declared, "would be worth several keels in our battle fleet." Certain that the State Department would never provide the necessary leadership, Elliott sought to bypass that department by creating an advisory committee on preclusive purchasing. State would be represented, as would the departments of War, Export Control, the Treasury, and others, but the committee would be chaired by someone from the NDAC; someone committed to a program of economic warfare.[13]

The fact that such a program of economic warfare violated the foreign policy Hull had established and Roosevelt had endorsed gave Elliott not the slightest pause. He proceeded to push his ideas through the NDAC, where they received much praise. Stettinius said Elliott's plan on "economic warfare is splendid." Following Roosevelt's reelection he brought it before the NDAC and was "completely successful in stirring up the whole Commission on the matter of economic warfare." Stettinius then redrafted Elliott's proposal for submission to the president. Less specific (and less candid) than the original Elliott draft, the NDAC proposal that went to Roosevelt on November 27, 1940 argued that a smaller, more efficient committee was needed to control economic warfare. Though it did not specify who would run the committee, the State Department's role was given skimpy treatment, a fact painfully obvious to its officers, who had no intention of letting the NDAC get away without a fight.[14]

Roosevelt did not immediately crush the NDAC's obvious power grab. Instead he returned the proposal for specific suggestions how the new agency might be organized. Before anything could happen, Roosevelt streamlined the NDAC in December, transforming it into the Office of Production Management.[15]

But Elliott would not give up. Early in 1941 he drafted a six-page, single-spaced memorandum urging his comrades in the OPM not to let the president forget his plan. The disastrous course of world events made access to supplies still more uncertain and stockpiling even more crucial, he reminded his colleagues. Moreover, the flow of goods to Japan left the "Pacific backdoor . . . wide open to an evasion of the British blockade" by Germany via transshipment through the Soviet Union. The State Department lacked the knowledge of industrial materials to understand economic warfare, he contended. "I cannot conceive that had that Department understood in the full the economic importance of cobalt to the Japanese war effort and perhaps to the German, it would have permitted two or three years supply to go through over our objections. I think it is merely a matter of not understanding that this material might be worth several battleships to Japan's war effort in the future." To stop such egregious errors, Elliott urged the establishment of a new agency to oversee economic warfare. Meanwhile, he said, "we should . . . act far more freely in this field."[16]

The time for action had passed. Elliott remained an outspoken and persistent enemy of the compliant policy Hull insisted upon, but he could not persuade his superiors to challenge that policy. NDAC chiefs had been excited by Elliott's early recommendations, but once the president had made clear his opposition to a program of economic warfare through a new agency, the NDAC staff was generally content to accept the ruling and follow orders. Only Elliott persisted, and he was an exceptional person who found himself increasingly restrained or ignored by his superiors. Moreover, with the reorganization of the NDAC into the OPM, Stettinius's Industrial Materials Division, which had been the center of economic warfare planning, became less important as Knudsen and Hillman rose to positions of prominence.[17]

No sooner had the NDAC/OPM bureaucratic coup failed than Hull faced another challenge, this time from Russell Maxwell, administrator for export control. Maxwell began his assignment in July 1940 with the rank of lieutenant colonel. He quickly rose to colonel, then brigadier general, and with his rise in rank he sought to expand his influence in the field of economic warfare. Originally his office was a purely administrative post intended to handle the licensing of exports. But Maxwell expanded his empire, annexing the small group studying economic warfare in the army's Industrial War College. Though as late as December 1940 he gave assurances that his agency was not a policymaking body, the new year and evidence that the OPM would not engage in economic warfare brought a different emphasis. By January Maxwell was talking about the parallels between economic and military warfare. He began measuring the impact of various embargoes against Japan, ostensibly as part of war plan preparations. By spring his staff concentrated on preclusive purchasing and other forms of economic warfare that preceded military conflict.[18]

At the end of April 1941 Maxwell was prepared to make his move, just as the NDAC had done the previous November. He proposed creation of a policy committee consisting of second-echelon officers from the departments of State, Treasury, and Justice, and the OPM. The idea found little if any support within the Roosevelt administration. Though it would mean a stronger policy toward Japan, even such a cabinet hawk as Morgenthau saw that its primary purpose was to further the influence and career of General Maxwell.[19]

In "attempting to encompass the entire field of economic defense," Maxwell had reached too far, and on May 2 Roosevelt cut him down. The president denied Maxwell control over the economic defense program and subsumed his office within the Office of Emergency Management. Maxwell lingered on, continuing his studies of Japanese economic vulnerability, until Roosevelt removed him from his post in September, ending one more challenge to Hull's control of foreign policy.[20]

A different kind of demand for stronger economic pressure on Japan came from the British, who were concerned about two factors: Japan buying strategic goods, which it shipped to Germany via the Soviet Union, and large Japanese purchases for stockpiling purposes. Both these problems could be resolved by imposing a system of rationing rather than a complete embargo. If a joint system of export controls led to closer Anglo-American cooperation in Asia, so much the better, from the British point of view; but not to State Department officials.[21] They were suspicious that Britain intended to lure the United States into a position where it would have to protect British interests in Asia, and particularly upset by the British willingness to bypass State and go directly to the NDAC, Export Control, and the Navy Department. Moreover, it seemed to many in the State Department that what Britain had in ample supply it was not interested in restricting. Hence, Britain would sell Japan the rubber it needed, but the United States would restrict export of the carbon black Japan needed to turn that rubber into truck tires—the British empire would sell iron ore and manganese to Japan, but the United States should ration the sales of the cobalt used to turn those materials into high-grade steels.[22]

Hull was not interested in doing Britain's dirty work and had no intention of imposing economic sanctions against Japan. However, those in the State Department who had been urging economic action against Japan (Green, Yost, and Feis in particular) took advantage of the British requests to press for restrictions, even to rallying support within the NDAC, Treasury Department, and Export Control. Moderates in FE urged caution and Hull refused to issue a blanket order. However, he was sensitive to the charge that Japan was buying for Germany, and by mid-June 1941, each of the sixteen items the British claimed had been going to Germany through Japan had been restricted. In some cases, as with carbon black and beryllium ore, Roosevelt had to personally intervene in order to get bureaucrats to deviate from their instructions and embargo exports of commodities in ample supply.[23]

Such minor restrictions were pinpricks that did nothing to stop Japan's aggression. The single commodity that would change the situation was oil and Hull personally saw to it that the flow of oil continued unabated. It was a task that required constant vigilance, because to those within the Roosevelt administration who saw Japan as the enemy and economic sanctions as the effective weapon at hand, oil exports to Japan were a national disgrace. The monthly rate of petroleum exports to Japan rose by one-sixth during the second half of 1940. Even more disturbing was the amount of gasoline going to Japan. In 1939 Japan had imported 1.2 million barrels of American gasoline. In the six months following the aviation gasoline freeze, it imported 3.4 million barrels, most of it near the 86 octane limit.[24]

These statistics, Japan's occupation of northern Indochina, and its joining of the Axis prompted another round of debate in the Roosevelt cabinet as hawks once again tried to staunch the flow of oil to Japan. Hull had won those fights in September and October 1940, but it was an endless battle; no sooner was one challenge overcome than another appeared. The next came from the British government, which feared that Japan was building such large oil stockpiles that it

The most outspoken opponent of oil sales to Japan was Petroleum Coordinator for National Defense Harold Ickes. (File 208-PU-98K-12, NA.)

would soon be relatively immune to any economic sanctions the Western powers could impose. Aware of Hull's opposition to any action that might appear hostile to Japan, the British suggested that restrictions be imposed by denying Japan access to tankers. Many American-owned tankers, flying under Liberian or Panamanian flags, were in the Pacific trade and might be persuaded to take their business elsewhere. Since Japan was already ordering more oil than it could transport in its own ships, the Anglo-American restrictions should prove very effective.[25]

British leaders had every reason to think the United States would endorse their plan. It would work, and it was relatively safe, since it did not involve an open break with Japan and by permitting normal, peacetime amounts of oil to reach Japan it would avoid provoking Japan to strike against the Indies. The British also timed their proposal to coincide with what they thought would be a newer, stronger policy following Roosevelt's election to a third presidential term.

Green, Yost, and Feis supported the British plan, but Hull resisted and FE followed the secretary's lead. In Japan's present frame of mind it would not take much to push it toward a rapid expansion against the Indies, and Hamilton concluded that "pending a clarification of the situation in Europe," such a Japanese move should "be prevented if at all practicable."[26] Perhaps because his department was so evenly divided on this matter, Hull did not reject the British proposal; he simply ignored it. In January the British were still waiting for a reply to their proposal, originally delivered to Hull in November. As massive amounts of oil flowed to Japan each week, the British grew impatient and approached the Navy Department directly, then asked Hull bluntly whether he intended to apply the tanker-control measures. Such tactics were ineffective. Hull had been operating in Washington too many years and felt too strongly about this issue to be swayed by either British or bureaucratic pressure. The most the British could extract was an agreement in principle to reducing exports to normal, prewar amounts; and Hull never did honor that agreement.[27]

What eventually compelled the Roosevelt administration to pull American-owned tankers out of the Pacific was American opposition not to Japan but to Germany. By the spring of 1941, German submarines were sinking British merchantmen faster than they could be built. "It is . . . not their financial difficulties which gives me most concern," Assistant Secretary of State Adolf Berle confided in his diary, but their "appalling" shipping losses. Roosevelt and his aides concluded that in this time of crisis American shippers could no longer enjoy the luxury of having their foreign-registered ships engaged in the lucrative Pacific trade when those ships were desperately needed in the dangerous North Atlantic run. Under orders from the president, the National Maritime Commission gave American shipowners a choice of "voluntarily" cooperating with the government by shifting their foreign-registered ships to the Atlantic trade or seeing strong government controls established. Roosevelt gave his orders on February 10, and by the end of March the Maritime Commission had persuaded owners to transfer two hundred ships into the Atlantic trade.[28]

Even before this, Japan's shortage of tankers prompted it to buy gasoline in steel drums and sometimes containers as small as five gallons. Seeing an opportunity to hurt Japan, hard-liners urged that the drums and containers be placed under licensing. Keeping to its traditional policy, FE (with Hull's blessing) agreed to accept such restrictions only if they were necessary for domestic economic reasons. Export Control, with discreet help from some State Department officials, was able to find such a basis by arguing that a shortage of tin as well as drums would occur if these items were not added to the restricted list. The embargoes were imposed, but were only a minor inconvenience to Japan.[29]

As oil sales to Japan continued, more and more voices were raised in protest. Henry Morgenthau and Harold Ickes railed against the trade, Vice-President Henry Wallace wrote Hull about it, Congress considered legislation to stop it, and the Washington bureaucracy increased its efforts to do something about it.[30] State's Division of Controls was the first to act.

When it came to oil exports, Controls had a mind of its own. Before Japan signed the Tripartite Pact and occupied northern Indochina in late September 1940, Green and Yost tried to have the definition of aviation fuel reduced to 70 octane. There was little chance they would be successful, since Hull, Welles, Hamilton, and the European Affairs Division of the State Department were all opposed to further restrictions on oil sales to Japan. When Hull faced down the cabinet hawks in late September, Yost understood that the cause was hopeless "for the present."[31] But these activists did not change their feelings, and by the spring of 1941 they were beside themselves with anger over the amount of oil flowing to Japan.

Fearing a total American embargo, Japan had obtained licenses for more than nine million barrels of gasoline, far more than it could physically export in a short time, and it was buying as much 86-octane gasoline as it could lay its hands on. With so many licenses outstanding, Yost suggested that Export Control establish a new and more comprehensive definition of aviation gasoline "*at once*." Then all existing licenses would be turned in for reissue under new regulations that would restrict Japan to two-thirds of its average imports during 1935–39. Yost's plan died just like all the rest of Controls' schemes. The proposal came at a critical point in Japanese-American negotiations, and Hull would not accept any move toward economic sanctions as long as the talks continued. The only action Controls was allowed to take was to withhold granting any more oil export licenses, an action that had absolutely no impact on Japanese purchases because of the large number of licenses Japan had already acquired.[32]

Hull was not opposed to denying Japan huge stockpiles of critical materials. But there was a vast difference between the way Hull approached that desired goal and the way Yost, Hornbeck, Feis, and other hawks did. Hull, and the majority of State's officers, favored "attrition of Japan's energies and resources by steps undertaken gradually on a basis designed to obviate creating the impression that they were in the nature of overt acts directed primarily at Japan." That was simply Hull's policy of non confrontation put into practice. Small, unobtrusive (and therefore ineffective) measures could be taken, but a restriction on the sale of oil to Japan went far beyond what Hull would accept. To embargo oil, Hamilton explained, would only encourage Japan to move into the Indies, and that would increase the likelihood of American involvement in Asian hostilites. Hornbeck did not agree, but his protests had no apparent effect. Nor did the rantings of Henry Morgenthau, who loudly denounced Hamilton as the key obstructionist "over there." Welles wanted to lower the octane level of restricted gasoline and so did Hornbeck, Morgenthau complained, but Hamilton was blocking it.[33] We can assume that Hamilton's influence was so formidable because he spoke with Hull's blessing.

While Hull managed to keep a tight rein on his own staff, he had more difficulty with other agencies, such as Export Control. That office was eager to add all lubricants to the embargo, not just aviation lubricants. Aware of Hull's opposition to any provocative action against Japan, Export Control suggested that the restrictions could be imposed while retaining the appearance of the old system so as not to disturb "certain people." Nor was Export control prepared to put the idea in a memorandum and simply send it over to the State Department, where it would surely die. Instead, it broached the matter to various agencies at a meeting within Export Control on April 23. The representative from the Army-Navy Munitions Board opposed the proposal, while the representative from the Tariff Commission endorsed it as a step to stopping all petroleum exports to Japan. That a representative from the Tariff Commission would actually debate the application of a total oil embargo against Japan is a shocking example of how many people in Washington thought they had some role to play in the conduct of American foreign relations. In this particular case, State's representative reported that Secretary Hull asked that petroleum products not be disturbed in any way and specifically that the subject be dropped "right now until the Secretary gave them the word." The matter was promptly tabled.[34]

If Hull could intimidate Export Control, he had little influence over Harold L. Ickes, long-time secretary of the interior and more recently petroleum coordinator for national defense. In that capacity Ickes was supposed to assure proper domestic supplies of oil, but he was sickened by the massive exports of oil to Japan and decided to do something about it. In June 1941, Ickes proposed to General Maxwell of Export Control that oil sales to Japan be cut off. Once again Hull intervened, but this time felt it necessary to bring Roosevelt into the dispute.

The president supported his secretary of state and chastised Ickes that oil exports were a very sensitive issue intimately involved with the conduct of foreign affairs and "so much a part of our current foreign policy that this policy must not be affected in any shape, manner or form by anyone except the Secretary of State or the President." By attempting to foster a different oil policy with the administrator of Export Control, Ickes was tampering with a foreign policy question that was "peculiarly entrusted to the President and under him to the Secretary of State," who were the only ones adequately informed to make decisions on foreign policy.[35] It was a point well taken, but one that was increasingly ignored by the Washington bureaucracy.

Thus, Hull found himself the moderate surrounded by militants. But his moderation was only relative. The secretary shared the dominant view in Washington that Japan was a bandit nation seeking to carve an empire out of Asia for purely selfish reasons and that it was totally unjustified in calling for a revision of the world order. Hull differed only as to when and how Japan should be resisted. He did not favor confrontation over China and he did not favor confrontation over Southeast Asia until the European situation should have improved. Thus, in July 1940 to June 1941, the first year he had the embargo power, Hull used it conservatively. While many commodities had been restricted, there was nothing approaching a structured program of economic warfare against Japan. Most of the embargoes were legitimate attempts to preserve badly needed supplies. A few were designed to prevent Japan from purchasing for Germany.

What Hull was willing to do, Hamilton explained in April 1941, was "to maintain a firm position in the Pacific and gradually to increase our pressures upon Japan and our aids to China." That reflected a change. The previous July Hull had thought the aviation gasoline and partial scrap embargo had gone too far. Now, eight months later, Hull was prepared to accept a program of preclusive purchasing. Yet in both circumstances Hull was guided by the intense desire "not to become involved in armed conflict with Japan at this time." As Hamilton explained, "It is of course regrettable that Japan has as large supplies of various commodities as she now possesses. But accumulation of those supplies cannot with warrant be regarded, it is submitted, as great an evil as certain other developments, such as war at this time with Japan."[36]

It was on this final point that Hull and his fellow moderates disagreed with the militants Hornbeck, Feis, Green, and Yost in the State Department and Morgenthau, Ickes, Knox, Stimson, Maxwell, Elliott, and others throughout the Washington bureaucracy. The militants thought the continued sale of supplies to Japan foolish at least and criminal at most. Blindly believing the United States could impose economic sanctions on Japan with impunity, or asserting that since war with Japan was inevitable nothing was gained by continuing to sell to Japan, the hawks pressed for action that would have pushed Japan and the United States into war. As long as Hull remained vigilant and was able to outmaneuver the militants, the United States would not force Japan into a choice between surrender and war. But one slip, one oversight on Hull's part and a small group of eager administrators, ignorant of the consequences of their actions, might ram through an economic sanction that could push Japan into a decision for war. Morgenthau had almost done that in

July 1940 when he tried to sneak through a gasoline embargo. It could happen again.

If Washington foreign policy managers could agree on anything, one might think, it would be the desirability of giving China enough aid to keep it in the war against Japan. Since December 1938 small, morale-boosting loans to China had helped tie down one million Japanese troops in China. During 1941 aid flowed more easily, including the establishment of the clandestine air force known as the Flying Tigers. But much of this support was illusory; small in amount and late in arrival, American aid to China was pathetically meager, just enough to keep China fighting. Rather than as an ally fighting a common enemy, the Roosevelt administration treated China as a pawn whose inexhaustible manpower would be sacrificed to keep Japan from moving into the important region of Southeast Asia.

The ususal way to sustain Chinese morale was to give China a loan whenever diplomatic or military news was particularly depressing. One loan was given in September 1940 upon the announcement of the Tripartite Pact; another was prepared in November, when Japan formally recognized, as the only official government in China, the puppet resigme of Wang Jingwei.[37] Hull had long dropped his opposition to loans and by 1941 he was willing to let China use the loan money to buy military equipment. The important thing was to keep China fighting. It was this change in attitude that permitted the rise of the American Volunteer Group, or Flying Tigers.

Originally, Hull had denied passports to Americans who sought to begin such service. But by the fall of 1940, Hull was approving passports to American pilots headed for China and actively endorsed the sale of military aircraft to China. This came as good news to the Chinese government, which had sent a delegation to win just such support. Headed by Claire Chennault (who would become famous as the leader of the Flying Tigers and during World War II as the commander of American air forces in China), the delegation walked the corridors of power in Washington to garner support for a five-hundred-plane Chinese air force.[38]

Morgenthau wanted to sell China bombers to reach out and blast Japanese cities and he tried to enlist Hull's support in this scheme. To Morgenthau's amazement, Hull had no objection, even saying he wanted to get five-hundred American planes to start from the Aleutian Islands and fly over Japan just once to teach them a lesson.[39] Morgenthau took Hull's flight of fancy too seriously and thought he had an ally when the secretaries of state, war, navy, and treasury gathered just before Christmas 1940 to discuss the matter of planes for China. But Hull said nothing at that meeting and the War Department shot down Morgenthau's bomber proposal.

Army Chief of Staff George C. Marshall bluntly told Morgenthau that diverting two dozen four-engine bombers from Britain to China in order to bomb Japanese cities was not a sound plan. The planes would all be destroyed in a month, he declared the damage done to Japanese cities would be small, and the British would have to put off strikes against important European targets. War Department's strategy did not envision bombing Japanese cities but providing China with enough pursuit planes to interfere with Japanese withdrawal from China. If that could be accomplished, Marshall argued, there would be "a big result in the vicinity of Singapore."[40] Once again, Europe came first, and American strategy called not for confronting Japan but for containing it. Many in Washington were prepared to fight Japan to the last Chinese soldier, it appeared.

Though lip service was given to the creation of a Flying Tigers group in China, it came about only slowly. Gradually during the spring and summer of 1941 pilots and mechanics were recruited and moved to China. But they remained small in number—fewer than 100 pilots and mechanics by September—and their supplies were inadequate.[41] The problem was that while everyone supported the idea of helping China no one wanted to give up anything to make that aid a reality.

Meanwhile, the United States threw its entire industrial capacity behind the anti-Axis struggle. In the spring of 1941 Congress enacted the Roosevelt program of lend-lease by which the United States would give certain countries the supplies they needed on credit. To find out what China required, Roosevelt sent White House aide Lauchlin Currie on a fact-finding trip to China. Currie returned two months later with glowing reports of China being at a crossroads between dictatorship and democracy.[42]

The immediate problem was getting aid to China. And to quote a Treasury Department study, "without strong support from policy making authorities, it is apparent that little action on Chinese requests by production and service representatives can be expected."[43]

To bring the bureaucracy into line with policy, Roosevelt asked Currie to coordinate supply efforts for China. Perhaps somewhat naively, Currie tried to reason with government supply officials. It was important for China to receive aid, he explained, because "Singapore is the key to the Indian Ocean, Australasia, and Oceana. It is as indispensable to the continuation of Britain's war effort as it is to Japan's dominance of the East." The best way to defend Singapore was to dispatch the fleet, but since that seemed unlikely, the only other way was to deter a Japanese move south by building up the Chinese air force, which could then threaten the flank of any Japanese southern thrust. Such arguments appealed to the Army-Navy Joint Planning Committee not because they thought Singapore so vital but because the plan obviated any need for Army or Navy to secure the region. The JPC endorsed the idea of the Flying Tigers.[44]

Currie's clout and the JPC endorsement were not enough to get anything done in Washington. Persistent obstructionism by low-level Washington bureaucrats easily blocked this national policy. At one point the assistant director of purchases in the Office of Production Management blocked the purchase of supplies for China on the grounds that the Burma Road was not adequate for transit, China had not repaid earlier loans, and the goods sent to China might fall into Japanese hands. His opposition was only overcome when Hornbeck drafted and Hull sent a stern reprimand that it was not the responsibility of the assistant director of purchases in the OPM to make policy or to question a "policy of this Government as made known clearly and repeatedly by those officials who have authority to declare and have declared the policy of this Government."[45]

Prying ammunition for China out of the army was even more difficult. For example, China needed .30 caliber bullets for the P-40 fighters it was receiving. Though the British were supposed to supply that ammunition, they never did, and the War Department said it had none to spare. Fighter planes without bullets were clearly useless, but nevertheless Marshall informed Currie on June 15 that there would be no .30 caliber ammunition for China. Currie appealed to Roosevelt's confidant, Harry Hopkins "If we don't get the ammunition over there there will be an international scandal and we might as well forget the rest of the lease-lend program for China. . . . I have come to the conclusion that the only hope is a directive from the President." Welles added his support to this cause and Hopkins urged Roosevelt to press for at least a token shipment to China. By the start of August, Army gave in. Noting that the president had directed some ammunition be sent to China and no one else was going to do it, Army agreed to a token shipment of one million rounds of .30 caliber ammunition and half a million rounds of .50 caliber.[46]

Yet it was impossible to get a presidential directive for everything on the Chinese shopping list, and without that clout little aid flowed. What supplies were available usually went to Britain first. In July 1941, for example, the Roosevelt administration authorized nearly 821,000 tons of aid to Britain, while shipping China barely 16,000 tons, 2 percent of the British share. Put more graphically, for every ton of aid shipped to Britain, the United States gave China forty pounds.[47] These figures simply reflected the dominant fact in Washington life that Europe was more important than Asia. The army was especially adamant on that point, and no amount of pleading from Hornbeck or Currie could alter its opposition.[48]

During World War II and since, Americans have assumed that the United States was heavily involved in China's effort to stop Japan even before the Japanese attack at Pearl Harbor. Such Hollywood films as *Flying Tigers,* starring John Wayne, have helped to perpetuate that myth. In reality, American aid to China was minimal. Even the Flying Tigers, which only consisted of a handful of planes, never saw combat before December 7, 1941.[49]

Though Hull managed to stave off the assaults launched by the sanctionists within the bureaucracy, Japan and the United States were sliding toward war. By the end of 1940, both Japanese and American diplomacy had backfired. Beginning in the spring of 1940 with Hull's stern warning to Japan about the status of the Netherland East Indies, the Roosevelt-Hull policy had consisted of a series of actions and statements designed to deter Japan from its southern expansion. The transfer of the fleet to Pearl Harbor in May, the aviation gasoline embargo in July, the loan to China and the scrap embargo of September, and the reinforcement of the fleet and the sudden withdrawal of American nationals from China in October combined to give Japanese leaders the clear message that Washington would defend Southeast Asia.

Japan was not deterred. Instead, it felt encircled and redoubled its efforts to move south and establish control over the resources and markets of the South Seas. Meanwhile, Japan sought to deter a confrontation by negotiating the Tripartite Pact. Since the pact called for Germany to declare war on the United States if the United States attacked Japan, Matsuoka hoped to deter Washington from confronting Japan as it pushed south. The wish in Tokyo was not to get into a war through the Tripartite Pact, but to avoid one.[50] Unfortunately, the pact only hardened the resolve of the hawks in the Roosevelt administration.

Deterrent diplomacy failed during 1940 because each power concentrated on threatening the other while doing nothing to allay the fears of the other. Tokyo, feeling encircled by a coalition of Western powers led by the United States, clung to its New Order. Washington, believing that Japanese domination of the South Seas and Singapore posed an intolerable threat to its own vital interests, warned then threatened Japan, but offered nothing constructive other than Hull's assurances that adherence to the dogmas of liberal commercialism would eventually solve all of Japan's problems.

In the spring of 1940, Hull had high hopes that Japan was hopelessly bogged down in China and that the combination of continued Chinese resistance and American diplomatic pressure would eventually bring Japan to its senses. By year's end he was still convinced that Japan was waging a losing battle in China, but he was no longer sanguine about the future. Even as it struggled in China, Japan demonstrated that it was hell-bent on expanding throughout Asia and nothing the United States said would deter it. Sanctions would bring on an early war; diplomacy would do no good. So Hull waited for the war in Europe to end, for Japan to stumble, or for war with Japan to come. When the commander of the United States Fleet asked the president if the United States would fight if Japan continued its expansion, Roosevelt responded that the nation would not fight over Thailand, Malaya, the Dutch East Indies, or even the Philippines, but the Japanese "could not always avoid making mistakes and that as the war continued and the area of operations expanded, sooner or later they would make a mistake and we would enter the war."[51] Roosevelt and Hull could see the war coming, they just did not know what to do about it.

CHAPTER EIGHT

REACHING FOR THE MOON: THE HULL-NOMURA TALKS

By 1941 war with Germany was inevitable. Having given up on a diplomatic solution to the German threat, Roosevelt placed the industrial power of the United States behind Britain and the naval resources of the nation against Germany in the Atlantic. By February, a 159-ship Atlantic Fleet was conducting increasingly aggressive "neutrality patrols." To Chief of Naval Operations Stark, "the question as to our entry into the war now seems to be when and not whether." He predicted it would come as early as April.[1]

The unanswered question was what Japan would do once the United States and Germany were at war. Japan had already capitalized on British and French weakness; might it not also try to take advantage of American preoccupation with a war against Germany to run wild over the Pacific or, even worse, attack the United States? Stark thought war with Japan could be avoided, but Hull was not so sure. After all, the Tripartite Pact, which Japan had signed the preceding September, called upon Japan to declare war against the United States if it attacked Germany or Italy. Since the conflict with Germany was not open to diplomatic solution the only possibility of avoiding war with Japan was to convince it to abandon its alliance with Germany and stop its program of southward expansion. That was not likely until moderate Japanese replaced military expansionists, which seemed a futile hope.

Then something remarkable happened—Roosevelt and Hull heard the startling news that Japanese leaders were prepared to abandon their policy of military expansion in favor of a path of peaceful commercial expansion characterized by the idea of the Open Door. The message came from the unlikely source of two Maryknoll priests, Bishop James E. Walsh and Father James M. Drought. The two men had recently returned from Japan and the story they told Roosevelt and Hull on January 23 bordered on the fantastic. In ordinary times the president would have thanked the priests for their efforts and perhaps, if they were lucky, encouraged them to continue their talks with Hull or one of the secretary's associates in the State Department. The entire interview would have lasted barely longer than the fifteen minutes for which it was originally scheduled. But these were not ordinary times, and as Roosevelt and Hull listened the interview grew to one hour and then two, and when it had ended the president and Hull wanted to hear more.[2]

Drought and Walsh claimed that American defense measures, economic pressure already applied, and pressure that could still be applied had convinced many Japanese leaders that Japan's national interest was no longer served by a policy of forceful expansion. In short, American warnings had worked. Japan, the two priests maintained, was prepared to make an abrupt change in its foreign policy. In return, Japan would require economic assistance from the United States as well as Western power recognition of Japan's special interest in East Asia (something similar to the special interests granted to the United States under the Monroe Doctrine.) In respect to China, Japan was allegedly prepared to withdraw as soon as the Chinese government could maintain order and would cooperate with Japan to suppress communism.

The problem in implementing all this, Drought and Walsh explained, was the opposition of the well-entrenched militarists. It would be necessary to negotiate in secret until a complete agreement had been reached. Presented with a fait accompli, the extremists in Tokyo would lose face and lose power, and the transformation would be complete.[3]

Many questions remained to be answered. What did Japan mean by a "special interest in East Asia"? Was cooperation to suppress communist activities a euphemism for continued Japanese occupation of China? Were the Japanese moderates really strong enough to overpower the extremists who outwardly, at least, dominated Japan's government? Admittedly, the Maryknoll fathers had good contacts in Japan, but had they properly interpreted what they had been told in Tokyo, or was their optimism born of wishful thinking?

"What do you think we should do?" the president asked Hull. True to form, the secretary turned to his associates for their considered opinion. They gave him only depressingly negative reports. "It seems clear that Japan's military leaders are bent on conquest—just as are Germany's," came the response. What Japan really wanted was a face-saving withdrawal from China that would allow it to "extend and accelerate" its southern expansion. "Results of a permanent value" had to come through a "regeneration" from within, not just a Japanese withdrawal from China. The Drought-Walsh proposal was not to be trusted.[4]

Hull rejected this advice. Putting aside his deep suspicion of Japan, he suggested to the president that Drought and Walsh should not be discouraged in continuing their efforts and that when the new Japanese ambassador, Nomura Kichisaburo, called on the president to present his credentials Roosevelt and Hull should talk to him about the matter. Roosevelt readily agreed. He and Hull were willing to gamble that the experts were wrong and that a diplomatic solution was possible.

A year earlier Grew had urged his government to take just such a gamble and offer Japan a small, symbolic concession following his talks with Nomura, then foreign minister. Hull had turned a cold shoulder to the proposal, arguing that he did not want to raise Japan's hopes for a settlement when there was no indication that an agreement was possible. But the intervening year had brought the fall of France, the signing of the Tripartite Pact, and increasing American involvement in the Atlantic, with war against Germany a probability. In that situation the fact that no one thought there was much of a chance of reaching a settlement with Japan was not a major obstacle to making the diplomatic effort. If there was just one chance in a hundred of averting a war with Japan, it was worth the effort.[5] From Hull's perspective, moreover, there were two international crises in the world, and only the Asian one was even remotely susceptible to diplomatic action. If he did not try to reach a settlement with Japan, Hull and his State Department would be relegated to the long-range planning and paper shuffling that characterized State during wartime. Partly because it was the only game in town, and partly because the world was on fire, Hull entered into the "Hull-Nomura talks."

When the president received Nomura on February 14 he wore a

During the spring of 1941, Hull devoted most of his time and energy in the search for an agreement with Japan. (File 59-JB-Hull-5, NA.)

"long face" to impress upon the ambassador the seriousness with which he viewed the deteriorating state of Japanese-American relations. After warning the ambassador of the risks in further expansion and in alliance with Hitler, Roosevelt invited Nomura to sit down with Hull and see "if our relations could not be improved."[6] During the next three weeks, an anxious Secretary Hull prodded Nomura to discuss "the questions which call for settlement by mutual agreement." But when Nomura met again with Roosevelt and Hull on March 14, there was still no indication of any Japanese interest in conducting talks. Hull, his patience wearing thin, bluntly told Nomura that if serious discussions were to take place, Japan had to make clear its interest in participating in them.[7]

These American overtures produced nothing, because Nomura had not come with instructions to reach a settlement with the United States. Assurances that Japan was prepared to abandon its expansionist policy were the product of Drought and Walsh's hopeful wishes, not a realistic assessment of Japanese feeling. The people who mattered in Tokyo had no interest in a settlement on anything other than Japan's terms, and by April Roosevelt and Hull's restrained pleas for talks were about to die for lack of Japanese interest. But Ambassador Nomura, like his counterpart in Tokyo, Ambassador Grew, was willing to take a chance rather than see the United States and Japan slide into war. The opportunity to break the impasse came on April 9 when Drought, Walsh, and two Japanese in Washington (dubbed the John Doe associates because they were never identified by name in the negotiations) submitted a draft proposal for reconciling all the outstanding differences between Japan and the United States: the status of China, the form of trade relations, the policy toward the European war.[8] At any earlier time during the Sino-Japanese War, Hull would have rejected the statement out of hand. It came through unofficial or at best semiofficial channels and it proposed terms that one American analyst characterized as having "all the marks of deception." But the document purported to have the support of moderate elements within Tokyo and Ambassador Nomura had associated himself with it. It also appeared at a most propitious time.

On April 3 Roosevelt had finally yielded to his secretaries of war and the navy and agreed to transfer substantial portions of the Pacific Fleet to the Atlantic. That would embolden the militarists in Tokyo and make a diplomatic settlement virtually impossible to achieve. Perhaps it was only coincidence, but the day following the April 9 draft proposal Roosevelt reversed himself and decided to leave the fleet at Pearl Harbor for the time being.[9] Roosevelt's decision gave Hull some time to see what he could do through negotiations, but it was also clear that speed was essential. Hull could no longer allow the situation to drag on. Unsatisfactory as it was, he had to begin his talks on the basis of the April 9 draft. Since Hull assumed that peace in Asia could come only if Japan was prepared to change its ways, the fundamental question was whether Japan was sincerely interested in doing that.

As the talks began, Hull set a firm yet not hostile tone. He described the liberal commercial world order and how once it was established all nations could be assured of equal access to markets and raw materials. He also identified four underlying principles on which that liberal commercial world order rested.

1 Respect for the territorial integrity and the sovereignty of each and all nations;

2 Support of the principle of noninterference in the internal affairs of other nations;

3 Support of the principle of equality, including equality of commercial opportunity;

4 Nondisturbance of the status quo in the Pacific except as the status quo might be altered by peaceful means.

If Japan could accept these, he told Nomura, an agreement would not be a problem. If Japan rejected any one of them, an agreement was not possible. With painstaking care, Hull explained to Nomura (whose English was poor) that if Japan was willing to accept the four principles, the United States was prepared to begin informal talks, taking the April 9 draft as a starting point.[10]

Hull had made his position clear and set the direction for the talks to follow. It was a path that could only end in failure. Hull's sine qua non for a settlement was Japan's abandonment of its New Order and return to the liberal commercial values it had accepted in the 1920s. It was asking too much of Japan. Hull could not establish a liberal commercial world order and until he could there was no hope of Japan abandoning its autarchic program. The transformation Hull desired would not occur until after Japan was ravaged by war and occupied by American troops and in a different world economic setting than 1941. To think that such a change could be brought about through honest talk and promises of economic cooperation, even if coupled with threats of economic sanctions, was to reach for the moon. The best diplomatic efforts on both sides might have fashioned a modus vivendi that might have prevented the outbreak of war in 1941 if it did not establish a lasting peace. But a comprehensive agreement along the lines Hull sought was unachievable, and a grave tactical error on his part. Yet when we examine Hull and the mood within the State Department at that time, the decision to seek a comprehensive settlement seems inevitable.

Cordell Hull had demonstrated that he could be flexible when he had to be, standing firm at one moment and backing down at another. But he was never happy dealing with limited problems; he was much more at home dealing with the underlying concepts and the fundamental questions of international relations. Given the choice, he would rather seek to end war and establish a real peace than merely treat the symptoms of a world at war. The John Doe associates' April 9 draft suited Hull's mood and temperament perfectly. It sought a fundamental agreement, one that would sweep away all the outstanding differences between the two nations and establish a lasting peace. It would be so fundamental and so sweeping in its scope that Japanese leaders would be unable to interpret it to suit themselves. This was important, because Hull, like everyone else in Washington, believed the Japanese were not to be trusted. Any agreement that was vague, open to interpretation, or limited in application was of little value. If the Japanese could work their way around it they would.[11]

Hull's insistence on a comprehensive agreement or none at all worried Nomura, who understood that his government was not prepared to accept the four principles Hull laid down as a sine qua non. That would mean an end to the talks, and that, he feared, would mean war. To avoid this, Nomura reported the four points to his government but also sent back the April 9 draft prepared by the John Doe associates as if it had been drafted at the State Department. Thus, the diplomatic negotiations began with a fundamental misunderstanding. What Hull saw as a partially acceptable proposal coming from individuals associated with the Japanese Embassy the Japanese government saw as an American proposal. When later negotiations found the United States demanding terms beyond those contained in the April 9 draft, it appeared to the Japanese that the United States was escalating its demands, and this misunderstanding undermined what little moderate influence there was in Tokyo.[12]

For the next ten weeks Hull, oblivious to all this, engaged in a fervent effort to find common ground for an agreement. He and Nomura held sixteen secret meetings, usually at Hull's apartment in order to avoid publicity. Again and again they went over the diplomatic ground to see if it was solid enough to support both nations. The talks failed. They never came close to being successful. But they offer a wonderful opportunity to see what Cordell Hull considered important, how much he would give up to preserve peace between Japan and the United States, and who was actually in charge of United States policy toward Asia during the spring of 1941.

This last question was quickly answered, when Hull kept the talks to himself. Welles was not involved—for the most part he was not even briefed on their progress. Secretaries Knox and Stimson remained in the dark; Stimson did not even know the discussions were going on until mid-May when he read summaries Nomura had sent to Tokyo that American intelligence had intercepted and decoded (a system called MAGIC.) Though the president was briefed on the progress of the talks, he rarely participated in them. To a remarkable extent this was Cordell Hull's show, and he intended to keep it that way.[13]

The talks quickly focused on two issues: the status of China and the Axis Alliance. On China the point of contention was withdrawal of Japanese troops. Japan insisted that the Chinese government must cooperate to suppress Communist activities in China and Japan must be permitted to retain some troops in China to cooperate in this anti-Communist operation. Hull believed that such a foot in the door would be a way for Japan to make peace in China without actually withdrawing or giving up any of its gains, and he emphatically told Nomura the United States would not accept an agreement that simply allowed Japan to extricate itself from its disastrous China campaign. Hull insisted there must be specific language stipulating the removal of all Japanese troops from China and not retaining any under the guise of maintaining order or suppressing Communists. China had been tying down Japanese armies nearly four years and Hull was not going to do anything to let Japan out of that mess unless it was a total, and therefore humiliating, withdrawal.[14]

The secretary's intransigence on this issue reflected less a devotion to ideals than a practical assessment of the situation. The American principle of nonrecognition, proclaimed by then secretary of state Henry Stimson in 1932 when Japan conquered Manchuria, prohibited Hull from recognizing any gains acquired through force or the threat of force. A Sino-Japanese settlement that left Japan in control of Chinese territory was a violation of that principle. Yet throughout the negotiations, Hull made it clear to the Japanese (as well as to Stimson) that Japan could stay in Manchuria but would have to give up everything else in China proper.[15] If this was a stand on principle it was a very selective application of that principle.

A more convincing explanation for Hull's position can be found in the prevailing departmental view that before there could be peace with Japan, moderates would have to cast out the military expansionists who sought to establish Japan's New Order at bayonet point. The word used within the department was *regeneration.* Hull hoped such a regeneration might take place if four years of fighting in China produced only a profitless and humiliating withdrawal for Japan, thus shaking the military and strengthening the moderates. Since Japan held Manchuria before the Sino-Japanese War began, allowing it to keep that province would do nothing to ease the humiliation the military must suffer before it could be overthrown. On the other hand, a face-saving withdrawal from China (one that would leave Japan in control of some areas of China conquered since 1937) would release Japan from its unwinnable war in China while leaving the same military expansionists in control of Japanese foreign policy. It was because Hull wanted to bring about a change within Japan, not because he was slavishly following the nonrecognition doctrine of 1932, that he insisted upon an abject Japanese retreat from China.

This does not mean Hull was a totally pragmatic and unprincipled statesman. Quite to the contrary, he was a person of great principle and rigid singlemindedness. But the principle he clung to was more fundamental than respect for the nonrecognition doctrine or friendship for China. Hull believed that the prosperity and progress of the United States and all the nations of the world were inextricably linked to the establishment of a liberal commercial world order. Stimson's nonrecognition doctrine was a means to that end. When it served its purpose, Hull would honor it. When, as in the case of these negotiations, it stood as an obstacle to peace, Hull was prepared to ignore it.[16]

The most telling criticism of Hull's negotiations over the issue of China was that he was reaching too far. He demanded Japanese withdrawal from China because it would break the power of the army in Tokyo. For that same reason, the Japanese army leaders would never accept a settlement on those grounds. But Hull did not moderate. The more the extremists gained power in Tokyo, the harder he pushed to have them toppled. The harder he pushed, the more they dug in their heels in resistance. During May and June the talks made no progress.

As the talks dragged on, Foreign Minister Matsuoka Yasuko showed himself to be an implacable enemy to Hull's policy by moving Japan closer to the Axis. On May 9, he cabled Nomura a truculent defense of Japan's involvement in the Axis, a note that Nomura wisely withheld from Hull but that Hull was able to read through the medium of MAGIC. The official Japanese reply to Hull's comments of a month earlier, which arrived on May 12, said nothing to make Hull optimistic.[17]

Nor was there encouraging news at home. This was the time when Feis pushed for a program of preclusive purchasing against Japan and Export Control was trying to expand the scope of the aviation gasoline embargo. When Secretary of War Stimson read of the talks in mid-May, he was "rather horrified" by the "terms of the negotiations."[18] Predictably, Stanley Hornbeck denounced the talks as a sham, pointing out that the May 12 Japanese draft offered much less than the original April 9 draft.[19]

Hull did not have much trouble handling such criticism. He was helped by the secret nature of the talks. Most members of the administration did not know they were going on and those who did had to keep their thoughts to themselves. While Stimson might be "rather horrified" by the terms Hull was offering Japan (presumably because Hull was disregarding the nonrecognition doctrine Stimson had authored in 1932), it was not a fit subject for debate in a cabinet session. Hornbeck, too, represented little worry to Hull. He was still the ranking Asian specialist in State, but had shown himself to be so virulently anti-Japanese that Hull had begun to ignore his advice. The more Hornbeck saw himself losing influence, the more strident he became and the more Hull kept him at arm's length.[20]

The president posed a different problem. Roosevelt approved of the talks, of course, but he was also under considerable pressure from hawkish advisers to move major elements of the Pacific Fleet into the Atlantic. They wanted him to order convoying of ships to Britain, a particularly dangerous action since it would mean battles between German submarines and American destroyers with loss of life on both sides. Roosevelt resisted that but he did agree to extend the aggressive "neutrality patrols" so far across the Atlantic that they overlapped the declared German war zone around the British Isles.

To help in the patrols, Roosevelt ordered one-fourth of the Pacific Fleet into the Atlantic in early May, just as Hull was reading Matsuoka's surly defense of the Tripartite Pact.[21]

It was a difficult time for Hull. With American power in the Pacific declining and Japan moving ever closer to the Axis, there seemed little chance for the talks to succeed. The long hours, the frustration in dealing with a Japanese government that was unresponsive to his offers, the need to keep both eyes on the hawkish Washington bureaucracy made Hull irritable and impatient. It was the British ambassador's bad luck to provoke Hull and receive the full force of the secretary's frustration.

The British had always been skeptical about the talks and dared to suggest that unless Hull was very careful, the United States might find itself maneuvered into a Japanese trap. Hull had already told Ambassador Halifax he was not optimistic about the success of the talks but that if there was one chance in twenty-five it was worth taking. So when he read the British government's warning, the secretary of state acted most undiplomatically. He might have to tolerate criticism by Ickes, Morgenthau, Stimson, and Knox but he did not have to accept it from the British, a nation whose Asian policy had been adorned with appeasement and humiliating retreats. When Hull summoned Halifax on May 25, the ambassador "found him in a state of pained and reproachful indignation. He very much resented what he evidently felt to be the implicit criticism in . . . my aide memoire . . . vis-à-vis his good faith with us or his sagacity in dealing with the Japanese. . . . [Hull] found it very difficult to accept what he termed a lecture from His Majesty's Government. . . . I have never seen him so disturbed."[22] As he berated Halifax, Hull justified the talks as offering a real chance that the power of Matsuoka and the pro-Axis group in Japan might be neutralized. He told Halifax that the American government "had very good information to show that Matsuoka was fighting a pretty lone hand for his full Axis policy in Japan, and that Hitler was, in his phraseology, beating him black and blue."[23]

Perhaps the wish had fathered the thought, but Hull did believe he could achieve one of the primary goals of the Hull-Nomura talks, the weaning of Japan from the Axis Alliance. Hull saw the Japanese government divided between Matsuoka and the pro-Axis forces on one side and Prime Minister Konoye and those who favored putting some distance between Japan and the Axis on the other. Though Matsuoka seemed to be firmly in control, intelligence reports indicated he was drinking heavily and becoming less stable. Hull believed that by acting reasonably in his talks with Nomura and by convincing the Japanese that the United States would inevitably enter the war against Germany, Japanese moderates might see the Axis as a detriment and topple Matsuoka and his group. The secretary did not think the moderates would give up Japan's New Order—this would not be the regeneration that must preceed a fundamental settlement; but he did think it possible that on the one issue of the Axis Alliance, some progress could be made.

"It is an awfully delicate thing," he confided to Wendell Willkie, the 1940 Republican presidential candidate. "I am trying to maneuver, to let them [the moderates] have a chance to assert themselves at Tokyo and see whether that crowd can succeed in controlling the situation." With peace hanging in the balance, Hull felt the pressure: "Of course, I'm watching with all the anxiety that a person can to see some daylight on that thing over there—in the Pacific." And if the situation were removed it would make you stronger? Willkie asked. "Oh, my good fellow," Hull responded breathlessly, "it would make a noise that could be heard on the northwest corner of the moon."[24]

To help push Japan away from the Axis, Hull stressed to Nomura the American determination to stop German expansion. When war came, Hull argued, it would be one in which Germany was the aggressor and the United States was acting in self-defense. This was important because the terms of the Tripartite Pact stipulated that if Germany attacked the United States Japan would not be obligated to enter the conflict. By repeatedly claiming that Germany was the aggressor and the United States the innocent victim, Hull was giving the Japanese leaders an easy way to remain neutral in the imminent German-American war.[25]

Though Hull did not know it, the United States did not have to fear Japan joining in when Atlantic patrolling erupted into open warfare with Germany. Japan's purpose in entering the Tripartite Pact was to deter the United States from confronting Japan in its march to the South, not provide an excuse for Japan to declare war against Washington. While the alliance required Japan to declare war against the United States if the United States attacked Germany, a secret letter from German ambassador Eugen Ott to the Japanese government at the time of the signing of the pact gave Japan full freedom to declare war or not as it chose. In other words, what the treaty required the secret protocol negated.[26]

Even had Hull been aware of that it would have brought him only small comfort. Pleased that Japan would not go to war over a German-American conflict, he would have held little hope for peace in the Pacific so long as the extremists were in control of Japanese policy, extremists who were intimately identified with the Axis Alliance. Japan's withdrawal from the Tripartite Pact would weaken the extremists and would demonstrate to Hull that the moderates had the power to do what they and the John Doe associates were saying they wanted to do. So even if the pact was a moot question in its international ramifications, Hull would have pressed for its re-nunciation because of its importance for internal Japanese politics.

This delicate diplomatic game failed to produce any measurable results. Matsuoka continued to endorse the Axis and Hull continued to warn Nomura that Matsuoka's language raised doubts about Japan's sincerity in seeking any reconciliation with the United States. Nor was there any indication of progress in the lengthy sessions conducted between second-level officers from the State Department and the Japanese Embassy.[27]

Hull was running out of time. In June, substantial issues still separated the two nations, and Hull knew that German armies were poised to strike at the Soviet Union.[28] Once Germany attacked Japan's age-old enemy, the pro-Axis forces in Tokyo would be vastly more influential. If the Japanese moderates hoped to succeed, they needed something to counter Matsuoka and his kind. With the support of Hamilton and Joseph Ballantine, the FE officer most involved with the talks, Hull decided to force the issue in a rather undiplomatic way.

On June 21, one day before the German invasion of the Soviet Union, Hull delivered to the Japanese ambassador the latest American proposal for an agreement along with an "oral statement" that concerned the Japanese leadership. Some Japanese undoubtedly wanted good relations with the United States, Hull said, but there were other higher officials (Hull never used Matsuoka's name) who were committed to supporting Nazi Germany and "the only kind of understanding with the United States which they would endorse is one that would envisage Japan's fighting on the side of Hitler." So long as such leaders maintained this attitude in their official position, Hull warned, there would be no basis for settling Japanese-American disputes.[29]

Hull had long believed Matsuoka had to leave before there could be an improvement in Japanese-American relations, but to make the point so bluntly was a desperate gamble that would almost certainly fail. Japan would surely protest this interference in the internal affairs of its government. Whom the government of Japan chose to conduct its foreign affairs was its business, not that of the United States. But Hull had nothing to lose. He dropped his bombshell and left town for a rest at White Sulphur Springs, West Virginia.

As predicted, the Japanese government protested Hull's oral statement. The secretary discreetly withdrew it; he had made his point. Surprisingly, the government of Prime Minister Konoye resigned on July 16, and when a new government was constitued the next day, it consisted of the same people, except that Matsuoka had been replaced by Vice-Admiral Toyoda Teijiro. On the face of it, this was a welcome change, and at any other time might have given Hull hope for a settlement. But by July 17 Japan had decided how it would respond to the German attack on Russia, and that decision boded ill for peace in the Pacific.[30]

At an Imperial Council meeting on July 2–3, Japanese leaders decided to strike south toward the rich oil, rubber, and tin resources of Southeast Asia and the Dutch East Indies. Because of MAGIC, the United States was soon aware that Japan intended to occupy the southern half of French Indochina as a staging area for its southern campaign. Such a challenge had to evoke an American response commensurate with the seriousness of the situation.[31] But this raised the old problem of precisely how important Southeast Asia was and what kind of response the United States should therefore make.

The strongest voices for moderation came from Hull and the admirals in navy, who feared that Roosevelt would order some action that might provoke Japan to attack. Hull spoke in terms of a $100 or $200 million loan to China coupled with economic pressure on Japan that would always be short of provoking war.[32] Navy Department officials also warned against economic sanctions because they would cause an immediate, severe psychological reaction among Japanese leaders and intensify that nation's determination to expand, an expansion that would probably involve the United States in war.[33]

Roosevelt understood the danger of being too hard on Japan, but he also felt the time for words had passed; it was necessary to act. He settled on a two-pronged response. On the military front, he would call the Philippine army into federal service, make Field Marshal Douglas MacArthur the commanding general of all U.S. Army forces in the Philippines, and begin a major reinforcement of Philippine

Dean Acheson believed the U.S. should stand up to Japan and he acted upon his beliefs. (File 208-N-37088-PMI, NA.)

defenses. On the economic front he would freeze all Japanese assets in the United States. If Japan could not withdraw any dollars from the frozen accounts, it could not buy any goods in the United States and trade would end. Mindful of Navy's warning to avoid provoking Japan, Roosevelt intended to make the freeze selective and release funds for the purchase of those goods the United States thought Japan ought to have. The shock of the Philippine buildup and the freezing order would be a potent warning to Japan, while at the same time the flexibility in releasing funds would avoid the confrontation Hull and the Navy Department feared.[34]

Responsibility for turning Roosevelt's ideas for a freeze into an actual plan fell to Sumner Welles, a man Roosevelt could trust. Welles began his efforts on Saturday, July 19, 1941, by sketching out a system that would release sufficient funds for Japan to purchase gasoline below 80 octane at amounts typical for the prewar years of 1935–36. Welles gave the task of drafting the detailed directions to Assistant Secretary of State Dean Acheson.[35]

Acheson had his own ideas about what should be done with Japan, and they did not include letting it get any oil. What he produced by Monday morning was not the plan the president had ordered or Welles had outlined but a sweeping embargo. Acheson intended to make the freeze total during the first few weeks, while a joint State-Treasury effort would establish a system by which Japan could only purchase oil in exchange for goods the United States needed, notably raw silk. Welles did not like what he read and deleted all the hard-line provisions Acheson had added. What the president had before him in the cabinet meeting of Thursday, July 24 was what he had asked for.[36]

In that cabinet meeting, Roosevelt reassured State and Navy officials that the freeze would not result in a total embargo, which might prompt Japan to strike at either the United States or the Indies. He explained that the freeze would be imposed without official comment but the licenses for exports would be granted in the normal manner. Funds for the export licenses would be released in accordance with the amounts Japan should be allowed to have; in the case of oil this was low octane in 1935–36 amounts.[37] It was a shrewd diplomatic and political action. The freeze announcement would satisfy that portion of the public which was increasingly upset that Japan purchased large amounts of gasoline on the West Coast while gasoline rationing was imminent on the East Coast. Diplomatically, the Japanese would discover that they could obtain some petroleum products and would hesitate to cut off this last source of oil by rash action. Roosevelt intended the freeze to be not the first blow in a program of economic warfare but a final warning, designed to bring Japan to its senses, not its knees. If Japan failed to stop its aggression, the freeze could be made total at a day's notice.

The announcement of the freeze was made following the close of business on Friday, July 25, but no details were available because Welles was busy drafting the administrative procedures. Working with Acheson and Treasury Department officials, Welles concluded that "the exportation to Japan of oil, gas, and petroleum products will be a matter to be dealt with on specific licenses. There will be no public announcement as to what action will be taken on such applications although for the time being such licenses will be automatically granted." Payment for these exports would come from blocked Japanese accounts.[38] Having reached this agreement, Welles began work on determining how much oil Japan would be permitted to import from the United States. On July 31 he reported to the president.

Welles's program conformed to Roosevelt's wishes. Oil exports to Japan would be permitted to purchase nonaviation petroleum products up to the amount it had purchased during 1935–36. Export Control would calculate just how much this was and issue a license. Then the joint State-Treasury-Justice Foreign Funds Control Committee (FFCC) would release just enough frozen dollars to permit the Japanese to purchase the oil licensed for export. Until Export control could make its calculations and issue the licenses, FFCC would simply hold, without action, any applications for funds that Japan might submit. Roosevelt approved the system and the appropriate agencies were notified.

Thus, by August 1 the decision had been made, procedures established, and the rather cumbersome bureaucratic machinery established.[39] But the system did not work. On August 1, Export Control notified the FFCC that Japan was entitled to 450,000 gallons of "not so good" gasoline and issued export licenses for $300,000 worth of diesel fuel. By the middle of August, these figures were substantially enlarged.[40] But Japan never got the oil it was entitled to purchase and the policy that was supposed to avoid provoking Japan was transformed into full-scale economic warfare that led to the attack four months later on Pearl Harbor.

It has been customary to assume that the freeze became a total embargo either because public opinion prevented, or continued

Japanese aggression did not justify, any relaxation of the embargo.[41] Neither explanation is accurate. That the freeze was never intended to be a total embargo was made clear at the time it was announced, so to ask why the freeze was not relaxed is to ask the wrong question. The real question is why the procedures that Welles drafted and Roosevelt approved were never followed. And the answer to that can only be found in the actions of the people who administered the freeze: the FFCC and particularly its chairman, Assistant Secretary of State Dean Acheson.

On August 5 Acheson met with his opposite members in the Treasury and Justice departments. When they saw how much oil Japan would be able to buy under the freeze guidelines, they agreed not to release funds to Japan for the purchase of items for which Export control had already issued licenses. Perhaps Acheson believed his actions were in keeping with the spirit of the freeze. More likely, these hawks believed they were doing the country a favor.[42]

Rather than blatantly denying Japan's requests the FFCC engaged in an administrative "run-around." Treasury officials later described the period as one when "the Japanese tried every conceivable way of getting the precious crude oil, but to each proposal the Division of Foreign Funds Control had an evasive answer ready to camouflage its flat refusal."[43]

Hull remained oblivious to what Acheson was doing. He had been resting away from Washington when the freeze was imposed and was kept posted by regular telephone conferences. When he returned to his office on August 4, he knew what the freeze consisted of, or thought he did, and made no effort to check up on Acheson's administration of the presidential order. Those were very busy days. Roosevelt was off in Newfoundland at a secret summit conference with Churchill. As we shall see in the next chapter, that conference raised some new diplomatic problems for the secretary, and no sooner were they resolved than other, more pressing ones arose. Hull had neither the time nor the inclination to peer over Acheson's shoulder. The only people in the State Department Acheson had to worry about were some junior officers in FE who were pushing him "very hard to let the oil be exported," claiming that he "had no authority to hold it up."[44] Assistant Secretary Acheson was not bothered by what some junior foreign service officers thought.

When Acheson briefed Welles in mid-August on the state of trade with Japan he noted that export licenses for petroleum products had been granted in accordance with Welles's instructions but that the

Treasury Department was asserting that Japan had enough dollars on hand to make release of frozen funds unnecessary. Acheson did not mention his role in all this, nor did he explain how insistent both he and Treasury were that Japan not get any oil. Not until September 4 did Hull become aware of what had happened, and then only because of something Nomura said. On September 5, Hull called in Acheson and discovered the extent of the "de facto" embargo. But by then it was too late. To have reopened the flow of oil after a month's cut-off would have sent the wrong message to Tokyo and reinforced the position of the Japanese hard-liners, who claimed that the United States would give in. All the secretary could do was order that no new restrictive measures be introduced and that the present attitude not be relaxed. "Whether or not we had a policy," Acheson wrote, "we had a state of affairs that would continue."[45]

Acheson was dead wrong. Japan could not allow that state of affairs to continue. Every day Japan consumed several thousand tons of stockpiled fuel oil. Eventually that stockpile would run dry and Japan would be left helpless. Long before that would happen, the Japanese would either have to persuade the Americans to reopen trade or seize the oil in the Netherlands and East Indies. In effect, the Acheson embargo placed a time limit on peace in the Pacific. But Acheson remained oblivious. He was not involved in policy formulation and paid little attention to the consequences of his actions concerning the freeze. Like Morgenthau and Ickes, with whom he associated, Acheson believed that Japan would never go to war with the United States, so the application of economic sanctions was safe. As late as a week before the Pearl Harbor attack, Acheson was still pressing Hull for a tough line against Japan and Hull had to rein him in by pointedly asking him if "he knew what the naval force could do in the Far East." Acheson had no idea, but it was just that sort of ignorance that gave him the arrogance to alter presidential orders.[46]

Acheson was not the first to try and change policy at the level of implementation. Morgenthau, Ickes, General Maxwell at Export Control, and a variety of people within the NDAC had given it a try. In each of those cases, however, Hull or Roosevelt had become aware of what was going on and intervened before any serious damage could be done to national policy. What was different about Acheson's exploit was that he got away with it. As a result, Japan and the United States were on a collision course that even statesmen of great flexibility would find it difficult to avoid. Cordell Hull was not a flexible man.

CHAPTER NINE

PLAYING OUT THE HAND

No one during the fall of 1941 wanted war with Japan. Navy preferred to concentrate on the Atlantic. Army said it needed a few more months before it would be ready in the Philippines. Hull had made the search for peace his primary concern for months. Roosevelt could see nothing to be gained by a war with Japan. Hawks such as Acheson, Ickes, and Morgenthau argued that their strong policies would avoid war, not provoke one. Even Hornbeck said the same thing, though he probably would not have been displeased by a Japanese-American war.

The problem confronting the Roosevelt administration was the method to follow to avoid war. Was it best to resume negotiations with Nomura, even though they had produced so little in May and June, or should the United States give Japan an ultimatum that one more step would mean war? Should Hull and Nomura conduct the negotiations or should Roosevelt and Prime Minister Konoye Fumimaro meet in a summit to cut through bureaucratic red tape and find grounds for an agreement? Should the diplomatic goal be a comprehensive agreement or just a limited, temporary one designed to postpone war? And what price would the United States be willing to pay to buy peace? The answers to those questions would determine whether the United States was going to plod along on a path that would end in war or have the energy and imagination to gamble on achieving a peace.

The freeze of Japanese assets had not signaled the end of diplomacy. Neither Roosevelt nor Hull was optimistic about achieving a diplomatic settlement, but Hull was prepared to make an effort. When the secretary returned to his office on August 4, he began preparations for reopening his talks with Nomura, suspended since June 21.[1]

Meanwhile, Roosevelt was meeting secretly in Newfoundland with Churchill, who was trying to move the United States away from talk and toward confrontation with Japan. The British worried that the sanctions the United States had recently initiated—to which Britain fully subscribed—would spark a Japanese attack on Britain's Asian possessions while the United States would sit by and do nothing. To prevent this Churchill and the British delegation urged Roosevelt to warn Japan that if it attacked a third power (i.e., Britain) Roosevelt would ask Congress for authority "to give aid to such a power" (i.e., declare war). Though Roosevelt dismissed such talk out of hand, Churchill did persuade him to accept a less militant ultimatum, warning Japan that any further expansion would compel the United States to take "any and all steps of whatsoever character it deems necessary in its own security notwithstanding the possibility that such further steps on its part may result in conflict between the two countries." Hull refused to accept this ultimatum. He rewrote it to leave out any reference to conflict and linked it with a more positive document proposing reopening the talks with Nomura. When Roosevelt returned to Washington on August 17, Hull easily persuaded him to substitute the weaker language for that agreed on with Churchill.[2]

Once again Hull managed to scuttle action that would provoke a confrontation with Japan. But as soon as he persuaded the president to abandon the British ultimatum, Nomura proposed something that threatened to snatch the entire question of Japanese-American relations out of Hull's hands.

The Japanese had grown very apprehensive about the future course of Japanese-American relations. The freeze and resulting end of trade caused great concern in Tokyo, as some Americans had predicted it would. Army leaders, who were always strongly anti-American, had become restless, while Navy leaders, who were usually more circumspect, recognized that time was running out. Prime Minister Konoye decided it was no longer possible to achieve a settlement with the United States through the painstaking discussions conducted by Ambassador Nomura and Secretary Hull. It would be necessary to break the diplomatic deadlock by a face-to-face meeting with Roosevelt.[3]   The idea of a conference with Konoye appealed to Roosevelt. Having just returned from the Atlantic Conference, where he and Churchill had fashioned the Atlantic Charter to guide the democracies through the coming struggle against the dictatorships, Roosevelt would have been less than human if he had not wondered whether something equally dramatic might come from a Pacific conference. More important, personal diplomacy appealed to the president, who had immense confidence in his ability to charm statesmen, even a prince of the royal house of Japan. If what was needed to assure peace in the Pacific was for the leaders to journey to Alaska or Hawaii to have a meeting of minds, Roosevelt was prepared, even eager, to go.[4]

Everything that made the leaders' conference appealing to Roosevelt made it appalling to Hull. From the moment he heard it proposed he opposed it, and not always for reasons of state.

Hull considered Japanese-American relations his peculiar domain and would have resented Roosevelt usurping him even under the best of circumstances. But the leaders' conference proposal came on the heels of the (to Hull) unsatisfactory Atlantic Conference, where Roosevelt had excluded his secretary of state and proceeded to deviate from the careful policy Hull had prescribed. If the president could do that much damage in the Atlantic Conference talking to a virtual ally, he could do much more in a Pacific conference with a virtual enemy. After four years of struggling to keep control of foreign policy, Hull would not yield it to Roosevelt without a fight.[5]

Beyond an understandable desire to protect his bureaucratic "turf," Hull had substantive reasons for objecting to the Roosevelt-Konoye meeting. A fundamental agreement with Japan was not possible, he believed, and the meeting would only produce a general agreement on vague principles that the Japanese would interpret differently from the Americans. The Chinese might feel betrayed and make a deal with Japan, Hull worried. If that happened, Japan could move some of its one million troops out of China against the British, the Dutch, or even the Americans.[6] As we shall see below, such a development would have been disastrous to the efforts in the western Pacific of the army and the navy.

Hull's assumption that the conference could not succeed in fashioning a settlement rested upon the deeply held suspicion of Japan that permeated all levels in official Washington.[7] This suspicion prompted Hull and company to interpret every Japanese position in the least charitable way. The Konoye government agreed to accept the principles of a liberal commercial order throughout the Southwest Pacific, but remained silent about China; Hull saw it not as a welcome first step but as a Japanese demand to establish its New Order in East Asia. Tokyo provided informal assurances that it would not invoke the Tripartite Pact against the United States; instead of welcoming them and urging still stronger ones Hull insisted that such assurances meant nothing and only a full renunciation would do. Recognizing that the terms of a Japanese-Chinese agreement would only block any agreement with the United States, Konoye omitted that issue from the talks; Hull saw the maneuver not as a sincere effort to find something on which the two countries could agree but as a trick, and insisted that the disposition of China was central to any peace in the Pacific. Hull did not doubt that Konoye could carry out an agreement along the lines he had specified—he doubted that Konoye could carry out an agreement along the lines *Hull* specified.[8]

From Tokyo, Grew bombarded the department with cables urging support for the Roosevelt-Konoye meeting and voicing optimism. But his advice did no good. After it was all over—after diplomacy had failed, the war had begun, Grew had been interned and then repatriated—he wondered why Konoye was not given more encouragement. "Could this have been due merely to the quibbling over formulas? Was the transcendent importance to our country of preserving peace to depend on the utterly futile effort to find mutually satisfactory formulas?"[9]

Grew was correct. Locked into his search for a comprehensive peace, Hull would not consent to a futile attempt to find a solution through summitry. But Hull did not call it "quibbling over formulas," nor did he see it as a choice between peace and war. These two men looked at the situation differently because they began with different perspectives. Grew thought Konoye sincere—Hull "knew" he was not.

Hull's skepticism rested partly on his traditional distrust of the Japanese and partly on a source of information that Grew did not even know existed—Hull was reading many of Japan's diplomatic messages. While these MAGIC intercepts did not provide the secretary with anything that would amount to a "smoking gun" in Konoye's hand, they did fuel his suspicion. The cables revealed that Japan could make no further concessions to the United States and was pinning its last hopes on an interview between Konoye and Roosevelt. To try to get an agreement "on questions of self-defense, occupation of China by Japanese troops and equal treatment in trade" would take too long, so the two leaders would identify the issues on which they could agree, "hold a conference for the discussion of these points and then issue a joint statement at the end and thus help create a more wholesome atmosphere between the two countries."[10]

Hull could welcome "a more wholesome atmosphere," but the messages indicated that Konoye was unable to accede to important American points even at a summit conference. That meant the conference would not be seeking a lasting peace, but only a superficial and temporary agreement. Hull was convinced that would demoralize China for no lasting benefit. Those were sufficient reasons for him to dig in his heals and resist Roosevelt's personal interest in the conference.

The president's original enthusiasm waned as Hull became more vocal in his opposition. By October Konoye was becoming desperate. While Grew continued to urge acceptance of Konoye's offer to talk, Hull saw his skepticism vindicated by a Foreign Office cable to Nomura on October 4 that said while Konoye accepted Hull's four principles "there may be differences of opinion when it comes to actually apply[ing] these four principles." It was the same old story. The real power in Japan was the military and Konoye was having to bend to it. Hull would do nothing to save the Konoye government. He would maintain his minimum demands and see if Konoye had the power to overrule the army. If he did, and Japan showed its willingness to withdraw from China, Hull would provide American good offices. If he did not, and it fell, it would simply substantiate what Hull believed all along.[11]

The crisis came on October 14, when Konoye insisted that the Japanese army agree to a withdrawal from China. The prime minister did not care if the concession was only temporary, to be followed by an agreement with China that would leave the troops in; what was needed was something to satisfy the United States. War Minister Tojo Hideki refused. Such a concession would only make the United States more difficult to deal with and China would never accept anything less. "I make no concessions regarding withdrawal!" Tojo bellowed. "It means defeat of Japan by the United States—a stain on the history of the Japanese Empire!" It was a test of strength between the army and the moderates, and Konoye lost. On October 15 Konoye's government fell, replaced by General Tojo as both prime minister and minister of war.[12]

Among American foreign policy managers, the moods ranged from pessimism to fatalism to a slight degree of optimism. The pessimists were upset that the moderates had clearly lost in Tokyo and now there was nothing to restrain the Japanese extremists. The fatalists concluded that the change in government did not make any difference, since the militarists had been in control all along. Grew sparked the optimism by reporting that in an unprecedented move, the emperor had personally intervened in a Privy Council meeting to instruct the army and navy ministers to abide by his wishes and pursue a peace policy. Tojo was selected as prime minister, Grew explained, because he was able to control the army. A rapprochement was still possible. That was what Hull wanted to hear. He saw this vindicating his policy of blunt talk to the Japanese and decided that with the emperor supporting the American position (something of an overstatement) there was a real chance for a comprehensive agreement. Just possibly, at this dark hour, the moderates might yet snatch power from the extremists. If they did, he told Stimson, "we will be in a wonderful position."[13]

It was wishful thinking. On November 4, MAGIC intercepted a cable to Nomura that gave little hope of a settlement. "We will call it evacuation; but though it would please the United States for us to make occupation the exception rather than the rule," the cable read, "in the last analysis this would be out of the question."[14] At the same time Grew was informing Washington that if Japan could not achieve a reconciliation with the United States it might launch an attack against American possessions in Asia. In his diary he worried that the more desperate Japan became the more likely it would be to undertake "an allout, do-or-die attempt, actually risking national hara-kiri, to make Japan impervious to economic embargoes abroad rather than to yield to foreign pressure." To believe that Japan would back down rather than go to war with the United States "is an uncertain and dangerous hypothesis upon which to base considered United States policy and measures."[15] It was an ominous situation. If Tojo was in earnest when he said Japan would not back down on stationing troops in China, and if Grew was correct that unless Japan could negotiate an agreement with the United States it would strike, then Hull's insistence on total Japanese withdrawal from China would result in war.

While all these diplomatic maneuverings were taking place, the army and navy developed a strategy for keeping Japan from moving against Singapore and the Indies. They would base bombers in the Philippines, making it too dangerous for the Japanese navy to bypass the islands. If Japanese ships tried to avoid the American bombers by steaming far to the east, they would come within range of the American Fleet at Pearl Harbor. Nor would Japan be able to successfully invade the Philippines, with so many soldiers tied down in China and with new American defenses constructed in the islands. So long as China remained in the war and once the Philippines had been fortified and staffed with bombers, Japan would be hemmed in and unable to strike. Then the army and navy could turn their full attention to the important war in Europe and the Atlantic.[16]

There was a healthy dose of wishful thinking in all this. It assumed that the B-17 Flying Fortress and the B-24 Super Flying Fortress were so devastating that Japan would fear to launch an attack against an archipelago equipped with a hundred or more such bombers. Moreover, it assumed that the Japanese high command would not attack until after that aerial buildup was complete. Yet the army had no other choice. Roosevelt had ordered that the Philippines be made into a deterrent and the bombers were the only thing that could possibly do the job. So army officers made a virtue out of necessity and B-17 fever swept through the ranks. Week after week the rhetoric increased until by October General L. T. Gerow, the War Plans Division chief, was flatly stating that air and ground units already sent to the Philippines or scheduled to be sent "have changed the entire picture in the Asiatic area. The action taken by the War Department may well be the determining factor in Japan's eventual decision and, consequently, have a vital bearing on the course of the war as a whole."[17] It was left to Secretary of War Stimson, however, to translate the added power of some B-17s into a revolutionizing development. In mid-October, Stimson wrote Roosevelt that the potential in the Philippines "bids fair to stop Japan's march to the south and secure the safety of Singapore, with all the revolutionary consequences of such action. . . . Our whole strategic possibility of the past twenty years has been revolutionized by the events of the world in the past six months. From being impotent to influence events in that area, we suddenly find ourselves vested with the possibility of great effective power." The sobering note was that the deterrent effect of the Philippines rested upon the successful completion of the defenses there. That would take time and military plan-

By the fall of 1941, Secretary of War Henry L. Stimson and Chief of Staff George C. Marshall (left) agreed that Japan had to be stopped and believed they had found a way to do so. (File 208-PU-194B-11, NA.)

ners were hoping Japan would not strike before the task had been completed. "As you well know," Stimson reminded Roosevelt, "the final success of the operation lies on the knees of the gods and we cannot tell what explosion may momentarily come from Japan."[18]

Army officers believed that the best way to deter Japan and thus avoid war was to take a firm stand through continued application of the embargo and reinforcement of the Philippines. But they had assumed that such efforts would always stop short of anything that would provoke war. Thus, anything that portended a break with Japan caused alarm in the armed services, especially in the Navy Department.[19] The same concerns applied to aid for China. Chinese resistance was an important part of the deterrence strategy, so aid should flow to China; the Flying Tigers could even be enlarged, but nothing should be done in China that would mean war with Japan. To go to war with Japan in order to keep China fighting so that China could help deter a war with Japan made no sense. Do not fight Japan for China, the Joint Board concluded, do not issue an ultimatum to Japan over China, continue support for China but do so short of risking war; and put off hostilities as long as possible, even if that requires making an agreement with Japan.[20]

By November, Cordell Hull's approach to Japanese-American relations no longer suited the national interest. The Tojo government refused to withdraw from China. Hull refused any agreement with Japan that did not include total withdrawal from China (except, of course, Manchuria.) Unless Japan could get an agreement it would strike south toward the Indies (the critical source for oil in any war with the Western powers.) American forces in the Philippines would be able to stop that Japanese drive, but only after a few more months of preparations and only if China continued to tie down one million Japanese troops.

If Hull persisted in his search for a comprehensive peace while continuing to impose economic sanctions, there would be a war for which the United States was not prepared. On the other hand, if he offered Japan a settlement in China that did not involve total withdrawal it would be a serious blow to Chinese morale and might cause the collapse of Chinese resistance. That would only increase Japan's ability to move against the Philippines and thus undercut the entire American military strategy for the South Pacific. The only hope was to shift the diplomatic effort from a search for a lasting, comprehensive agreement to the negotiation of a temporary agreement that

Four years of diplomatic effort had brought the United States and Japan to the brink of war by November 1941, and Cordell Hull faced the most difficult decisions of his career. (File 208-PU-9600-2, NA.)

would buy a little time. Hull had to stop trying to find a just and lasting peace and start trying simply to avoid war.

Just about everyone except Cordell Hull understood what had to be done. The Japanese government, Roosevelt, and some Japan officers in the State Department all proposed abandoning the search for a comprehensive agreement in favor of negotiating a temporary agreement, what the diplomats called a modus vivendi (from the Latin, a way of living). Such an agreement was not intended to resolve Japanese-American tensions, only buy time.

Japanese leaders suspected that Hull and Roosevelt were trying to drag out the talks in order to further deplete Japanese resources before the inevitable war began. But the emperor's insistence on searching for a peaceful solution to Japanese-American differences compelled the Tojo government to make one more effort. First it would try plan A—reach an accord on the vexing issues of southern expansion, the Tripartite Pact, and Japanese troops in China. If that did not work (and no one expected it would), Nomura could offer plan B, a modus vivendi that specified that the United States would sell Japan some oil.[21]

No sooner had Roosevelt (through the medium of MAGIC) read of Japan's interest in postponing a war than he outlined his own plan, a six-month agreement with no movement of armaments on either side, during which Japan and China would discuss peace. Stimson objected because the freeze on armaments would prevent the improvement of American defenses in the Philippines, which was Army's primary purpose in postponing a clash with Japan.[22] Rather than come up with a revised plan, Roosevelt did nothing. Hull showed no interest in it, so the American government waited for the Japanese to make their offer.

Japan's plan A did not offer much. Japan promised to accept a liberal commercial world system provided it was "applied uniformly to the rest of the world as well." It was impossible to extend liberal commercialism to the entire world in the best of times, and certainly not while a war raged through Europe. (Perhaps the Japanese leaders were trying to make the point that Japan should not be held to standards that much of the world ignored.) The second part of Plan A contained assurances that Japan would interpret the Tripartite Pact entirely independently; that is, it would not be dictated to by Germany. Nomura explained that his government could not say more in black and white, but he urged Hull "to 'read between the lines' and to accept the formula as satisfactory. You will agree with me that where there is no mutual confidence and trust, a thousand words or letters would not be a satisfactory assurance."[23]

Unfortunately, there was no "mutual confidence and trust" between Japan and the United States, a condition reinforced by the contrast between what Hull heard Nomura say and what he read via MAGIC. Nomura said Japan was ready to ignore the pact; secret cable traffic indicated that Japan was about to renew it, on November 25. Of course, there was no inherent contradiction between these two points, since Nomura was giving assurances that Japan would not invoke the pact against the United States in the event of a German-American war. Still, given the mood in Washington, it looked like Japanese duplicity. Nor did the third part of plan A, Japanese withdrawal from China, give any evidence of Japanese moderation. Japan would leave some troops in Inner Mongolia and on Hainan Island, Nomura said, but would withdraw the remainder within two years of a Sino-Japanese peace; a peace negotiated without American participation.[24]

Though Hull rejected plan A, he made no counter proposal. The secretary remained passive, suggesting nothing. It was as if when Hull moved away from dealing with fundamental issues he was at a loss as to how to proceed. A form of paralysis overcame the State Department, with Hull showing no initiative and Hornbeck reassuring everyone that the best thing to do was what was being done: applying firm pressure on Japan with no break in diplomatic demands. It was the only wise policy, Hornbeck said in literally dozens of memoranda, and it would be safe—Japan would not go to war with the United States.[25] It was further down in State that the first rumblings of an initiative were heard. FE officers, who had been most anxious over the way Acheson had transformed the freeze into an embargo, were worried by the lack of progress being made in the talks. The Japanese offer of November 10 and Hull's unwillingness or inability to alter national policy forced some of FE's officers to act. Joseph Ballantine was the primary instigator.

Ballantine, who had served as Hull's principal assistant during the eight months of the Hull-Nomura talks, understood their futility better than anyone. He had also demonstrated an amazing degree of flexibility and sensitivity toward Japan. In May, as the talks were just getting under way, Ballantine suggested that the United States might want to encourage both China and Japan to enter into peace talks with the United States acting as the "post office." Moreover, Ballantine thought the president should suggest an armistice with no troop movements. This amounted to Japan and China talking peace while Japan continued to occupy large amounts of Chinese soil, a situation hardly in keeping with traditional American policy. Ballantine had an even more unorthodox suggestion the following July. Japan did have a legitimate grievance against the Anglo-Saxon powers, he concluded, which had excluded it from "economic and commercial opportunities in the Asiatic dependencies of white powers." As long as that situation persisted, he noted to his colleagues, "it would be difficult to eradicate the deep-seated feeling among Japanese that white nations, especially the Anglo-Saxon powers, are exploiting Asiatic peoples to their own advantage."[26]

Now, on November 11, Ballantine took his knowledge of Japan, his sensitivity to Japanese problems, and his willingness to dissent from the conventional wisdom and, with the assistance of fellow FE officer Max Schmidt, released a memorandum calling for a new direction in Japanese-American negotiations. The language of this recommendation was cautious, even tentative, as befitted a proposal that went far beyond anything Hull had been prepared to consider during the preceding eight months. In self-deprecating tones, Ballantine and Schmidt humbly suggested that it was "almost certain" there was no chance for a comprehensive agreement with Japan, and therefore it seemed reasonable to see if a temporary agreement could be reached in order to gain time, time Hull needed to achieve his lasting peace.[27]

Ballantine and Schmidt paid lip service to the principles which Japan was supposed to accept, and on which Hull laid such great stress, but the heart of the plan consisted of the United States asking Japan and China to begin peace talks. Japan would offer China an armistice and when the talks began the United States would refrain from sending any further military supplies to China. Japan, for its part, would refrain from expanding its forces in Indochina. Once a peace had been negotiated, the United States would gradually reopen trade with Japan in coordination with Japan's withdrawal from China.

Peace was slipping away and Hull knew it.[28] But he did nothing. He neither accepted nor rejected the Ballantine-Schmidt proposal, nor did he show any indication of preparing his own plan. As a result, he had nothing constructive to offer Nomura when he spoke with him on November 15. The secretary seemed tired and irritable, complaining that "the new Government in Japan seems to take the attitude that we must reply at once to their points, but . . . we do not feel that we should be receiving ultimatums of such a character from the Japanese government under circumstances where the United States has been pursuing peaceful courses throughout and the Japanese Government is the one which has been violating law and order."[29]

This was Hull's personal nadir. The secretary had gone over the requisite points for an agreement so many times that there was nothing more to say. He did not believe Japanese leaders when they said they wanted good relations with the United States. He did not like the idea of a modus vivendi or any type of temporary agreement, as proposed by Ballantine and Schmidt, because he did not think it would achieve anything of a lasting nature. Diplomacy was dead in the water.

At this moment of greatest despair and inaction, a bold new proposal emerged, one designed to break the deadlock and draw the nations back from the brink of war.

The original plan came from Harry Dexter White, special assistant to Secretary of the Treasury Morgenthau. White had drafted it not in November but the previous June, after he had followed Hull's diplomacy for some time. To his colleagues in the Treasury Department, White excoriated Hull's "pathetic" diplomacy for its

> 19th century pattern of petty bargaining with its dependence upon subtle half promises, irritating pin pricks, excursions into double dealing, and copious pronunciamentos of good will alternating with vague threats—and all of it veiled in an atmosphere of high secrecy designed or at least serving chiefly to hide the essential barrenness of achievement. . . . Where modern diplomacy calls for swift and bold action, we engage in long drawn out cautious negotiation; where we should talk in terms of billions of dollars, we think in terms of millions; where we should measure success by the generosity of the government that can best afford it, we measure it by the sharpness of the bargain driven; where we should be dealing with all-embracing economic, political and social problems, we discuss minor trade objectives, or small national advantages; instead of squarely facing realities, we persist in enjoying costly prejudices; where we should speak openly and clearly, we engage in protocol, in secret schemes and subtleties.[30]

The indictment had had the ring of truth in June and was even more telling in November.

The specifics of White's proposal amounted to a diplomatic revolution by which Japan and the United States would move from enmity into a symbiotic relationship. Such an improbable shift would be accomplished by (1) removing military pressure through transferring the fleet from the Pacific to the Atlantic; (2) removing economic pressure through resuming normal trade with Japan; and (3) building a positive relationship by renouncing American extraterritorial rights in China, stabilizing the Yen-dollar exchange rate, giving Japan a major loan to rebuild its economy, buying Japanese shipping, and asking Congress to remove the Japanese exclusion provision of the 1924 Immigration Act. White based this sweeping program on the contention that Japan and the United States had no inherent conflicts in Asia and if Japan could be assured of access to raw materials it would prefer to live in peace with the United States. For its part, Japan would abandon its China venture and withdraw all its troops from China (though it could keep troops in Manchuria), give China a major reconstruction loan, sell up to 50 percent of its shipping to the United States, and sign a nonaggression pact with the Asian powers. FE seized upon this proposal, translated it into the proper diplomatic language, and enthusiastically endorsed its adoption.[31]

While the FE version of this plan circulated through the War and Navy departments for their comments, Ambassador Nomura and newly arrived special envoy Kurusu Subaru presented their plan of last recourse, plan B. Japan would remove its troops from southern Indochina and pledge to make no further expansion in Southeast Asia. In return the United States would withdraw the freeze, help Japan obtain the oil it needed in the Netherlands East Indies, and cut off aid to China. Once a Sino-Japanese peace had been concluded, Japan would withdraw its troops from all of Indochina.[32] In effect, plan B called for the two countries to return to the status quo ante July 1941, with the added proviso that the United States withdraw all support from China.

Though plan B was clearly unacceptable Hull made up his mind to prepare a response. He approached Roosevelt, who on November 21 sketched the rough outlines of a counterproposal: Japan would refrain from sending any additional troops south or into Manchuria and would agree not to invoke the Tripartite Pact in the event of a German-American war. In return the United States would resume trade in some oil and rice and would introduce Japan and China to talk peace, but would not participate in those talks.[33]

On November 21, then, there were two separate proposals emerging from the Roosevelt administration. The FE version of the Harry

Dexter White proposal presented a dramatically different basis for a comprehensive Japanese-American agreement and Roosevelt's proposal suggested specific terms for a temporary agreement. On November 22 these two items merged into a single document that included a modus vivendi intended to prevent a break in relations while a larger agreement would remove the reasons for a conflict.[34]

Perhaps it was a naive plan that was too radical for Tokyo, the Congress, or the American people to accept. Almost certainly it came too late to be successful. But it was still an exciting moment. At the eleventh hour, with the nations at the verge of warfare, a handful of innovative people several levels down in the foreign policy bureaucracy offered a dramatic alternative to their chief's lethargic diplomacy. But before their plan could see the light of day, less flexible officials drew all its teeth. Each department, each office that reviewed the draft took exception to one provision or another. Hull did nothing to defend the proposal and every objection resulted in its further gutting. What emerged was barely a shadow of its original self.

The provision that allowed Japan to keep troops in Manchuria if the Soviets reduced theirs in Siberia would favor Japan and therefore hurt the Russians, army officers objected, and State Department officials deleted it. Admiral Stark objected to reducing naval forces in the Pacific, and State cut that section. Furthermore, Stark said, it was an insult to ask Japan to sell any ships to the United States, so that part should be deleted. It was. As the proposal made the rounds within the State Department, it was mutilated beyond recognition. The American pledge to seek repeal of the Japanese exclusion provisions of the 1924 Immigration Act was deleted. All reference to a two-billion-yen loan to Japan was cut. Finally, a provision was added requiring Japan to renounce the Tripartite Pact.[35]

The only sign of flexibility left in the proposal by November 22 was an offer to remove the freezing order once peace talks between Japan and China had begun. By November 24, even this had been retracted; the new wording called not for a removal but a *modification* of the freeze so that Japan could exchange some of its goods for American supplies, notably raw silk for prewar amounts of oil and other goods. (It was the same plan Acheson had suggested in July, a proposal Welles and Roosevelt had rejected as being too restrictive. But what was too restrictive in July was too liberal in November.) When in doubt, State Department officers chose the more conservative path. When Hull worried that the Chinese would be unhappy even with the watered-down proposal, he deleted any reference to the United States asking Japan and China to begin peace talks.[36]

It was not much of a document that the best foreign policy minds in Washington had created. The bold proposal that originated with Harry Dexter White and was carried on by FE had been reduced to a cautious, palid one. Such caution had served the nation well in earlier years, when Navy spoke of defending the national honor in China, when Roosevelt toyed with a "quarantine," when friends of China demanded economic sanctions, when overzealous administrators sought to "tighten the screws" on Japan. In those circumstances, caution had worked to avoid confrontation with Japan—now caution was working to bring it on.

The triumph of bureaucratic rigidity over boldness occurred on the morning of November 26, when Cordell Hull gave up on diplomacy and decided to "kick the whole thing over." Rather than presenting the anemic modus vivendi, the secretary gave Nomura and special envoy Kurusu a robust statement of the extreme American position.[37]

Since it was the final document handed to the Japanese, the November 26 statement has received attention it does not deserve. It was not a diplomatic document, not even an ultimatum. It was a statement for the record, which Hull knew could never be the basis for continued negotiations. When Nomura and Kurusu protested the harsh terms Hull showed no intention to negotiate. To Kurusu's question whether the United States was interested in a modus vivendi, the secretary replied simply that he had done his best in the way of exploration. Lamely placing the blame on the agitated state of public opinion, Hull gave the Japanese diplomats no hope. In fact, Hull placed so little importance on the November 26 statement that when the British ambassador came by the next day Hull called it simply something general and could not lay his hands on a copy to show him.[38]

In respect to war or peace, Hull's decision of November 26 made no difference. The bureaucracy had so restricted the proposed modus vivendi that it stood no chance of being accepted in Tokyo. What the November 26 note illustrates is that after nearly four years and five months of trying to bring peace to the Pacific, Hull had given up. As he told Stimson the next day, "I have washed my hands of it and it is now in the hands of you and Knox—the Army and the Navy."[39]

To understand why Hull finally gave up and accepted war with Japan we must examine the mood within the Washington foreign policy establishment throughout November, and Hull's reaction to the events of November 23–25 in particular.

A strong sense of fatalism surrounded everything Hull did in November. At a cabinet meeting early that month the talk was of war with Japan and rallying public opinion, not avoiding war. State Department officials had given up any hope of a settlement with Japan and talked only of buying some time.[40] The only hope of postponing war was the proposed modus vivendi. On November 22, Hull called in the representatives of Britain, China, Australia, and the Netherlands. For two and a half hours he explained how he hoped to strengthen the hands of the moderates in Japan by presenting the now much-modified White/FE proposal. But to do that he needed time, and that meant offering Japan a modus vivendi, a three-month agreement by which Japan would withdraw its fifty thousand troops from southern Indochina and limit its troops in northern Indochina to twenty-five thousand. In return, Japan would receive some modest amounts of oil. Hull did not think there was more than one chance in three that the Japanese would accept the American proposal, but if they did it would postpone war and give the American military the time it desperately needed.[41]

While the diplomats consulted their governments, Hull learned that time had almost run out. MAGIC revealed that Japan had set November 29 as the absolute deadline: "After that things are automatically going to happen." Roosevelt warned: "We must all be prepared for real trouble, possibly soon."[42] So it was under the press of time that Hull called back the British, Australian, Dutch, and Chinese representatives on November 25 to see what their governments thought of his proposal. The Chinese ambassador objected to Japan leaving twenty-five thousand troops in Indochina under the proposed agreement. Of the Western powers, only the Dutch representative had received instructions from his government. Hull was bitterly disappointed. He lectured those present on the value of postponing a war. Although Asia was more important to their countries than to the United States, he complained, they expected his government to take the lead in militarily defending the entire area. Sounding like a hurt child, Hull reported: "I was not sure that I would present it to the Japanese Ambassador without knowing anything about the views and attitude of their Governments. The meeting broke up in this fashion."[43]

The next day the news was no better. The British responded with an ambiguous statement that offered to support the United States whatever it decided to do yet raised some questions about the wisdom of leaving Japanese troops in Indochina. Most disappointing was the Chinese government, which strongly objected to the modus vivendi and warned that should it be imposed, there could be dire consequences in China.[44]

Hull was trapped in a diplomatic crisis from which he saw no escape. On the one hand, if he went ahead with the proposal to Japan and China felt betrayed and collapsed, he would have lost a major Asian ally and markedly increased Japan's ability to conquer Southeast Asia, since the army and navy had made Chinese resistance a key to their strategy. On the other hand, if he withheld the proposal it was clear that Japan was going to move South in a matter of days, and Philippine fortifications were not yet sufficient to withstand an assault. The army and navy were pleading for a little more time, and Stimson thought the proposal adequately safeguarded American interests. Yet when Roosevelt, Stimson, Knox, Marshall, Stark, and Hull met in the White House on November 25, the talk was about the imminent Japanese attack and what might be done to make sure that Japan fired the first shot. Though Stimson had no objections to offering Japan one more chance, there was no pressure to make the effort.[45]

Cordell Hull was showing classic symptoms of what is nowadays called "burn-out." He was an idealistic person who sincerely believed that the system he espoused would bring peace and prosperity to the peoples of the world, and week after week, month after month he had been working toward that end. But in November he was no closer than he had been the previous March. During the past few weeks he had been working sixteen-hour days and the strain was showing. Physically, emotionally, and mentally exhausted, isolated within the Roosevelt administration, receiving no support from the British or Chinese, Hull felt helpless in the pursuit of a hopeless task. He would let Stimson and Knox, War and Navy, worry about it.

CHAPTER TEN

WHAT WENT WRONG

With the end of diplomacy on November 26, the United States braced itself for war. Army and Navy officials warned their commanders throughout the Pacific that talks had broken off and a Japanese attack should be expected at any time. The question was where Japan would strike and what the United States should do about it.

Policy managers believed that Japan would move south against Singapore, the Dutch East Indies, and possibly the Philippines, areas national policy declared vital to American national interests, and they set about preparing the paperwork, and the public, for American entry into the war.[1]

But what would the United States do if Japan avoided the South Pacific and moved west instead? Suppose it attacked Kungming, the Burma Road, and Thailand? Would the United States fight to save that region? The answer was No. Stimson thought it might be best to confront further Japanese aggression wherever it took place, but more practical thinking prevailed.[2] The line against Japanese expansion was drawn through the South Pacific to Singapore, not the land mass to the north. There was nothing surprising about this. American policy during the preceding four years had demonstrated that the United States saw no vital interests in China or Indochina. Nevertheless, there were those whose love of China or whose hatred of Japan was so intense that they considered this American policy an

egregious error. Stanley Hornbeck was one such person and he left
no doubt about his feelings:

> We saw Japan take Formosa.
> We helped Japan take Korea.
> We let Japan take Manchuria.
> We let Japan take Rehe.
> We let Japan take Beiping—and Shanghai and Nanjiing and Hank-
> ou and Guangzhou.
> We forgave Japan's sinking of the *Panay*.
> We forgave Japan's bombing of the *Tutuila*.
> We have observed Japan's bombing of civilians in China, her driv-
> ing of 30 million Chinese from their homes, her rapings of women and
> her torturings of men and children.
> We have tolerated Japan's taking in China of American lives, her
> assaulting and injuring of American men and women and children,
> her bombing and destruction of American missions and hospitals and
> schools, her ruining of American enterprises, her strangling of Amer-
> ican trade, her interference with American officials and tampering
> with American mails, etc., etc., etc.
> And now there is talk about *drawing "lines"* and saying: "You must
> not cross these lines; you must not immediately and directly jeopar-
> dize the British and the Dutch and the American strategic positions in
> the Far East; but (the sponsors say it by implication and tacit assent)
> you may continue to endanger our nationals and to bomb our prop-
> erties and to destroy our interests in China and have your armies and
> your energies and your resources freed of their commitment there: so
> long as you keep within *those limits* you may assume that we won't
> use force to stop you.[3]

Given a half-century of American refusal to defend China from
Japanese incursion, it is ironic that it was the issue of China that in
the final hours of negotiations stood as an insurmountable obstacle
between Japan and the United States. To understand why, we must
not look to the sanctity of treaties or the burden of the clean record
that had characterized American relations with China for decades.
China loomed large in Hull's thinking during the final days of peace
because the Roosevelt administration had put itself in a position
where its diplomatic goals exceeded its military means, thus forcing
it to depend too much upon China.

We might trace the origins of this problem to the Five Power
Treaty of 1922, to the absence of naval building during the 1930s, to
the fall of France and the British retreat from Asia in 1940, or to the
more recent gap between a war plan that stressed the Atlantic and

Europe and foreign policy that defined the East Indies and Singapore as vital. Whatever the reasons, by 1941 the United States needed China as much as China needed the United States, or more. Only if China continued to engage a million Japanese troops could American and British forces in the South Seas hope to contain the Imperial Japanese army and navy. It was the reality of American weakness that placed Hull in such a difficult position. He was not thinking about sanctity of treaties when, on November 26, he made a decision that, in effect, chose war with Japan rather than the collapse of China.[44]

In retrospect, Hull probably made the wrong decision on November 26. China was not going to collapse if Hull offered the modus vivendi to Japan. Presidential assurances and shipment of military supplies would have kept up Chinese morale and left open a chance, a slim chance, to avoid war. Hull's decision was the result of emotional, physical, and mental exhaustion. In human terms it was understandable. But to dwell on it is to give it a significance it does not deserve. By November 26, Cordell Hull was a man in the middle of an ocean wondering what straw he should grasp. The important question is how he got there.

The Japanese-American conflict grew out of two mutually exclusive views of world order. Japan, seeing itself as a poor nation surrounded by richer and more powerful nations, sought to gain security through the establishment of a New Order. By dominating the political and economic life of East Asia, then Greater East Asia, and ultimately Greater East Asia and the South Seas, Japanese leaders hoped to assure safe access to the markets and raw materials vital to Japan's role as a great nation. American leaders could agree that a secure source of raw materials and markets was essential for all nations, but they flatly rejected Japan's autarchic approach. Americans favored the liberal commercial world order, characterized by free trade and free investment. If Germany succeeded in establishing its autarchic order over Europe and Japan over Asia, the world would be set back 750 years, or so Roosevelt and Hull believed. The United States would never accept Japan's New Order in Greater East Asia and the South Seas. It was learning to live with Japan in China, but expansion farther south was intolerable.

Since each nation equated its own system with national survival it is tempting to conclude that this was a conflict not susceptible to peaceful resolution and that it could be resolved only on the field of battle. Yet neither side wanted to fight the other. Japanese leaders looked upon the massive economic and military resources of the United States and concluded that almost anything would be better than a war with such a great power. American leaders, while not respecting the Japanese, saw America's real interests in Europe and wished to avoid war in Asia. This mutual desire for peace meant an opportunity for diplomacy.

The purpose of diplomacy is to find a way for nations with conflicting interests to resolve their differences other than on the battlefield, and if not to resolve those differences at least to learn to coexist with them. By this criterion, American foreign policy managers failed. During a period of more than four years they were unable to guide either American or Japanese policy in a direction that would avoid war.

Where did American leaders go wrong? Or phrased more discreetly, how might they have acted differently?

To begin with Cordell Hull and his staff approached Japan with strongly held preconceptions. They could not see Japan, they could not understand what Japan was saying, they could not believe that any Japanese leder was both sincere and capable of delivering on promises. This negative view of Japan and the Japanese led Hull and company to make many tactical errors. When, as early as 1938, Grew warned that the Japanese people would never turn on the military and that sanctions would only unite the nation, Washington ignored his advice. When Grew and Foreign Minister Nomura negotiated the first tentative steps toward an understanding in December 1939, Hull turned a cold shoulder. When Ballantine noted in the summer of 1941 that Japan had legitimate complaints about its treatment at the hands of the Western powers, his advice caused not even a ripple within State. It fell to someone from the Treasury Department, Harry Dexter White, to draft a plan that recognized Japan's legitimate economic needs and proposed to meet them. And when the State Department was finished with that proposal it offered Japan nothing and demanded much.

Though Hull turned a deaf ear to the voices of conciliation in the administration, he also refused to heed those who called for confrontation. As Ickes, Maxwell, Stimson, Knox, Morgenthau, Leahy, Davis, and even the president discovered, when Hull set his mind to something he was a formidable opponent. Though he won the vast majority of his battles with the hawks of the Roosevelt administration, neither Hull nor the president managed to maintain control over the constantly growing and increasingly complex foreign policy bureaucracy. By losing control over the execution of policy, they lost control over the direction the nation moved.

None of the bureaucratic sleights of hand that proliferated during 1940 and 1941 was critical. But the cumulative effect of these little actions moved the United States further toward economic sanctions than Hull or Roosevelt intended. As a result, Japan felt increasingly encircled, and responded by expanding into the resource-rich areas of Southeast Asia. When it moved into southern Indochina in July 1941, and Dean Acheson transformed Roosevelt's financial freeze into sweeping economic sanctions, the damage to American foreign policy was irreparable. This is not to say that without Acheson's machinations there would have been no war. But in the summer of 1941 time was the critical factor. If a confrontation with Japan could have been put off to the spring of 1942 it might have been avoided indefinitely, because by then American military power would have been much greater and German victory in Europe less certain. Acheson and the others who moved the nation toward economic warfare denied the United States that time.

As the two nations inched their way along the road to Pearl Harbor, Hull committed his most serious tactical error. He tried to establish a lasting peace with Japan through the negotiation of a comprehensive agreement. To the secretary, peace was not merely the absence of war but the maintenance of fair, decent, and equal relations between nations. But to achieve a diplomatic agreement that would bring about a change of that magnitude was beyond Hull's grasp. In 1938 and 1939 that did not seem to make much difference because the United States could afford to wait for Japan to see the futility of its chosen path of conquest. Hull and Roosevelt saw a war coming in Europe, but they did not foresee the collapse of France with the resulting disruption of the world balance of power. That event, more than any other, outmoded the policy of waiting for Japan to undergo a regeneration of spirit before reaching an agreement. That was the time when Hull should have set aside his search for a comprehensive peace and begun working on a limited understanding, something to avoid war. If he could not bring himself to do this in June 1940, then he should have done so in October, after Japan moved closer to the Axis and into Indochina. An even better opportunity to shift the focus came with the Hull-Nomura talks in the spring of 1941. Or if Hull was waiting for a position of strength to seek a compromise, he had it in August when the freeze was imposed and the talks reopened. In September 1941, when Hull learned that the freeze had cut off Japan's access to oil, the secretary had all the incentive he needed to change his diplomatic objective.

Through all these events Hull tenaciously held to his goal of a sweeping agreement with Japan on fundamentals. This policy was not inspired by a slavish devotion to the sanctity of treaties or a sentimental attachment to China—it was the result of Hull's belief that anything less would be a futile appeasement of Japan.[5] The fact that it was pragmatic, however, did not make it wise.

If the secretary had so little faith in temporary agreements as to shun becoming involved in them, then Roosevelt should have intervened to change the focus of Japanese-American talks. But the president never did so, and permitted his secretary of state to lead the nation along a diplomatic path that could only end in tragedy.

Roosevelt's failure of leadership might be explained by any of a number of factors. He too was deeply suspicious of Japanese intentions. He was also preoccupied with the pressing matters of Europe and did not have the time to devote to Asian affairs. Moreover, to take charge of the negotiations with Japan meant taking them away from Hull, who jealously guarded his territory. Beyond all these reasons, the problem of Japanese-American relations was clearly a diplomatic question, and Roosevelt was not comfortable with the intricacies of diplomacy. He enjoyed meeting with Churchill and would have enjoyed meeting with Konoye. He liked to think in terms of a quarantine, naval blockades, and simple economic sanctions. The stuff of which the negotiations with Japan were made did not suit him.

A variety of factors brought Cordell Hull to that point on the morning of November 26, 1941 when he gave up on diplomacy and accepted war. The American faith in the liberal commercial world order and Japan's attempt to establish a New Order in Asia at the point of a gun assured Japanese-American tension. In responding to this tension, the Roosevelt administration failed to employ diplomatic efforts that were consistent with American national interest. The rigidly anti-Japanese Washington mind-set and Cordell Hull's fixation with a comprehensive settlement made diplomacy ineffectual. Even had Hull and Roosevelt been more sensitive to Japan's concerns and more flexible in their diplomatic negotiations, they still faced the problem of a bureaucracy that was out of control. The president and the secretary of state had a policy, but so did Morgenthau, Ickes, Stimson, Knox, Acheson, Grew, Welles, Hornbeck, Maxwell, Yost, Green, Leahy, Stark, and the rest. As a result, the course Roosevelt and Hull charted was not the one that the nation followed. Perhaps stronger control over the bureaucracy would have made no difference, but the chaos that characterized the execution of American policy left no chance for success.

GLOSSARY

Throughout this work, the *pinyin* spelling of Chinese words has been employed. The following list may help those who are more familiar with the traditional spelling.

Beiping	Peiping
Yangzi	Yangtze
Chongqing	Chungking
Guangzhou	Canton
Gulangsu	Kulangsu
Hankou	Hankow
Jiang Jieshi	Chiang Kai-shek
Jiujiang	Kiu Kiang
Kungming	Kunming
Nanjing	Nanking
Rehe	Jehol
Shandong	Shantung
Shanghai	Shanghai
Tianjin	Tientsin
Xianggang	Hong Kong
Xiamen	Amoy

ABBREVIATIONS USED IN NOTES
AND BIBLIOGRAPHY

ACNPJA	American Committee for Non-Participation in Japanese Aggression
CINCAF	Commander-in-Chief, Asiatic Fleet
CNO	Chief of Naval Operations
FE	Far Eastern Division, Department of State
FO	Foreign Office, Great Britain
FR	U.S. Department of State, *Foreign Relations*
FDRL	Franklin D. Roosevelt Library, Hyde Park, N.Y.
JAH	*Journal of American History*
LC	Library of Congress
MVHR	*Mississippi Valley Historical Review*
NA	National Archives
NDAC	National Defense Advisory Commission
OCS	Office of the Chief of Staff, U.S. Army
OA	Operational Archives, Navy Yard, Washington, D.C.
ONI	Office of Naval Intelligence
PPC	Presidential Press Conferences, FDRL
PPF	President's Personal Files, FDRL
PSF	President's Secretary's Files, FDRL
PHA	U.S. Congress, *Pearl Harbor Attack*
PHR	*Pacific Historical Review*
RG	Record Group, National Archives, Washington, D.C.

.

USDOD   U.S. Department of Defense
USNIP   *U.S. Naval Institute Proceedings*
WPD   War Plans Division

Unless otherwise indicated, diaries are housed in the author's papers—the Leahy diary in the Leahy papers, the Stimson diary in the Stimson papers, etc.

Unless otherwise indicated, all items cited in footnotes are telegrams.

N O T E S

Introduction

1. Potter, "Compromise and Secession," 105–6.
2. Hornbeck lecture to Army War College, Jan. 13, 1939, "Policy, 36–41" file, Hornbeck papers.

Chapter 1

1. Johnson to Hull, July 8, 1937, *FR Japan,* I:314–15; Grew diary, 99:3251ff; Yarnell letter to Murfin, July 7, 1937, folder #1, "Far Eastern Situation," CINCAF correspondence, personal, Yarnell papers.
2. Ballantine memo, July 14, 1937, file 793.94/8725, RG 59: Hornbeck memo, July 19, 1937, *FR 37,* 3:204; Vincent memo, July 20, 1937, file 793.94/9723 1/2, RG 59: Peck to Hull, July 20, and Lockhart to Hull, July 27, 1937, *FR 41,* 3:268, 273.
3. Hornbeck memos, July 12, 14, 16, 1937, *FR 37,* 3:144, 167–70, 189, July 12, 1937, file 793.94/8735, RG 59. For statements urging moderation see Hull memo, July 12, 1937, file 793.94/8761, RG 59, and Hornbeck memo, July 10, 1937, *FR 37,* 3:134.
4. FE memo, Feb. 16, Hull to Bingham (London), May 24, 1937, *FR 37,* 3:959, 104; Grew letter to Wilson, May 13, 1937, vol. 83, Grew papers. On Navy see Yarnell letter to A. J. Johnson, July 7, 1937, folder #1, "Far Eastern Situation," CINCAF correspondence, personal, Yarnell papers; Pelz, *Race,* chs. 1 and 5; Richardson, *Treadmill,* 15–17, 137. On Roosevelt see Farley, *Jim Farley's Story,* 34; McIntire, *White House Physician,* 109; Range, *Roosevelt's World Order,* 6–7; Burns, *Lion and the Fox,* 261; Roosevelt, *This I Remember,* 235; Welles, "Roosevelt and the Far East," 33.

5. Griswold, *Far Eastern Policy;* Cohen, *America's Response to China;* and Iriye, *Across the Pacific.*

6. Hull letter to Vice-president Garner, Jan. 8, 1938, *FR Japan,* 1:430; CINCAF annual report, Aug. 30, 1937, file FFb/A9-1, box 2187, general correspondence, Sec. of the Navy, RG 80; Richardson *Treadmill,* chs. 5 and 14, and Pelz, *Race,* ch. 14.

7. Jonas, *Isolationism.*

8. Statement drafted at Hull's request, late Sept. 1937, folder 309, box 72, Hull papers; Hull statement and memo, July 16, 1937, *FR Japan,* 1:326, 321.

9. Vincent memo, July 27, 1937, Hull to Grew, July 21, 29, 1937, *FR 37,* 3:279–80, 237, 297.

10. The statement is in *FR Japan,* 1:326. See also Feis letter to Frankfurter, Oct. 6, 1937, Frankfurter papers.

11. Moffat diary, July 14, 1937; draft statement prepared by Hugh Wilson at Hull's request, late Sept. 1937, folder 309, box 72, Hull papers.

12. Press release, Aug. 23, 1937, *FR Japan,* 1:355–57. See also Wilson, *Disarmament,* 58–59, Moffat diary, July 31, Aug. 23, 1937.

13. Hornbeck memo, Aug. 16, 1937, *FR 37,* 3:422–23; Hull press release, Aug. 23, 1937, *FR Japan,* 1:355–57.

14. FE memo, Aug. 7, 1937, file 890.00/57, RG 59; Hull to Grew, Aug. 7, 1937, Grew to Hull, Aug. 10, 1937, *FR 37,* 3:353, 368.

15. Johnson to Hull, Aug. 12, 1937, *FR 37,* 3:386.

16. Hornbeck memo, Aug. 12, 1937; *FR 37,* 3:380–81.

17. Hull to Johnson, Aug. 12, 13, 1937, *FR 37,* 3:388, 395. For an earlier example of the Roosevelt administration ignoring the principle of nonrecognition in order to protect important American commercial interests, see Clauss, "Roosevelt and Manchukuo," 595–611.

18. For examples of early feelings that the war could be contained and quickly settled, see Hull memo, July 26, 1937, *FR 37,* 3:264; R. Walton Moore letter to William Bullitt, July 22, 1937, "Bullitt/37" folder, box 3, Moore papers; Grew diary, 99:3283, 100:3288; Hornbeck memos, July 15, 24, 1937, files 793.94/9010, 8988, RG 59. For examples of concern that Japan dominate East Asia, see Berle, *Navigating,* 135–38; FE memos, Sept. 18, 25, Oct. 2, 16, 1937, file 793.94/10043, 10672, RG 59; Hornbeck memo, Aug. 10, 1937, *FR 37,* 3:371–72. On concern for a Japanese-German-Italian alliance of "bandit" nations, see Hugh Wilson letter to Grew, Oct. 18, 1937, "Joseph C. Grew" folder, Wilson papers. On the importance of principles see Messersmith memo, Oct. 11, 1937, file 711.00/759, RG 59; Wilson letter to Grew, Oct. 18, 1937, "Joseph C. Grew" folder, Wilson papers; Stimson diary, Nov. 7, 1937.

19. Adams letter to Johnson, May 24, 1938, Johnson papers; Stimson diary, Nov. 7, 1937; Moffat diary, Oct. 4, 13, 1937. FE's George Atcheson wrote Nelson Johnson on Nov. 16, 1940: "Our best wishes to you for all the times and, as Stanley would have us say, also in and with regard to Christmas. With wishes over and above and in addition to these, for New Year" (Johnson papers).

20. Hornbeck memos, Sept. 4, 1937, "Policy, 36–41" folder, Hornbeck

papers; Sept. 4, Oct. 1, 1937, file 793.94/9860, 10705, RG 59; Sept. 4, 1937, *FR 37*, 4:306; Eden, *Facing*, 603; Stimson diary, Nov. 7, 1937.

21. Herbert Feis, chief of State's Economic Affairs Division and part of the anti—Japanese camp, considered Under Secretary of State Sumner Welles one of the idealists. Yet Welles called himself a realist and in practice was not particularly involved in these Asian questions. Stimson diary, Nov. 7, 1937; Wilson letter to Grew, Oct. 18, 1937, "Joseph C. Grew" folder, Wilson papers.

22. Wilson, *Disarmament*, 59, 68; Wilson letter to Grew, Oct. 18, 1937, "Joseph C. Grew" folder, Wilson letter to Bullitt, Sept. 9, 1937, "William C. Bullitt" folder, Wilson papers.

23. On the value of such meetings and Hull's desire to have them see Moffat diary, July 31, Sept. 7, 1937; Acheson, *Present*, 20; Hamilton letter to Johnson, March 4, 1938, Johnson papers; Cecil Gray letter to Hornbeck, Sept. 29, 1965, "Acheson, Dean" folder, Hornbeck papers. See also Moffat diary, Oct. 4, 1937.

24. Berle, *Navigating*, 137–38; Hull memo, Sept. 23, 1937, *FR 37*, 4:31; Wilson, *Disarmament*, 67–68; Wilson letter to Grew, Oct. 18, 1937, "Joseph C. Grew" folder, Wilson papers; Moffat diary, Oct. 1, 1937.

25. Various memos, Sept. 3 to Nov. 1, 1937, file 693.002/362–92, Hamilton memos, Dec. 1, 1937, file 693.002/405, 448. Gauss to Hull, Dec. 1, 1937, file 693.002/408, RG 59; Brit. aide memoire, Nov. 26, 1937, *FR 37*, 3:882.

26. Hornbeck memo, Aug. 30, 1937, file 793.94112/19, RG 59; Leahy diary, Aug. 31, 1937; Moffat diary, Sept. 1, 1937; Hull to Herschel Johnson (London), Sept. 1, 1937, *FR 37*, 4:441–42; Hamilton memo, Sept. 15, 1937, file 793.94112/87, RG 59.

27. Hornbeck memo, Aug. 9, 1937; *FR 37*, 4:618–19; MacKay memo, Aug. 11, 1937, file 893.51/6440, RG 59; Green memos, Sept. 20, 30, Oct. 1, 1937, *FR 37*, 4:536–37, 539–41.

28. Yost memo, Aug. 4, 1937, file 893.20/605, Hull to Gauss, Aug. 17, 1937, file 793.94/9389, Hornbeck memo, Aug. 10, and Welles memo Aug. 11, 1937 (with Hull's comments added), file 893-20/606, Messersmith memos, Sept. 1, 1937, file 893.20/615, and Aug. 20, 1937, file 393.1115/1380, Spencer memo, Aug. 20, 1937, file 793.94/9510, Hamilton memo, Oct. 22, 1937, file 793.94/10801, RG 59; Hull to Johnson, Sept. 15, 1937, *FR 37*, 4:528–30.

29. Borg, *Crisis*, 338–46; Dallek, *Roosevelt*, 146.

30. Feis letter to Frankfurter, Oct. 6, 1937, box 325, Frankfurter papers; Roosevelt press conference, Sept. 4, 1937, 10:197, PPC, FDRL; Spencer memo with Hamilton comment, Aug. 18, 1937, file 793.94111/39, RG 59; Borg, *Crisis*, 349; *Time*, Oct. 4, 1937, 17–18. For Hull's keeping open the U.S. Court, see FE memo, Sept. 1, 1937, file 172/829, RG 59.

31. Hull to Johnson, Sept. 2, 1937, *FR 37*, 4:301–2; CNO, Sept. 2, 1937, file QW17 (370817), box 4010, RG 80. State estimated that in July 1937 there were 10,500 U.S. nationals in China. There was real concern in State that these nationals might be caught in the fighting. See Moffat diary, Sept. 1, 1937; Leahy diary, Sept. 3, 1937. By November 6, 1937 there were 4,600 nationals remaining. See Hull letter to Garner, Jan. 8, 1938, *FR Japan,*

1:429–30. For Hull's interest in applying a moral embargo on munition sales to Japan and China see Wilson, *Disarmament,* 62.

32. Borg, *Crisis,* 346–49. The president's order is in *FR Japan,* 2:201.

33. Green memos, Sept. 13, 16, 1937, *FR 37,* 4:527–28, 533–34.

34. Hornbeck memo, Sept. 4, 1937, file 793.94/9860, RG 59; Grew to Hull, Aug. 27, Hull to Grew, Sept. 23, 1937, *FR 37,* 3:485–88, 505–8; Moffat diary, Oct. 27, 28, 1937.

35. Hamilton memo, Sept. 20, 1937, *FR Japan,* 1:502; Moffat diary, Oct. 4, 1937.

36. On fear of appearing to "gang up" on Japan and keeping Britain at a distance see various items in *FR 37,* 3:160–61, 205, 235, 289–90, 328. On distrust of the British see Hornbeck memo, July 31, 1937, "Dept. of State" file, Hornbeck papers; Moffat diary, July 20, 29, 31, Aug. 4, 6, 1937; Eden letter, Sept. 15, 1937, file 20667/A6896/448/45, FO 371.

37. Moffat diary, Oct. 1, 2, 4, 1937; Wilson, *Disarmament,* 67–68; State memo to British Embassy, Oct. 5, 1937, *FR 37,* 3:582–83. See also Moffat diary, July 29, 1937, and Hull to Grew, Sept. 14, 1937, *FR 37,* 3:524.

38. Hornbeck memo, Sept. 3, Wilson memo, Sept. 2, 1937, *FR 37,* 4:9–12; FE memo, Sept. 3, 1937; file 793.94/9941, RG 59; Moffat diary, Aug. 31, Sept. 17, 1937.

39. Moffat diary, Sept. 22, 23, 1937; Hornbeck draft to Harrison (Geneva), Sept. 24, 1937 (not sent), "Morgue" folder, Hornbeck papers; Hull to Harrison, Sept. 24, 28, 1937, *FR 37,* 4:33–34, 43.

40. Wilson and Hornbeck memo, Sept. 28, 1937, file 793.94/10299, RG 59. Undated draft, folder 309, Hull papers. Moffat diary, Sept. 28, 1937; press release, Sept. 28, 1937, State, *Bulletin;* Hull to Harrison, Sept. 28, 1937, *FR 37,* 4:42–45.

41. Text of the speech is in *FR Japan,* 1:379–83. See also Norman Davis draft Sept. 6, 1937, box 51, Davis papers, and State's draft Sept. 28, 1937, *FR 37,* 4:42–44. Wilson claims the "sting in the scorpion's tail" originated with the president. Wilson, *Disarmament,* 69.

42. Moffat diary, Oct. 5, 1937.

43. For an example of Roosevelt's disdain for the minutae of diplomacy, see Moffat diary, Sept. 18, 1937. On Roosevelt's intentions see Ickes, *Diary,* 2:213, 223, 277; Phillips diary, Oct. 26, 1937; Borg, *Crisis,* ch. 13; Roosevelt press conference, Oct. 6, 1937, no. 400, 10:247ff, PPC, FDRL. Roosevelt's interest in naval blockades is treated in Haight, "Naval Quarantine," 203–26, and "Aftermath," 248. For Roosevelt's instructions and the debate in State, see Berle, *Navigating,* 140–41; Moffat diary, Oct. 8, 10, 1937; Long, *Diary.* Oct. 13, 1937; Wilson, *Disarmament,* 69.

44. Borg, *Crisis,* 400–5; Hornbeck memo, Oct. 6, 1937, box 2, Davis papers.

45. Moffat diary, Oct. 11, 28, 1937, Hamilton memo, Oct. 12, 1937, *FR 37,* 3:596–600; Wilson, *Disarmament,* 69–70.

46. Davis memos, Oct. 19, 20, 1937, box 5, Davis papers; Haight, "Aftermath," 243–48; Borg, *Crisis,* 405–8; Cole, *Roosevelt & Isolationists,* 246–47; Dallek, *Roosevelt,* 150–53; Jacobs, "Quarantine Speech," 499–502.

47. Wilson letter to Grew, Nov. 16, 1937, "Joseph C. Grew" folder,

Wilson papers. The only public statement coming out of State after Oct. 5 was an endorsement of a league denunciation of Japan as violating the Nine Power Treaty and State's moderates drafted it in as unprovocative language as possible. See *FR Japan,* 1:384–97. Wilson letter to Grew, Oct. 16, 1937; "Joseph C. Grew" folder, Wilson papers. Moffat diary, Oct. 6, 1937. For a fine summary of departmental diplomatic actions during October see Borg, *Crisis,* 408–14. Borg attributes the conciliatory actions of State to an "administration" policy, while it seems to me that the officers of State followed a policy quite different from what the president had in mind.

48. Welles to Davis, Oct. 30, 1937, *FR 37,* 4:23–24; Moffat diary, Oct. 31, 1937. See also Feis letter to Frankfurter, Oct. 25, 1937; box 325, Frankfurter papers.

49. Moffat diary, Sept. 15, 29, Oct. 12, Nov. 3, 13, 1937; Berle, *Navigating,* 141; personality portrait drafted by British embassy in Washington, 1939, file 22834/A5562/5143/45, FO 371.

50. Details of this conflict between State and the delegation are in file 793.94 Conference, RG 59; Moffat diary, Oct. 30–31, 1937, Hamilton memo to Hornbeck, "Max Hamilton" folder, Hornbeck papers; Stimson diary, Nov. 7, 1937, Welles to Davis, Nov. 1, 1937, *FR 37,* 4:134. The final draft of the opening speech is printed in *FR Japan,* 1:404–8.

51. Clive to FO, Nov. 9, 1937, file 21017/F9385/6799/10, FO 371.

52. Davis to Hull, Nov. 10, 1937, Hull to Davis, Nov. 12, 1937, *FR 37,* 4:176/77, 180.

53. Holman minute, Nov. 12, 1937, file 21017/F9385/6799/10, FO 371; Welles memo, Nov. 13, 1937, *FR 37,* 4:154; Lee, *Britain,* ch. 3.

54. Davis to Roosevelt and Hull, Nov. 14, 17, 1937, Hull to Davis, Nov. 15, 1937, *FR 37,* 4:183–88; Moffat diary, Nov. 13, 19, 1937; *New York Times,* Nov. 16, 1937, 3. The conference adjourned Nov. 24, 1937. The final declaration is in *FR Japan,* 1:417ff.

55. Hornbeck letter to Grew, Dec. 20, 1937, Hornbeck papers.

56. Grew to Hull, Nov. 18, 19, 1937; Hull to Grew, Nov. 19, 1937, *FR 37,* 3:690–97, 699–701; Heinrichs, *Ambassador,* 460ff.

57. Moffat memo, Dec. 2, 1937, Welles memo, Dec. 8, 1937, *FR 37,* 4:235, 776; Bullitt letter to Moore, Dec. 17, 1937, "Bullitt–1937" folder, Moore papers; Hornbeck letter to Grew, Dec. 28, 1937, Hornbeck papers. See also Heinrichs, *Ambassador,* 253–54, Borg, *Crisis,* 462ff.

Chapter 2

1. Johnson letter to MacMurray, July 20, 1937, MacMurray papers; Johnson letter to Adm. Brooks Upham, Dec. 7, 1937, Johnson papers; Johnson to Hull, Dec. 8, 1937, *FR 37,* 3:778.

2. FE memo, Dec. 11, 1937, file 890.00/72, RG 59.

3. Koginos, *Panay Incident;* Perry, *Panay Incident;* Heinrichs, *Ambassador,* 255–59; Borg, *Crisis,* 486ff; *FR Japan,* 1:532–47; Moffat diary, Dec. 15, 1937.

4. Wheeler, *Prelude;* Pelz, *Race;* and Heinrichs, "United States Navy."

5. Yarnell letter to J. Weldon Jones, Apr. 1, 1937, Harvey Overesch, July

23, 1937, "Far Eastern Situation" folder, CINCAF correspondence, personal, Yarnell papers; Yarnell letter to Leahy, Aug. 10, 1937, Johnson papers.

6. Yarnell letter to Johnson, Oct. 22, 1937, Johnson papers; Yarnell memo, Nov. 7, 1937, "Yarnell" folder, Hornbeck papers and "Navy Department" file, PSF, FDRL.

7. Leahy diary, Aug. 29, 30, 31, 1937; Wilson, *Disarmament*, 60; Moffat diary, Sept. 1, 1937. Hornbeck favored the ship transfer. See Hornbeck memo, Sept. 4, 1937, *FR 37*, 4:306.

8. Yarnell to Navy Dept., Sept. 22, 1937, file 393.1115/1057, RG 59.

9. Roosevelt memo to Hull, Oct. 2, 1937, Hull memo to Roosevelt, Oct. 4, 1937, *FR 37*, 4:362–64.

10. Leland P. Lovette letter to Yarnell, Oct. 2, 1937, box 4, Yarnell papers; Wilson memo to Hull, Sept. 22, 1937, file 393.1115/1057, RG 59. On the warning to Yarnell see Leahy diary, Sept. 24, 1937; Sec. of the Navy to Yarnell, Sept. 24, 1937, file QW 17 (370922), box 4010, RG 80.

11. Lovette letter to Yarnell, Oct. 2, 1937, box 4, Yarnell papers; Wilson memo to Hull, Sept. 22, 1937, file 393.1115/1057, RG 59.

12. Leahy diary, Oct. 2, 30, 1937; Hamilton memo, Oct. 28–30, 1937, *FR 37*, 3:646–48.

13. Leahy diary, Dec. 12, 13, 1937.

14. Moffat diary, Dec. 13, 1937; Moffat letter to Grew, Dec. 18, 1937, vol. 12: Moffat papers; Leahy diary, Dec. 14, 16, 1937.

15. Morgenthau diary, 103:20ff; Ickes, *Diary*, 2:274.

16. Treasury's concern is in various memos in Morgenthau diary, 87:156ff, 274ff, 383, and in "FFC Programs: Embargo, etc." folder, box 21, RG 56.

17. Lee, *Britain*, 91.

18. Morgenthau diary, 103:53ff.

19. Ibid., 248; Lee, *Britain*, 91.

20. *FR Japan*, 1:523, 549–51; Lee, *Britain*, 92.

21. Roosevelt advice on blockading Germany in 1936 is in a memo of conversation with Arthur Sweetzer, May 29, 1942, Sweetzer papers. Roosevelt's involvement with things naval is in Richardson, *Treadmill*. On Roosevelt's interest in a naval blockade of Japan see Haight, "Naval Quarantine."

22. Ickes, *Diary*, 2:274; Morgenthau diary, 103:59ff; Lee, *Britain*, 90–91; Haight, "Naval Quarantine," 209–11.

23. Lee, *Britain*, 89–90; Moffat diary, Dec. 15, 1937.

24. Cadogan, *Diaries*, 31–35; Lee, *Britain*, 93.

25. Leutze, *Bargaining*, 17–28; Haight, "Naval Quarantine," 219–24; Cadogan, *Diaries*, 33–40; Borg, *Crisis*, 510–12; Welles memos, Jan. 8, 13, 1938, *FR 38*, 3:7–8, 19.

26. Haight argues the British blocked Roosevelt's naval proposals and forced the president to adopt an alternative method of blocking the Axis, i.e., providing France with aircraft. I do not credit Roosevelt with such determination nor the British with such influence. Haight, "Naval Quarantine," 225–26.

27. FE memo, Jan. 22, 1938, file 890.00/77, RG 59; Hornbeck memo, Feb. 16, 1938, folder 114, Hull papers.

28. Grew diary, March 1938, 3716–19; Grew letter to Hornbeck, April 12, 1938, memo to George Sumner, March 9, 1938, Grew letter to Hornbeck, Jan. 19, 1938, vol. 91, Grew papers.

29. Hornbeck letter to Grew, Dec. 20, 27, 1937, Hornbeck papers. For State's lack of concern for Japanese "excuses" see FE memo, Apr. 8, 1938, file 611.9412/55, RG 59.

30. FE memo, Jan. 22, Apr. 2, 23, June 4, July 9, 1938, file 890.00/77, Ballantine memo, Jan. 25, 1938, *FR 38*, 3:53; Spencer memo, Jan. 27, 1938, file 693.001 Manchuria/33, Jones memo, Apr. 13, 1938, file 893.62222/6, Adams memo, July 7, 1938, file 693.001/348, Jones notation on dispatch no. 320 from Tianjin, Aug. 26, 1938, file 793.94/14041, RG 59; Hornbeck memo to Hull, July 11, 1938, Hornbeck papers.

31. Feis letter to Frankfurter, Jan. 18, 1938, box 325, Frankfurter papers; Grew letter to Hornbeck, March 17, 1938, vol. 91, Grew papers.

32. Hornbeck memo, Jan. 3, 1938, "Japan policy" folder, Hornbeck papers; various reports for 1938 and 1939, files 893.00 P.R./141–64, RG 59; Johnson letter to Thomas Lamont, Feb. 8, 1938; to Anne Archbold, Feb. 16, 1938, Johnson papers; Johnson letter to Hull, Feb. 17, 1938, Hull to Johnson, March 18, 1938, Hornbeck memo to Hull, May 27, 1938, folders 103–4, Hull papers; FE memo, March 5, 1938, file 890.00/83, RG 59; Ballantine lecture to Naval War College, Nov. 5, 1937, 46ff, WPD, RG 38.

33. Johnson to Hull, March 4, 1938, *FR 38*, 3:115–16. This view was supported by marine captain Evans Carlson, who spent much time with the Chinese Communist armies. Carlson letters to Missy LeHand, March 3/4, 31, 1938, file 4951, PPF, FDRL. Distretti, "Attachés."

34. Ballantine memo, May 4, 1938, file 793.94/13081 1/2, RG 59.

35. Grew letter to Hornbeck, March 22, 1938, vol. 91, Grew papers; Ballantine memo, Aug. 1, 1938, Hornbeck memo, Aug. 2, 1938, file 793.94119/435, RG 59. A similar but more moderately phrased explanation of this view is in Hornbeck letter to Cadogan, April 13, 1938, *FR 38*, 3:153.

36. FE memo, June 14, 1938, file 611.9431/160, RG 59.

37. Hull to Grew, June 25, 1938, *FR 38*, 3:204–5; Vincent memo, July 6, 1938, file 893.6363/161, RG 59. Hull, Jan. 15, Feb. 3, 1938, *FR 38*, 4:236, 646; Hamilton memo, Jan. 21, 1938, Welles memo to French charge, Feb. 16, 1938, FE memos, March 2, May 10, 18, June 17, 1938, file 693.002/ 453, 516A, 532, 640, 656, 661, 699, RG 59; Grew diary, 113: 3737; Hull to Grew, May 2, 4, 14, 1938, *FR 38*, 3:690–91, 698–99, 711, Grew to Hull, May 7, 1938, *FR 38*, 3:706–7; Feis memo, May 11, 1938, file 893.5151/ 506, RG 59. The ineffectiveness of diplomatic protests is revealed in FE memo, May 19, 1938, file 893.5151/461, RG 59; Hull, July 16, 1938, *FR 38*, 4:28. On July 4, 1938, Grew presented to the Japanese government a list of more than 250 unsettled incidents involving Japanese authorities and American interests in China, *FR 38*, 3:211.

38. Compare the final version of Hull to Grew, March 31, 1938 in *FR 38*, 4, with the draft version in file 893.5151/428, RG 59.

39. FE memo, Apr. 16, 1938, Trade Agreements Div. memo, May 6, 1938, file 611.9431/158, RG 59. Activists in State were unhappy with these findings. See Walter Adams letter to Johnson, May 24, 1938, Johnson papers.

40. The boycott movement is described in Shepardson, *World Affairs*, 224. The weakness of the movement was noted by *Business Week*, Dec. 4, 1937, 25, 27. See also Janeway, "Japan's Partner," 1–8 and "Japan's New Need," 338–40.

41. Letters protesting Japanese atrocities are in file 894.24/148ff, RG 59. The impact of these letters is testified to in Hamilton's letter to Johnson, June 3, 1938, Johnson papers, Stimson letter, June 9, 1938, Stimson papers.

42. Hornbeck's views on Japan are in Hornbeck letter to Iohnson, March 21, 1938, Johnson papers; Hornbeck memo, Jan. 3, 1938, Hornbeck papers. His views about public opinion are in letters to Johnson, Dec. 31, 1937, Apr. 20, 1938, Johnson papers; Hornbeck memo, July 25, 1938, *FR 38* 3:426. On Japan being a paper tiger see Hornbeck letter to Grew, Feb. 17, 1938, Hornbeck letter to Bullitt, May 9, 1938, Hornbeck papers. Hornbeck was not averse to helping those who shared his view to get into print and stir up a "little healthy excitement over some of these China–Japan problems." Hornbeck letter to Johnson, Jan. 20, 1938, Johnson papers; McCarty, "Hornbeck," 159–60; Hornbeck memo to Hull, March 26, 1938, "Adolf A. Berle 1938–1941" folder, Hornbeck papers.

43. Moffat diary, June 10, 1938.

44. Text of the moral embargo letter is in *FR Japan 1931–41*, 2:201–2. See also Atwater, *American Regulation*, 233; National Munitions Control Board, *Second Report*, 80

45. Vincent memos, July 6, 1938, file 893.6363/161, RG 59; July 23, 1938, *FR 38*, 3:234–37. Approving statements by Hornbeck, Welles, and Hull are attached to the original of this memo in file 793.94/13729, RG 59.

46. Schuler memo, Aug. 5, 1938; with reference to Grew dispatch no. 3100 dated July 11, 1938, file 793.94/13585, FE memo, Aug. 10, 1938; file 611.9431/161, FE memo, Aug. 6, 1939, file 890.00/105, RG 59. Hornbeck letter to Bullitt, Aug. 11, 1938, Hornbeck papers; Hawkins memo, July 30, 1938, *FR 38*, 3:244–46.

47. Hornbeck letter to Johnson, July 30, 1938, Hamilton letter to Johnson, Sept. 15, 1938, Johnson papers; Hull to Lockhart (Shanghai), July 9, 1938, *FR 38*, 4:398.

48. Johnson letter to Hamilton, Aug. 13, 1938, Johnson papers; Johnson to Hull, July 12, 1938, file 393.1115/3383, RG 59.

49. Vincent memo, July 13, 1938, file 393.1115/3383, RG 59; Leahy diary, July 23, 1938; Hornbeck letter to Johnson, July 29–30, 1938, Johnson papers.

50. Leahy diary, July 9, 18, 23, 1938.

51. Hull to Johnson, July 24, 1938, *FR 38*, 4:158–59.

52. Hull to Johnson, Aug. 1, 1938, *FR 38*, 4:165; Acting Sec. of Navy Edison letter to Hull, Aug. 15, 1938, file P9–2/EF16, RG 38; Tulley Shelley memo of phone conversation with Hamilton, Aug. 30, 1938, ONI memo, Aug. 30, 1938, file QW 17, box 4010, RG 80; FE memo, Aug. 30, 1938, Hamilton memo, Sept. 3, 1938, *FR 38*, 4:178–79, 182; Leahy diary, Aug. 19, 1938, FE memo, Aug. 20, 1939, file 890.00/107, RG 59.

53. Craig memo to CNO, Nov. 3, 1937, file Orange 2720-105, box 183, Operations Division, WPD, RG 165. See also Morton, "War Plan ORANGE," and Doyle, "U.S. Navy."

54. Burnett memo to Sec. of War, May 3, 1938, file "Philippine Islands," box 148, Sec. of War, general correspondence, 1932–42, RG 107; Hornbeck memo to Welles and Hull, Feb. 2, 1938, Hornbeck papers.

55. Krueger memo, Nov. 27, 1937, file Orange 2720-105, box 183, Operations Division, WPD, JPC to JB memo, Nov. 30, 1937, ser. 617, file JB 325, undated WPD memo commenting on Navy draft OP-12-B-6 which draft is dated Dec. 16, 1938, ser. 634, file JB 325, RG 165. See also Manchester, *American Caesar*, 180–83. WPD memo, Jan. 19, 1939, file A16-3/EG54 ser. 1, WPD, RG 38. Clark memo to Crenshaw, April 17, 1939, ser. 634, file JB 326, RG 165.

Chapter 3

1. Lee, *Britain*, ch. 6; Lowe, *Great Britain*, ch. 2; Clifford, *Retreat*, ch. 10.

2. For State's concern see FE memos, Sept. 17, Oct. 8, 1938, file 890.00/111, 114, RG 59. On the British position on Manchukuo see Cadogan letter to Hornbeck, Feb. 17, 1938, *FR 38*, 3:147–48.

3. Grew's message is in *FR Japan*, 1:785–90. Grew commented on the forcefulness of the statement, Grew diary, 119:3881ff, Grew papers.

4. Konoye's speech is in *FR Japan*, 1:478–81.

5. Grew letter to William Carey Crane, Dec. 23, 1938, vol. 91, Grew papers; FE memos, Nov. 10, 17, 1938, file 890.00/119, 120, RG 59; Moffat diary, Nov. 5, 1938.

6. Consideration of commercial sanctions was never extensive enough to approach being a plan. Hamilton memo, Oct. 10, 1938, *FR 38*, 4:62–65; Livesey memo, Oct. 10, 1938, Feis memo to Hamilton, Nov. 1, 1938, file 611.9431/183 1/2, 164 1/2, RG 59; Sayre, Hawkins, Livesy, Hamilton memo, Dec. 5, 1938, *FR 38*, 3:406–9; Adams memo, Jan. 21, 1939, file 893.5151/1347, RG 59. See also Moffat diary, Nov. 5, 1938.

7. Harry Dexter White memo, March 16, July 12, 1938, folder 189, box 62, RG 56; Morgenthau diary, box 127, 109; H. H. Kung letter to K. P. Chen, Aug. 30, 1938, folder D, box 33, Arthur Young papers.

8. For Export-Import Bank attitudes see Hornbeck memo, Aug. 11, 1938, file 893.51/6676, RG 59. State's views are in Hamilton memo, July 2, 1938, file 893.51/6638, RG 59; Hornbeck memo, July 15, 1938, *FR 38*, 3:538–39; Hornbeck letter to Bullitt, Aug. 11, 1938, "Bullitt" file, Hornbeck papers; Moffat diary, Sept. 6, 1938.

9. Feis memo to Hull, Sept. 22, 1938, *FR 38*, 3:562; Morgenthau diary, 142:352. The quotation is in a Harry Dexter White memo, Oct. 10, 1938, folder #3, "China," White papers. For Roosevelt's need for assurances see Arthur Young memo, Nov. 2, 1938, folder D, box 33, Young papers; Feis memo to Hull, Nov. 12, 1938, *FR 38*, 3:568. The development of the credit proposal is described in Adams, "Road to Pearl Harbor," 81–85.

10. Hamilton memo, Nov. 13, 1938, *FR 38*, 3:569.

11. Hornbeck memo, Nov. 14, 1938, *FR 38*, 3:573.

12. Hull memo to Roosevelt, Nov. 14, 1938, *FR 38*, 3:574–78. Hull also delivered a copy of Hornbeck's memo, which memo is filed in the "China 1938–1944" file, box 4, diplomatic correspondence, PSF, FDRL. Adams, "Road to Pearl Harbor," argues that Hull included Hornbeck's memoran-

dum because he was indecisive on this issue. More likely, Hull included Hornbeck's position paper because it reflected a strongly held minority view within State. The important thing is that Hull argued strongly and successfully against that course of action.

13. Pratt, *Hull*, 2:9, 19–20. Adams letter to Johnson, May 24, 1938, Johnson papers; Berle, *Navigating*, March 31, 1939, 205–6.

14. Morgenthau diary, 153:302–3.

15. Grew to Hull, Nov. 29, 30, 1938, *FR 38*, 3:397, 399; State memo Dec. 5, 1937, *FR 38*, 3:406. Morgenthau diary, 153:302–3. White memo, Dec. 6, 1938, "FFC Programs: Embargo, Etc." folder, box 27, RG 56.

16. Grew to Hull, Dec. 1, 14, 1938; State memo, Dec. 5, 1938, Brit. aide memoire, Dec. 7, 1938, Welles memo, Dec. 9, 1938, Brit. aide memoire, Dec. 7, 1938, *FR 38*, 3:400–402, 406ff, 416–17, 582, 581–82.

17. Welles to Hull, Dec. 2, 1938, Hull to Welles, Dec. 4, 1938, *FR 38*, 575–77.

18. Hornbeck memo, Nov. 14, 1938, *FR 38*, 3:572–73; FO, Jan. 4, 1939, file 23409/F11/11/10, FO 371. Adams, "Road to Pearl Harbor," 87–92, argues that the tung oil credit constituted a change in U.S. policy because it reflected a willingness to stop Japan even at the risk of war. I do not believe the evidence supports such a conclusion.

19. Hornbeck memo, Dec. 22, 1938, *FR 38*, 3:425–77; Welles to Hull, Dec. 20, 1938, Hull to Welles, Dec. 23, 1938; *FR 38*, 4:104–6. The final version of the note appears in *FR Japan*, 1:820–26.

20. The Oct. 6, 1938, the 1932, and the 1915 protests are in *FR Japan*, 1:785–90, 76 and *FR 15*, 105–11.

21. Hamilton lecture, Jan. 6, 1939, "Max Hamilton" folder, Hornbeck papers.

22. Vincent memo, Jan. 20, 1939, file 793.94/14694, RG 59. All but the first paragraph of that memo, in which Vincent cites Lippmann, is in *FR 39*, 3:483–85.

23. Adams memo, Jan. 21, 1939, file 893.5151/1347, Jan. 27, 1939, file 794.94/14653 1/2, RG 59.

24. Hornbeck memos, Feb. 25, March 8, 1939, *FR 1939*, 3:507–12, 655–56. Hornbeck's attitude toward Vincent's viewpoint is revealed in Hornbeck's notation on Vincent's memo, notation dated Jan. 20, 1939, file 793.94/14694, RG 59.

25. Adams memo, March 25, 1939, file 711.94/1263, RG 59; Jones memo, Feb. 15, 1939, Grew dispatch, Jan. 7, 1939, Jones memo, Apr. 20, 1939, Salisbury memo, Jan. 30, 1939, *FR 39*, 3:478, 481, 530–33, 496–97; Sturgeon memo, Dec. 1, 1938, *FR 38*, 3:234.

26. Grew dispatch to Hull, Jan. 13, 1939, received Feb. 6, 1939, *FR 39*, 3:1–3.

27. Roosevelt press conference, Apr. 8, 1939, no. 537, 13:260ff, PPC, FDRL.

28. The Roosevelt administration did not consider Japan's claim of sovereignty over the Spratly islands worthy of strong action. When the French and British came to the United States seeking joint economic pressure on Japan, they received sympathetic words but no action. See various items, *FR 39*, 3:1–116, 528–30, 641–42, Mallet to FO, Jan. 23, 28, with attached

minute dated Jan. 31, 1939, file 23409/F671/11/10, FO 371. See also Dallek, *Roosevelt,* 178–92.

29. American Committee, *America's Share,* 74; *Town Meeting of the Air,* Feb. 23, 1939, 6–7; Gallup, ed., *Gallup Poll,* 1:159–60. See also Friedman, *Road from Isolation;* Cohen, *Chinese Connection,* 212–13.

30. Moffat diary, Apr. 10, 17, 1939.

31. Moffat diary, Apr. 10, 12, 1939; Hamilton memo, March 7, 1939. *FR 39,* 3:515; Dallek, *Roosevelt,* 184; Divine, *Illusion,* 231–85.

32. Price letter to Stimson, Aug. 3, 1939, letter file, ACNPJA papers.

33. Grew to Hull, Feb. 8, 1939, Hull to Grew, Feb. 10, 1939, *FR 39,* 3:6–9, 11.

34. FE memo, Apr. 3, 1939, file 611.9431/4–1139, Sayre memo, undated, file 711.942/171, FE memo, Apr. 28, 1939, file 711.942/170 1/2, Hornbeck memo, May 12, 1939, file 711.942/634, RG 59; Sayre memo, May 11, 1939, *FR 39,* 3:536–37; Hosoya, "Miscalculations," 99, believes the effort to redraft the treaty was undertaken as part of a program of economic warfare rather than for sincere commercial reasons.

35. Hamilton memo, Jan. 27, 1939, Hornbeck memos, Feb. 6, March 10, 1939, Jones memo, May 3, 1939, Hull, May 4, 1939, *FR 39,* 3:494–95, 504, 376–78, 198, 399–400; Vincent memo, Feb. 10, 1939, file 893.51/6821, Economic Affairs Division memo, March 23, 1939, file 693.1115 Manchuria/1, RG 59. State quietly informed American bankers "that the present would be an inopportune moment, an especially inopportune moment" for publicly withdrawing from the consortium. Hornbeck letter to Lamont, May 8, 1939, Lamont letter to Hornbeck, June 12, 1939, file 893.51/6916, 6921, RG 59; Cohen, *Chinese Connection,* 218–19. Welles to Peck, March 21, 1939, Green memo, May 29, 1939, *FR 39,* 3:744–45, 670; Adams memo, Jan. 23, 1939, file 893.51/6772, RG 59.

36. Vincent memo, March 23, 1939, file 711.00/1238, RG 59. Moffat diary, Feb. 17, 1939. For the burden of work the department labored under see Stimson letter to Hornbeck, March 7, 1939, Hornbeck letter to Stimson, March 8, 1939, Stimson papers; Hornbeck letter to Peck, May 8, 1939, box 334, Hornbeck papers.

37. Langer & Gleason, *Challenge,* 104; Hull, *Memoirs,* 1:630.

38. Vincent memo, Apr. 19, 1939, Jones memo, Apr. 21, 1939, Ballantine memo, Apr. 24, 1939, MacKay memo, Apr. 26, 1939, Hamilton memo, April 28, 1939, file 711.00/1360, RG 59.

39. Gauss to Hull, March 1, 1939, *FR 39,* 4:11–12. See also various Gauss reports, *FR 39,* 4:1–12.

40. Gauss to Hull, May 6, 1939, *FR 39,* 4:36–40.

41. Hull to Grew, May 12, 1939, Hull to Peck, May 19, 1939, Hull to Gauss, May 22, 1939, *FR 39,* 4:46–47, 53–56, 58–59.

42. Tianjin developments in *FR 39,* 4:172ff.

43. Dooman to Hull, June 24, 26, 1939, *FR 39,* 198–99, 201–3; Lee, *Britain,* ch. 7; Lowe, *Great Britain,* ch. 3; Reynolds, *Anglo—American,* 58–62; Shai, *Origins of the War,* ch. 6.

44. Welles statement is in June 16, 1939 minutes of the Standing Liaison Committee, RG 353; Moffat diary, June 15, 1939; Hull to Caldwell (Tianjin), June 13, 1939, Hull to Dooman, June 19, 1939, *FR 39,* 4:177, 185;

Berle, *Navigating,* 228–29. Treasury's concern is in White memo to Morgenthau, July 10, 1939, folder 189, box 62, acc. #69A-4707, RG 56.

45. Hull to Dooman, June 24, 1939, Dooman to Hull, June 26, 1939, *FR 39,* 4:197–98, 201–3; Berle, *Navigating,* 230–31.

46. FE memo, July 6, 1939, file 890.00/152, Adams memo, July 6, 1939, file 793.94/15241, RG 59. The draft note as approved by Roosevelt is in file 711.94/1287 1/2, RG 59.

47. Hull to Dooman, July 1, 1939, Dooman to Hull, July 3, 1939, Hamilton letter to Grew, July 4, 1939, Grew memo, July 6, 1939, *FR 39,* 4:213–21.

48. Dooman to Hull, July 21, Aug. 4, 1939, *FR 39,* 4:224–25, 231.

49. Dallek, *Roosevelt,* 188–96; Langer & Gleason, *Challenge,* 153–59; Cole, *Roosevelt & Isolationists,* 311ff, 346–51; Hull, *Memoirs,* 1:635–38; Moffat diary, July 26, 27, 1939; Roger Sherman Greene letter to Price, July 25, 1939, letter file, ACNPJA papers; Ruth Bacon memo, Feb. 9, 1940, file 711.942/573, RG 59; minutes, July 26, 1939, Standing Liaison Committee, RG 353; Lindsay to FO, July 31, 1939, file 23569/F8216/12/36, FO 371; Ballantine lecture at Naval War College, Oct. 17, 1939, 27, WPD, RG 38.

50. A Gallup poll published on August 30, 1939 showed 71 percent of the respondents favoring the abrogation notice. Gallup, ed., *Gallup Poll,* 1:177.

Chapter 4

1. Grew memo to Dooman, Crewswell, Smith—Hutton, Oct. 12, 1939, Grew diary, 128:4127ff; Craigie, Oct. 16, 1939, file 23405/F11083/1/10, FO 371.

2. Grew diary, 127:4107ff; Gallup, ed., *Gallup Poll,* 1:177. On congressional opinon see Libby, "Irresolute Years," 157–58.

3. Hart semimonthly newsletter, Aug. 16, 1939, file FF6/A9-5 (390703) Secretary's general correspondence, RG 80; Ballantine, Naval War College lecture, Oct. 17, 1939, 2–3, RG 38. For the view that Japan would compromise only minor points see Hornbeck memo, Sept. 2, 1939, FE memo, Oct. 11, 1939, file 711.94/1302, 1392, RG 59. For views on the Japanese character see Treasury memo, Jan. 1939, folder 83, "China: Japanese Conflict," box 56, RG 56; Ballantine memo, May 18, 1939, Vincent memo, April 7, 1939, Salisbury memo, Feb. 28, 1939, files 793.94/14878 1/2, /14719, Hornbeck memo, April 4, 1939, file 793.94119/533, RG 59.

4. FE memos, May 24, 1939, file 894.00/856, RG 59, June 7, 1939, *FR 39,* 3:181ff; Hornbeck memo, Sept. 6, 1939, Hornbeck papers; Hornbeck memo to Hull, Sept. 16, 1939, *FR 39,* 3:250–51.

5. Grew diary, 127:4098; Hull memo, Sept. 7, 1939, *FR Japan,* 2:12–14.

6. Hornbeck memo, Sept. 14, 1939, Hornbeck papers.

7. Grew diary, 127:4083, 4127. Actually, Roosevelt was wrong, it would not be easy to intercept the Japanese fleet. See General Board memo to Sec. of Navy, Aug. 31, 1939, file "Navy Dept. 1938–39," PSF, FDRL.

8. For the origins of the speech see Grew letter to Hamilton, July 30, 1939, file 611.9431/7–3039, RG 59; Grew diary, 128:4108–9. For the purpose of the speech see Grew diary, 128:4127ff; Craigie to FO, Oct. 16, 1939, file 23405/F11083/1/10, FO 371.

9. The speech is printed in *FR Japan*, 2:19–29.

10. See ch. 3.

11. Grew memo, Nov. 4, 1939, *FR Japan*, 2:31–34; Grew to Hull, Nov. 4, 1939, *FR 39*, 3:593–95; Heinrichs, *Ambassador*, 296–300.

12. For example, Johnson to Hull, Oct. 17, 1939, and Jones memo, Oct. 6, 1939, *FR 39*, 3:286–88.

13. Grew to Hull, Nov. 28, 1939, Grew dispatch to Hull, Dec. 1, 1939, received Jan. 10, 1940, *FR 39*, 3:602–13.

14. FE memo, Dec. 2, 1939, file 711.94/1386, RG 59; Hull to grew, Dec. 8, 1939, *FR Japan*, 2:47; Hull memo, Dec. 15, 1939, *FR 39*, 3:98–99.

15. Grew to Hull, Dec. 18, 20, 1939, *FR 39*, 3:622, 624–25.

16. Grew to Hull, Dec. 18, 1939, *FR 39* 3:622.

17. Hull to Grew, Dec. 18, 20, 21, 1939, *FR Japan*, 2:190–95, *FR 39*, 2:625–26; Hornbeck memo, Dec. 19, 1939, file 793.94112/301, RG 59; Berle diary, Jan. 21, 1940; Hosoya, "Tripartite Pact," 195–200.

18. Heinrichs, *Ambassador*, 297–301; Hornbeck letter to Grew, Dec. 9, 1939, Hornbeck papers.

19. Ballantine Naval War College lecture, Oct. 17, 1939, 44–45, WPD, RG 38; FE memos, Oct. 24, Nov. 6, 19, 1939, file 793.94/15423, 15494, 15462, RG 59; Hornbeck memo to Stimson, Nov. 7, 1939, Stimson papers; Hull to Bullitt, Dec. 2, 1939, file 793.94/15517, RG 59; Hull memo to Roosevelt, Nov. 1, 1939, Welles memo, Nov. 21, 1939, *FR 39*, 3:712–13, 321.

20. MacVitty to Hull, Aug. 6, 1939, *FR 39*, 4:146–47.

21. Welles to Dooman, Aug. 23, 1939, Dooman to Hull, Aug. 24, 1939, *FR 39*, 4:148, 152–53.

22. MacVitty to Hull, Sept. 10, 12, 15, 26, 1939, Hull to MacVitty, Sept. 25, 1939, *FR 39*, 4:158–69; British consul at Xiamen to the British ambassador at Shanghai, Oct. 30, 1939, file 24663/F34/32/10, FO 371. The final agreement was signed on October 17 and both Japanese and American troops were withdrawn on the same day. MacVitty to Hull, Oct. 17, 1939, *FR 39*, 4:162–63. See also Capt. John Staples to ONI, Sept. 8, 1939, file P9–2/EF16, ONI general correspondence, RG 38. Clarke minute, file 24663/F34/32/10, FO 371.

23. Johnson (London) to Hull, Aug. 17, 21, 1939, Dooman dispatch to Hull, Aug. 25, 1939, Hornbeck memo, Sept. 1, 1939, Brit. aide memoire, Aug. 31, 1939, *FR 39*, 4:233–42; Hull to Bullitt, July 28, 1939, *FR 39*, 3:695; Hornbeck memo, Aug. 1, 1939, file 893.515/1410, Hamilton memo, Sept. 12, 1939, file 893.51/6988, RG 59; MacKay memo, Sept. 14, 1939, *FR 39*, 4:243–44; Peck to Hull, Jan. 12, 13, 1940, Hull to Peck, Jan. 13, 1940, Chin. aide memoire, Jan. 29, 1939, Dept. memo, Feb. 8, 1940, *FR 40*, 4:840–45, 854. For the final settlement see Brit. aide memoire, April 15–16, 1940, *FR 40*, 4:849–50. The final agreement was signed in June 1940.

24. Gauss to Hull, Aug. 24, Sept. 1, 1939, *FR 39*, 4:71–72. For why the British withdrew, see Brit. aide memoire, Aug. 29, 1939, *FR 39*, 3:215–17; Dooman to Hull, Sept. 5, 1939, *FR Japan*. 2:9–10; Kirk to Stark, Sept. 10, 1939 in Kittredge, "Naval Relations," 266; Bullitt to Hull, Sept. 11, 13, 15, 1939, Kennedy to Hull, Sept. 11, 1939, *FR 39*, 3:242–45, 247, 249–50.

25. Hull memos, Sept. 15, 1939, *FR Japan*, 2:12–13; *FR 39*, 3:238n;

Lothian to FO, Sept. 17, 1939, file 23551/F10253/4027/61; Kerr (Shanghai) to FO, Sept. 11, 18, 1939, files 23251/F10522/3918/10, 23456/F10321/84/10, FO 371.

26. Denning minutes Sept. 11, 1939, file 23521/F9939/3918/10, Brennan minute, Sept. 21, 1939, file 23456/F10321/84/10, FO 371; Brit. aide memoire, Sept. 19, 1939, French aide memoire, Sept. 20, 1939, U.S. aide memoire, Sept. 27, 1939, Bullitt to Hull, Sept. 30, 1939, *FR 39*, 3:256–59, 266–70, 272.

27. Hull to Gauss, Sept. 17, 1939, Gauss to Hull, Dooman to Hull, Sept. 19, 1939, Hull to Gauss, Sept. 21, 30, 1939, *FR 39*, 4:79–83, 89–91. Actually, the British retained a token military presence believing that once Roosevelt had obtained cash and carry in October he would be more forceful. Roosevelt got his cash-and-carry program but he did not become more forceful. Denning minutes, Oct. 6, 1939, file 23533/F10764/6457/10, Scott and Brenan minutes, Oct. 23, 1939, File 23456/F11166/84/10, FO 371; Hornbeck memos, Oct. 20, 28, 1939, and Brit. aide memoire, Oct. 30, 1939, *FR 39*, 3:291–95, 305, 307; Lothian to FO, Sept. 27, 1939, file 22838/A6639/6483/45, Kerr to FO, Nov. 10, 1939, with Clarke minute of Nov. 15, 1939, file 23569/F11815/1236/23, FO 371.

28. Hornbeck letter to Grew, Dec. 9, 1939, Hornbeck papers; Wilson letter to Castle, Dec. 20, 1939, case 1, Wilson papers; Legal Affairs Division memo, Oct. 2, 1939, Grady memo to FE, Oct. 17, 1939, file 611.9431/182 1/2, RG 59.

29. Hornbeck memo, Sept. 14, 1939, Hornbeck letter to Peck, Oct. 24, 1939, Hornbeck's notes on a luncheon given by Stimson, Nov. 9, 1939, "Henry Stimson" file, Hornbeck papers.

30. FE memo, Aug. 10, 1939, Legal Affairs memo with Hamilton comment, Oct. 2, 1939, Grady memo, Oct. 17, 1939, files 611.9431/177 1/2, 182 1/2, RG 59.

31. Hornbeck urged suspending generalized treatment of Japanese imports, ruling on each item individually. Hamilton disagreed and the idea was rejected. Hiss memo, Nov. 29, 1939, file 611.9431/196 1/2, Hornbeck memo with atached Hamilton memo, Dec. 19, 1939, file 711.942/428 1/2, RG 59.

32. Hornbeck memo, Nov. 16, 1939, file 611.9431/127 1/2, FE memo, Nov. 20, 1939, State memo to Roosevelt, Dec. 11, 1939, Roosevelt memo to Hull, Dec. 15, 1939, file 711.942/411, 412A, 409, RG 59; Hull letter to Hopkins, Dec. 15, 1939, *FR 39*, 3:617–18.

33. Hull memo to Roosevelt, Dec. 11, 1939, Roosevelt memo to Hull, Dec. 14, 1939, file 711.942/412A, 413, RG 59. Langer & Gleason, *Challenge*, 308; Morgenthau, *China*, 1:74–76. For Hull's instructions see Hull to Grew, Dec. 21, 1939, *FR 39*, 3:625–66.

34. Various memos, Sept. 18–21, 1939, *FR 39*, 3:545–47; FE memo, Oct. 24, 1939, file 711.942/304, RG 59. State also discouraged "good will" tours by Japanese to the United States. See Hamilton memo to Hull, Sept. 21, 1939, *FR 39*, 3:547; Hornbeck memos, Sept. 22, 1939, file 711.94/1306, 1307, RG 59.

35. Hull, *Memoirs*, 1:638. On December 2, 1939 the moral embargo was extended to materials from which planes were constructed. Though it was

aimed at the Soviet Union, it also affected Japan. Moffat diary, Nov. 16, 1939, State Dept. press releases, Dec. 2, 15, 1939, *FR Japan,* 2:202–3; Morgenthau, diary, 228.8; Morgenthau, *China,* 1:74–76.

36. Green memos, Nov. 15, 19, Dec. 14, 19, 1939, files 894.24/742, 759, 767, 764, RG 59; Hull, *Memoirs,* 1:729; State Dept. press release, Dec. 20, 1939, *FR Japan,* 2:203–4.

37. Ickes, *Diary,* 3:96; Hull memo, Jan. 31, 1940, *FR Japan,* 2:53.

38. Hornbeck draft of Roosevelt letter to Grew, Jan. 15, 1940, file 711.94/1420, RG 59. Grew received the letter Feb. 14, 1940 and was pleased by it, though he recognized it was drafted in State. Grew diary, 131:4290. See also Greene letters to Price, Feb. 6, 16, 1940, ACNPJA; Sansom and Brenan minutes, Feb. 6, 15, 1940, Lothian to FO, Feb. 24, 1940, file 24708/F924, F1398/193/61, FO 371.

39. Grew letter to Hornbeck, Jan. 31, 1940, vol. 98, Grew papers.

40. Grew letters to Hornbeck, Feb. 11, 1940, Forbes, Feb. 10, 1940, vol. 98. Roosevelt, Jan. 16, 1940, vol. 99, Grew papers; Grew diary, 100:4254.

41. Hornbeck memo, Jan. 16, 1940, Ballantine memo, Jan. 15, 1940, *FR 40,* 4:960–61; Hornbeck letter (with Hamilton and Ballantine) to Grew, Feb. 1, 1940, file 711.94/1396, RG 59. Hornbeck memo, Feb. 7, 1940, Hornbeck memo, Feb. 3, 1940, "Joseph C. Grew" file, Hornbeck papers. British observations are in Brenan minute, Feb 15, 1940, Warner minute, March 30, 1940, Howe minute, March 4, 1940, file 24708/F924, F1643, F924/193/61.

42. Various documents in *FR 40,* 4:637–47; Hull memo, Oct. 20, 1939, file 893.0146/721, RG 59; White memos, Sept. 26, Nov. 22, 1939, Cotton memo, Oct. 3, 1939, unattributed memo, c. Nov. 30, 1939, Hanes memo, Dec. 1, 1939, folder 253, box 68 (acc. #69A–4707), RG 56; Morgenthau, *China,* 1:17–18, 55; Hornbeck letter to Grew, Feb. 11, 1940, file 711.94/1396, RG 59.

43. Hull, *Memoirs,* 1:912.

Chapter 5

1. Japanese embassy press release, Apr. 15, 1940, *FR Japan,* 2:281; Grew diary, 134–4346.

2. Hull press release, Apr. 17, 1940, *FR Japan,* 2:281–82; Long, *Diary,* 81–82; Moffat diary, April 17, 1940, Harry Price letter to Stimson, April 25, 1940, ACNPJA papers; Grew diary, 134–4346; Grew to Hull, April 20, 1940, *FR Japan,* 2:283–84.

3. For documents on the transfer see *PHA,* pt. 1, 260, 304. Washington's concern that Japan was getting ready to move south is in Kittredge, "Naval Relations," 153; Tokyo military attaché to G-2, April 24, May 14, 1940, files 2063-357/29, 30, RG 165.

4. Stark letter to Richardson, Sept. 24, 1940, *PHA,* pt. 14, 932; Richardson, *Treadmill,* 332–33. Wolthuis, *U.S. and Netherland, Indies,* 67–68 argues that lack of naval power held back the United States. While power is always a factor, Hull consistently opposed anything provocative when it came to mobilization or deployment of ships. See State memo to Sec. of the

Navy, March 30, 1940, CNO file A4-3/FF6, RG 38. Richardson, *Treadmill*, 162–63; Berle, *Navigating*, 228–30; R. S. Crenshaw memo to CNO, Sept. 1, 1939, folder A16, WPD, ser. 1, RG 165; Stark letter to Richardson, March 15, 1940, *PHA*, pt 1, 258–59.

5. Long, *Diary*, 81; Hull memo, Apr. 17, 1940, *FR Japan*, 2:281–82; Kittredge, "Naval Relations," 267; Wolthuis, *U.S. and Netherland Indies*, 37–38.

6. Roosevelt press conference, no. 645–A, May 23, 1940, 15:364, PPC, FDRL; minutes, Advisory Committee on Problems of Foreign Relations, May 31, 1940, case 1, Wilson papers.

7. *See* ch. 3, n. 27 for earlier statement. Roosevelt press conference no. 636–A, April 18, 1940, 15:283, PPC, FDRL; Hull memo, Apr. 20, 1940, *FR Japan*, 2:283–84; Hull to Grew, May 30, 1940, *FR 40*, 4:336–37.

8. Hamilton memo, May 6, 1940, file 711.94/1506, RG 59.

9. Clayton speech before the National Cotton Council, Jan. 28, 1941, Clayton papers.

10. Dallek, *Roosevelt*, 226–29; Frank Knox letter to Annie Knox, June 15, 1940, Knox papers.

11. Hornbeck memo, Dec. 11, 1939, memo to Welles, Jan. 31, 1940, Hornbeck papers; Hornbeck letter to Nelson Johnson, Dec. 22, 1939, Hornbeck memo, Jan. 10, 1940, "Peace Planning Subcommittee" file, box 331, Hornbeck papers.

12. Wilson memo, Jan. 22, 1940, "Peace Planning Subcommittee" file, box 331, Hornbeck papers; Wilson diary, March 1, May 20, 1940, Wilson letter to Grew, March 9, case 4, Wilson papers.

13. Wilson memo, May 31, 1940, "Advisory committee on Problems of Foreign Relations," case 1, Wilson papers.

14. Long, *Diary* 107; Berle, *Navigating*, 316; Kittredge, "Naval Relations," 98; Wilson memo, "Advisory Committee on Problems of Foreign Relations, May 31, 1940, case 1, Wilson papers.

15. For operations of the navy in the Atlantic see Abbazia, *Roosevelt's Navy*, 33–35, 62–85. Crenshaw memo, May 15, 1940, file EF/48-1, May 22, 1940, file A4-3/FF1, CNO file, RG 38; Richardson testimony, *PHA*, pt. 1, 292; War Plans Division memo, May 22, 1940, folder A16-3, WPD ser. 1, RG 165; C. W. Cooke, memo, May 22, 28, 1940, CNO file A14-6, John P. Jackson memo, June 19, 1940, CNO file A14-4, RG 38; Crenshaw memo, June 17, 1940, folder A16-3, WPD ser. 1, RG 38. Even as Stark justified the transfer of the fleet to Hawaiian waters, he was thinking of detaching some cruisers to reinforce the Atlantic. See Stark letter to Richardson, May 22, 1940, *PHA*, pt. 14, 938–39.

16. Yarnell memo to CNO Sept. 2, 1939, folder A16-3, War Plans Division, ser. 1, RG 38; Strong memo, Sept. 19, 1939, file 3887-2, WPD, RG 165. For later examples of Army's feeling see McCabe memo, Sept. 29, 1939, G–2 file 2657-H-500, Strong memo March 2, 1940, WPD file 4192-3, G-2 memos "Summary of Far Eastern Documents," Jan. 8, July 20, 1940, G-2 Far East Branch, box 965, RG 165. But Army's disenchantment with fighting in the Pacific preceded Sept. 1939. See War Plans Division memo, Aut. 21, 1939, file 4192-1, Strong memo, Aug. 21, 1939, file 4192-2, Spaatz memo, Sept. 1, 1939, file 3748-18, WPD, RG 165.

17. Tirana memo, May 23, 1940, Pasvolsky file, box 1, RG 59.

18. Grew diary, 135:4382; Grew to Hull, June 4, 1940, *FR 40* 4:342–44; Grew letter to Hornbeck June 10, 1940, letters, vol. 98, Grew papers.

19. Berle memo, June 4, 1940, file 711.94/1563, RG 59.

20. Hull to Grew, June 4, 1940, *FR 40*, 4:345–46; Heinrichs, *Ambassador*, 309.

21. Grew memo, June 10, 1940 and Grew to Hull, June 12, 1940, *FR Japan*, 2:67–69, 77–78.

22. Stanton (Nanjing) to Hull, June 14, 1940, *FR 40*, 4:356–58.

23. Hull to Grew, June 15, 1940, *FR 40*, 4:353–56; Hamilton memo attached, file 711.94/1532, RG 59.

24. Grew Memo, June 28, 1940, *FR Japan*, 2:89–92.

25. Hull to Grew, July 4, 1940, *FR 40*, 4:381–87.

26. Hornbeck memo to Welles, May 18, 1940, Hornbeck papers; Hornbeck memo, May 24, 1940, *FR 40*, 4:333–36; Hornbeck memo, June 6, 1940, file 711.94/1564, RG 59; Hornbeck memos, June 3, 17, 24, 1940, Hornbeck papers.

27. Hornbeck memo to Hull, June 19, 1940, Hornbeck papers. See also Hornbeck memo to Hull, May 24, 1940, *FR 40*, 4:333–36, and unpublished portions in file 711.94/1669, RG 59; Wilson memo of May 31, 1940 meeting of the Advisory Committee on Problems of Foreign Relations, case 1, Wilson papers; Hornbeck memo to Welles, June 1, 1940 and Hornbeck memo, July 17, 1940, Hornbeck papers; Hornbeck memos, June 14, 15, 1940, file 811.20 Defense (M)/102 and 103, RG 59.

28. Butler, *Grand Strategy*, 2:328–39; Kittredge, "Naval Relations," 93; Deputy Chief of Naval Staff memo, Apr. 16, 1940, file 24716/F2885/2739/61, FO 371; Reynolds, *Anglo-American*, 135–36. Brit. aide memoire, June 27, 1940, *FR 40*, 4:365–67. For the British effort to persuade the U.S. and enlist Hornbeck's help, see Hornbeck memos, June 19, 20, 1940, *FR 40*, 4:359–61; Washington to London, June 24–28, 1940, file /24725/F3465/23/23, FO 371: War Cabinet Joint Planning Committee memo "J.P. (40) 300," June 25, 1940, file 24722/F3530/3530/61, FO 371.

29. Hull memo, June 28, 1940, *FR 40*, 4:369–72.

30. FE memo, May 31, 1940, file 711.94/1509, RG 59; Grew memo, June 10, 1940, *FR Japan*, 2:67–69; Kittredge, "Naval Relations," n128–29.

31. Ickes, *Diary*, 3:175–76; Berle, *Navigating*, 316; Green memo to Hull, June 4, 1940, *FR 40*, 4:573.

32. Friedman, *Road from Isolationism*, 33–36; Price letter to Stimson, Apr. 25, 1940, ACNPJA; Stimson diary, May 3, 1940; Hornbeck memo to Welles, May 6, 1940, "Welles, Sumner" folder, Hornbeck papers.

33. Rosen, *Combined Boards*, 3–6. Presidential proclamations during July placed many items under license. See *FR Japan*, 2:211–17. For a list of materials under license by the next summer see "Materials on Various Critical Lists" memo, file 115.1, Shipping Import Section, Priorities Division, Office of Production Management, NDAC, RG 179.

34. Ickes, *Diary*, 3:194–95; Stettinius report, May 30, 1940, file 013.3107, Industrial Materials Division minutes, June 14, 1940, file 013.3105, box 17, NDAC, RG 179. The organization of the NDAC is set forth in U.S., Executive Office of the President, *Government Manual, Fall*

1940, 52–58. For a critical view of the type of people who ran the NDAC see "Space and time: Newsletter of Advertising," a mimeographed publication dated Aug. 28, 1940 edited by David A. Munro, "J. Edgar Hoover" file, box 640, Stettinius papers.

35. Industrial Materials Division minutes, June 24, 1940, file 013.3105, box 17, NDAC, RG 179; "Aviation Gasoline" memo, July 16, 1943, box 77, Stettinius papers.

36. Industrial Materials Division minutes, June 28, July 3, 1940, file 013.3105, box 17, NDAC, RG 179; Stettinius memo to Roosevelt, June 28, 1940, "Industrial Materials—Stettinius" folder, box 8, NDAC, RG 220.

37. Roger Sherman Greene letters to Katie Greene, July 1, 11, 1940, Greene papers; Hornbeck memos, July 13, 19, 1940, *FR 40*, 4:583–86; Division of Controls memos, July 17, 18, 1940, file 894.24/1036 and 1040, RG 59; Hornbeck memos, July 18, 19, 1940, file 811.20 (D) Regulations/ 163, 164, RG 59.

38. Lothian to FO, July 19, 1940, file 27471/F3634/677/23, FO 371; Morgenthau memo to Roosevelt (drafted by Harry Dexter White), July 19, 1940, Morgenthau diary, 284:122.

39. Morgenthau diary, 284:214; Stimson diary, July 19, 1940.

40. The War Dept.'s message is in Morgenthau diary, 186:234. Morgenthau's message is in Morgenthau diary, 285:185. The president's order is in Green memo to Export Control, July 22, 1940, file 811.20 (D) Regulations/ 152D, RG 59.

41. For the aviation gasoline embargo see ickes, *Diary*, 3:274; Welles, "Roosevelt and the Far East," 33; Gaston memo (Treasury) to Col. Maxwell of Export Control, July 25, 1941, item 171, tab D1, box 994, RG 169; Alger Hiss (Hornbeck's administrative assistant) letter to Hornbeck, July 26, 1940, "Alger Hiss" folder, Hornbeck papers; Morgenthau-Ickes conversation in June 1941 recalling the events of July, 1940, Morgenthau diary, 415:82–83.

The issue of scrap is more complicated. There had been debate over embargoing scrap iron and steel and the NDAC was examining whether it was necessary. But there seemed to be a two- or three-year supply of scrap available and there was no economic need for licensing iron and steel scrap exports. Roosevelt press conference #657, July 2, 1940, 16:7, PPC, FDRL; Industrial Materials Division minutes, June 28, 1940, file 013.3105, box 17, RG 179; Green memo of conversation with Perkins, July 3, 1940, file 811.20 (D) Regulations/32, ECCP minutes, July 12, 19, 1940, file 611.0031 Executive Committee/782, Veatch memo, July 19, 1940, Hornbeck covering memo, July 20, 1940, file 811.20 (D) Regulations/150, RG 50.

Nevertheless, Herbert Feis claims that the State Department included in its draft proclamation on July 22: " . . . the very best grade of scrap iron and steel and that Morgenthau changed that from a limited embargo to all scrap iron and steel" (*Road*, 91). This is not borne out by the evidence. The draft proclamation that Joseph Green of State's Division of Controls sent to Col. Maxwell made specific reference to the president's order and itemized aviation motor fuel, tetraethyl lead, and aviation lubricating oil. It did not mention scrap (Green memo, July 22, 1940, file 811.20 (D) Regulations/ 152D, RG 59). Moreover, Morgenthau knew that the original presidential order did not include scrap, for on the following day, July 23, he phoned Stettinius and asked, "If either the President or I should ask you on an hour's notice to give us a justification for clamping an embargo on scrap iron, how long would it take you?" Stettinius said he could have that information by Thursday and on Friday the 26th he sent Stimson statistics showing that scrap exports were actually declining, including those to Japan. Though the record does not show any definite action by Morgenthau to put scrap on the list, it seems likely that he acted on scrap at the same time he acted on gasoline and probably with Stimson's cooperation (Memo, July 23, 1940, box 91 Stettinius papers; Stettinius memo to Stimson, July 26, 1940, "Embargo" folder, box 3, Sec. of the Army subject file, RG 107).

42. The proclamation is in *FR Japan*, 2:216–18. Morgenthau diary, 287:154ff; Roosevelt press conference no. 663, July 26, 1940, 16:62–63, PPC, FDRL. This series of events has been described by various historians with slightly differing interpretations. See Anderson, *Standard*, 129–35; Dallek, *Roosevelt*, 238–40; Feis, *Road*, 88–94; Langer & Gleason, *Challenge*, 719–23.

43. Stimson diary, July 26, 1940; Ickes, *Diary*, 3:273; Lothian, Aug. 6, 1940, file, 25212/W935B/9160/49, FO 371.

44. Bates memo, Oct. 1, 1940, file 400.1393/205-5.1, Army-Navy Munitions Board, RG 225; Miles memo, G-2, July 25, 1940, Sec. of the Army subject file, "Embargo" folder, box 3, RG 107; Ward memo to Asst. Chief of Staff, July 26, 1940, file 19440-50, OCS, RG 165; Strong memo, July 26, 1940, file 4344, WPD, RG 165; Anderson, *Standard*, 144.

45. Harriman memo, Aug. 1, 1940, file 400.1393.205-5.2, Army-Navy Munitions Board, RG 225; Stettinius memo of Aug. 1, 1940 NDAC meeting, "Misc. Records" binder, box 90, Stettinius papers; Feis memo, Aug. 1, 1940, Yost memo, Aug. 2, 1940, file 811.20 (D) Regulations/162, 255; C. C. Monrad and Robert E. Wilson memo, Aug. 2, 1940, file JJ7-6, CNO, RG 38; Anderson, *Standard*, 135–37.

46. Hiss letter to Hornbeck, Aug. 5, 1940, "Alger Hiss" folder, Hornbeck papers. For figures on Japanese gasoline imports from the United States, see ch. 7:24n.

47. Hull memo to Roosevelt, Sept. 12, 1940, file 811.20 (D) Regulations/564, RG 59.

48. Anderson, *Standard*, 142–52.

Chapter 6

1. Grew to Hull, July 26, 1940, *FR Japan*, 2:105–6.

2. Thomas P. Hart to Stark, July 24, 1940, folder 14, Hart papers; Grew to Hull, Sept. 12, 1940. *FR 40*, 4:599–602; Grew diary, 139:4509, 4525, 4533; Grew testimony, *PHA*, pt. 2, 584; Heinrichs, *Ambassador*, 315–16. See also Hamilton memo to Welles, Aug. 6, 1940, *FR 40*, 4:422; FE memo Aug. 8, 1940, file 890.00/212, RG 59.

3. Hosoya, "Tripartite Pact," 208–9.

4. Hart to Stark, Aug. 20, 1940, folder 14, Hart papers. For British considerations on withdrawal, see Chiefs of Staff to War Cabinet, June 25,

1940, Ashley Clarke minute, June 26, 1940, file 24722/F3530/61/61, and FO of Australian government, July 2, 1940, file 24725/F3543/23/23, FO 371. For State-Navy plans see Stark to Roosevelt, June 28, 1940, file EF16, CNO, RG 38.

5. See Aug. 12–23, 1940, *FR 40*, 4:762–87, FE memo, Aug. 15, 1940, file 890.00/213, RG 59.

6. Hull to Grew, Aug. 23, 1940, *FR 40*, 4:788–91; Knox to Hull, Aug. 24, 1940, file EF16, CNO RG 38; Stark to Hart, Sept. 21, 1940, Hart to Stark, Oct. 3, 1940, folder 14, Hart papers.

7. Stark letter to Richardson, Sept. 24, 1940, *PHA*, pt. 14, 961.

8. Unsigned, uninitialed, and unsent memo of Aug. 19, 1940, Hornbeck papers.

9. Ickes, *Diary*, 3:297–99, 314, 322, 330; Roger Greene letter to Harry Price, Sept. 6, 1940, ACNPJA. For Morgenthau's arguments see Morgenthau, *China*, 1:183–88; Hornbeck memo, Aug. 15, 1940, file 811.20 (D) Regulations/383, RG 59; Lothian to FO, Aug. 2, 1940, file 25212/W9160/49/49, FO 371. Knox was also involved in these discussions. See Morgenthau, *China*, 1:193–96; memo, Aug. 14, 1940, "Embargo" file, Sec. Army subject file, box 3, RG 107; Anderson memo, Aug. 30, 1941, and covering letter from Knox to Forrestal, same date, file JJ7, CNO files, RG 38.

10. Morgenthau, *China*, 1:175–76, 208–11, 225; Berle diary, Sept. 7, 18, 23, 1940, box 212; Hornbeck memo, Aug. 15, 1940, *FR 40*, 4:666–67; Hornbeck memo to Hull, Sept. 19, 1940, Hornbeck papers; Berle memo, Sept. 13, 1940, *FR 40*, 4:668.

11. Yost memos, Aug. 30, Sept. 27, 1940, file 811.20 (D) Regulations/477, 562. Apparently the free granting of licenses was the plan from the very start. See Hiss letters to Hornbeck, July 30, 31, 1940, "Alger Hiss" folder, Hornbeck papers.

12. Industrial Materials Division minutes, July 3, 17, 1940, file 013.3105, box 17, NDAC, RG 179; Industrial Materials Division Progress Reports, June 26–Aug. 15, 1940, "NDAC" folder, box 85, Hopkins papers; *Iron Age*, Aug. 14, 1940, 82D; NDAC minutes, Aug. 14, 1940, box 1, Sept. 11, 1940, box 3, RG 220; Yost memo, Aug. 14, 1940, copy of Batt (NDAC) memo to Stettinius, Aug. 22, 1940, file 811.20 (D) Regulations/266, 558.

13. Scrap prices rose nearly 11 percent in six weeks of 1940. See *Iron Age*, Aug. 1, 1940, 91, Sept. 5, 1940, 91, Sept. 19, 1940, 116. For *Iron Age* concern see Aug. 15, 1940, 86, Aug. 22, 1940, 52, 54, Sept. 9, 1940, 91. Henderson's arm-twisting of the steel industry is apparent from *Iron Age*, Oct. 10, 1940, 133, Oct. 17, 1940, 98, Dec. 26, 1940, 75; press release, Jan. 7, 1941, "Steel Scrap" folder, box 15, NDAC, RG 220.

14. The preparation of the embargo is seen in Henderson notation on NDAC meeting of Sept. 5, 1940, "Diary notes" folder, box 36, Henderson papers, FDRL; Price memo to Yost, Aug. 31, 1940, Yost memo, Sept. 4, 1940, Fishburn memo, Sept. 5, 1940, Feis memo, Sept. 6, 1940, Maxwell letter to State, Sept. 7, 1940, file 811.20 (D) Regulations/ 382, 555, 370, 556, 503 respectively. The delay and subsequent working out of a system is revealed in Morgenthau, *China*, 1:198; Berle diary, Sept. 7, 1940, box 212; Morgenthau diary, 305:51; Hull memo to Roosevelt (drafted by Feis) Sept.

12, 1940, Tower memo (NDAC) to State, Sept. 12, 1940, Green memo, Sept. 13, 1940, file 811.20 (D) Regulations/564, 479, 533, RG 59.

15. Feis, *Road,* 112; Langer & Gleason, *Undeclared War,* 34; Schroeder, *Axis Alliance,* 2, 15, 23–24; Butow, *John Doe,* 180–81; Craigie, *Japanese Mask,* 102; Pratt, *Hull,* 2:467; Esthus, *Enmity,* 80.

16. Berle, *Navigating,* 338; Adams memo, Aug. 31, 1930, file 711.94/1295, RG 59; Lothian to FO Sept. 27, 30, Oct. 1, 1940, and attached minutes, file 24709/F4534 and F4462/193/61. FO 371; Hull memo, Sept. 30, 1940, *FR 40,* 4:159–60.

17. Stimson diary, Sept. 27, 1940.

18. The quote is from Yost memo, Sept. 28, 1940, file 811.20 (D) Regulations/900, RG 59. For cabinet talk about reducing octane level of aviation gasoline see Ickes, *Diary,* 3:339.

19. Douglas, "A Bit of American History." Henry Douglas was a member of the staff of LC who worked with the ACNPJA to research and write several articles favoring economic pressure on Japan.

20. Stimson diary, Oct. 1, 2, 3, 1940; box 371, Frankfurter papers; Morgenthau, *China* 1:235–38; "Embargo" folder, box 3, Sec. Army subject file, RG 107; file 197a, "Misc. Japan," PPF, FDRL.

21. Roosevelt showed his support for Hull when he told Morgenthau on October 2, to leave the oil question to Hull (Morgenthau diary, 318:121–27 and Anderson, *Standard,* 153). This was quite a shift from a statement in early September that since oil issues had been going through Morgenthau, Roosevelt wanted them to continue to do so. See Morgenthau, *China,* 1:198; Long, *Diary,* 137, 139, 140; Ickes, *Diary* 3:346; Stimson diary, Oct. 8, 1940; Lothian to FO, Oct. 4, 1940, file 24709/F4556/193/61, Butler to FO, Oct. 16, 1940, file 24710/F4758/193/61, FO 371. Dallek, *Roosevelt,* 242–43, argues that Roosevelt's shift away from his natural inclination to get tough with Japan was caused by his concern for events in the Atlantic and his desire to be reelected in November.

22. *FR 40,* 4:235–55 for this diplomatic correspondence. Also Lothian to FO, Oct. 7, 1940, files 24709/F5467, F4615/193/61, FO 371; Berle diary, Oct. 4, 6, 1940, box 212; Long *Diary,* 138; Stimson diary, Oct. 8, 12, 1940, Stimson letter to Roosevelt, Oct. 12, 1940, "Stimson" folder, box 175, Patterson papers.

23. Hull memo, Oct. 8, 1940, *FR Japan,* 2:225–28.

24. Yost memo, Nov. 15, 1940, file 811.20 (D) Regulations/1151; Morgenthau, *China,* 1:242–43; Ickes, *Diary,* 3:388; Stimson diary, Nov. 29, Dec. 13, 1940, Berle diary, Dec. 8, 1941, box 212. For a while in early October, Roosevelt toyed with the idea of placing a picket line of ships around Japan to force it to stop its aggression. It was typical Roosevelt dreaming and reflected his fantasies but not his policy. See testimony, *PHA,* pt. 1, 265, 305.

25. Hull memo, Oct. 5, 1940, *FR 40,* 4:167–68; G-2 summary of Oct. 14, 1940 report from Horinouchi to Tokyo, "Reports Japanese," file box 962, G-2 Far East Branch, RG 165.

26. Loomis memo, Oct. 8, 1940, file 3251–37, WPD, RG 165.

27. McNarney memo, Oct. 7, 1940, Strong memo, Oct. 10, 1940, file

3251–37, WPD, RG 165; General Council meeting memo, Feb. 19, 1941, binder 16, box 888, OCS, RG 165.

28. Anderson memos, Oct. 8, 26, 1940, Gerow memo, Nov. 20, 1940, Anderson memo, Nov. 26, 1940, files 3251–37, 35, 39, 38 respectively, WPD, RG 165; Joint Planning Committee report to Joint Board, Dec. 10, 1940, file J.B. no. 325, ser. 670, box 1944, JB, RG 165; General Council meeting memo, Feb. 19, 1941, binder 10, box 888, OCS, RG 165.

29. Stark letter to Richardson, Sept. 24, 1940, *PHA*, pt. 14, 961; Stark memo to Hull, Oct. 8, 1941, *PHA*, pt. 16, 2216–18; Stark memo, Oct. 11, 1940, Kirk memo, Nov. 13, 1940, "Admiral Ghormley Conference Data," ComNavEu file, RG 38.

30. Stark letter to Richardson, Nov. 12, 1940, "Admiral Ghormley Conference Data," ComNavEu file, RG 38.

31. For the Plan Dog report see Kittredge, "Naval Relations," n252ff; correspondence, Navy Dept. file, PSF II, FDRL. See also Miner, "United States Policy," 60–79.

32. In his Plan Dog, Stark argued that Japan would not attack and left his assessment of the unimportance of the South Seas to other documents. See n31 above, undated and unattributed memo, Executive #4, no. 5, WPD, RG 165; Stark to Hart, Nov. 12, 1940, *PHA*, pt. 14, 973; and documents in "Admiral Ghormley Conference Data" file, ComNavEu, RG 38.

33. Stimson diary, Nov. 11, 12, 1940. On Knox see Australian legation from Washington, Oct. 17, Nov. 5, 1940, file 24710/F4936/193/61 and 24728/F5004/60/23, FO 371. Butler to FO, Nov. 13, 1940, file 24710/F5134/193/61, FO 371; Hornbeck comments attached to Plan Dog, folder 140, box 48, and Hornbeck memo, July 19, 1943, folder 312, box 73, Hull papers. Hornbeck's study, "The Importance of Singapore to the defense of the British Isles and the British Empire and to the Interests of the United States," did not appear until Dec. 4, 1940. See Hornbeck memo, Dec. 4, 1940, Hornbeck papers, Hornbeck letter to Stark, Dec. 5, 1940, file EF13-13, CNO, RG 38. For examples of early British desire for strong U.S. support, see Reynolds, *Anglo-American*, 145–55; FO to Lothian, Oct. 3, 1940, file 24736/F4493/626/23, Churchill minute, Oct. 4, 1940, file 27428/F4634/60/23, FO 371; Kittredge, "Naval Relations," n219, n225. Apparently, Hornbeck kept the British representatives thinking the Roosevelt administration was closer to taking action than it really was. See Halifax to FO, Sept. 5, Oct. 2, 19, 1940, files 24709/F4821/193/61, 24710/F4821/193/61, 24736/F4533/626/23, Halifax to FO, Jan. 30, 1941, file 27760/F524/9/61, FO 371.

34. Reynolds, *Anglo—American*, 182–85. Records of these talks can be found in "Admiral Ghormley Secret" and "Admiral Ghormley Conference Data," ComNavEu, RG 38; Kittredge, "Naval Relations," ch. 14; file 4402-89 B.U.S. (J) (41) 6 and 13, and WPD Exec. #4, no. 11, WPD, RG 165.

35. Undated memo, WPD exec. #4, no. 11, WPD, RG 165; minutes of 6th meeting, Feb. 10, 1941, B.U.S. (J) (41), "Admiral Ghormley, U.S.-British Staff Conversations," ComNavEu; Hart, "Narrative of Events, Asiatic Fleet, Leading Up to War and from 8 December 1941 to 15 February 1942," RG 38. For a discussion of how the British and American naval strategy

conflicted during 1940–41 see Leutze, *Bargaining,* chs. 14, 15; Barclay, "Singapore Strategy," 59–61; and Miner, "United States Policy," chs. 3, 4.

36. Watson, *Chief of Staff,* 124; Quinlan, "United States Fleet," 163–66; Marshall memo, Jan. 17, 1941, WPD Exec. #4, no. 11, WPD, RG 165; Kittredge, "Naval Relations," 357; minutes of 11th meeting, B.U.S. (J) (41), file "Admiral Ghormley, U.S.-British Staff Conversations," ComNavEu, RG 38.

37. Ward memo, Sept. 11, 1940, misc. conferences, binder #3, box 887, OCS, RG 165.

38. Watson, *Chief of Staff,* 124.

39. Actually the drafting fell to Hornbeck's assistant, Alger Hiss. Roosevelt to Grew, Jan. 21, 1941, *FR 41,* 4:6–8. Ironically, Grew was so pleased by the response that he wrote Hornbeck of what Roosevelt had written! Grew letter to Hornbeck, Feb. 25, 1941, Grew diary, 144:4793–96, and vol. 111, letters. On the gap between civilian and military perceptions of Southeast Asia, see Miner, "United States Policy," 79–101.

40. Grew despatch to Hull, Feb. 26, 1941, *FR Japan,* 2:137–43. For a similar Roosevelt letter, also written by Hornbeck, see Roosevelt letter to Francis B. Sayre, Dec. 31, 1940, in Cole, *Roosevelt & Isolationists,* 490–91.

41. Stark memo to Roosevelt, Feb. 5, 1941, folder 1, entry 50, ser. 7, Turner papers; Stark memo to Knox, Jan. 17, 1941; file A16-3/FF, ser. 1, WPD, RG 38.

42. Grew drafted this just before Dooman returned from Washington so he was not influenced by what Dooman had to say. Grew to Hull, Feb. 7, 1941. See Grew diary, 144:4801, 4849ff; Halifax to FO, Feb. 9, 1941, file 27962/F709/523/23, FO 371.

43. Stimson diary, Feb. 10, 1941; Marshall memo to Gerow, Feb. 26, 1941; WPD Exec. #4, no. 11, WPD, RG 165; Stark memo, Apr. 7, 1941, Turner memo, Apr. 10, 1941, Schuirman memo, Apr. 10, 1941, folder 2, entry 50, ser. 7, Turner papers; Stark letter to Hart, Apr. 19, 1941, folder 15, Hart papers.

Chapter 7

1. Berle, *Navigating,* 344, 355; Hull, *Memoirs,* 1:902. An overview of Hull's troubles in this respect is in Pratt, "Ordeal of Cordell Hull."

2. White memo, Aug. 13, 1940, "War Policy" folder, no. 15, White papers. Stimson was upset with the disorganized way economic policy was created and executed. Morison, *Turmoil,* 421–27.

3. Hiss letter to Hornbeck, July 31, 1940, "Alger Hiss" folder, Hornbeck papers. Yost memo, Aug. 24, 1940, Green letter to Export Control, Sept. 18, 1940, file 811.20 (D) Regulations/500, RG 59.

4. Yost memo, Sept. 28, 1940, file 811.20 (D) Regulations/900, RG 59. For an example of Controls efforts to stop export of gasoline to Japan, see n33 below.

5. The paper chase on machine tools is particularly convoluted, with contradictory statements. It appears that despite what Green claimed in the spring of 1941, the restrictions on machine tool exports were first and

foremost aimed at serving domestic economic needs. For details see: Green memos, Apr. 9, 1941, Nov. 29, 1940, file 811.20 (D) Regulations/3504, 855, RG 59; Long, *Diary,* 155; Machine Tool Priority Committee minutes, Feb. 12, 1941, file 400.174/216.2–13.3, Army-Navy Munitions Board, RG 225. Evidence that machine tools were in great demand domestically is Lothian to FO, Oct. 1, 1940, file 24709/F4534/193/61, FO 371; Knudsen speech before Army Ordnance Association, Oct. 8, 1940, quoted in *Iron Age,* Oct. 17, 1940, 83. Hull's concern that nothing be done that upset Japan is apparent in Green memo to Export Control, Oct. 10, 1940, Maxwell (Export Control) to Green, Oct. 11, 1940, file 811.20 (D) Regulations/ 603A, 618, RG 59. For the amount of machine tool export licenses granted during the fall of 1940, see Yost memo, Nov. 15, 1940, file 811.20 (D) Regulations/1151, RG 59; "Administration of Export Control, July 2, 1940–October 31, 1940" report, file 400.1393/205-5.1, Army-Navy Munitions board, RG 225.

6. European Affairs Division memo, Oct. 23, 1940, file 811.20 (D) Regulations/996, RG 59.

7. Memo, Dec. 31, 1940, file 811.20 (D) Regulations/1048, RG 59; "Record Book" entry, Dec. 17, 1940, box 102, Stettinius papers.

8. Welles memo to Will Clayton, Dec. 27, 1940, file 811.20 Defense (M)/928A, Feis memos, Dec. 12, 1940 and Feb. 1, 1941, files 811.20 Defense (M)/855, 1259, RG 59.

9. Hamilton memo, Feb. 22, 1941, file 811.20, Defense (M)/1512, RG 59.

10. Clayton memo to Forrestal, Feb. 11, 1941, folder 41-2-11, box 8, Clayton papers; Jones letter to Hull, Feb. 23, 1941, file 811.20 Defense (M)/1291, Collado memo, Feb. 24, 1941, file 811.20 Defense (M)/1513, Hamilton memo, Feb. 28, 1941, file 811.20 Defense (M)/1633, RG 59.

11. Hull memo (drafted by Feis) to Jones, Jan. 29, 1941, Jones memo to Hull, Feb 2, 1941, Feis memos to Hull, Apr. 1, 3, 1941, Hull letter to Jones, April 26, 1941, "National Defense — Strategic and Critical" folder, box 19, RG 234; Jones letter to Roosevelt with presidential notations, June 12, 1941, folder 41-6-12, box 8, Clayton papers. Feis memo to Hull with Hull "OK CH", Apr. 3, 1941, "National Defense — Strategic and Critical" folder, box 19, RG 234.

12. Elliott memo to Stettinius, Oct. 4, 1940, "W. Y. Elliott" folder, box 635, Stettinius papers.

13. Elliott memo and letter to Blackwell Smith, Nov. 1, 1940, Smith draft memo to Stettinius, Nov. 1, 1940, "Advisory Commission" folder, box 625, Stettinius papers.

14. Harriman memo to Stettinius, Nov. 1, 1940, Stettinius memo to Harriman, Nov. 6, 1940, Hoff memo to Smith, Nov. 6, 1940, "Advisory Commission" folder, box 625, transcript of conversation, Nov. 18, 1940, "Record Book," box 102, Stettinius papers; Elliott memo to Stettinius, Nov. 14, 1940, file 115.2, box 780, RG 179; draft memo for Roosevelt, Nov. 20, 1940, memo for Roosevelt, Nov. 27, 1940, "Advisory Commission" folder, box 625, Stettinius papers.

15. NDAC memo to Roosevelt, Nov. 27, 1940, file 811.20 Defense

(M)/849; Stettinius notes, Nov. 28, 1940, box 102, Stettinius papers; Dallek, *Roosevelt*, 256. Stimson was instrumental in getting this reorganization established. See Morison, *Turmoil*, 510–11.

16. Elliott memo to Harriman, Jan. 10, 1941, file 112.02, box 760, RG 179.

17. Grady memo, Nov. 29, 1940, file 811.20 Defense (M)/849, Steinbower memo, Jan. 7, 1941, Hornbeck memo, Jan. 27, 1941, files 811.20 (D) Regulations/1016, 2112, RG 59.

18. For how Export Control originally operated see Yost memo, Dec. 19, 1940, Green memo, Jan. 24, 1941, file 811.20 (D) Regulations/983, 2111, RG 59; Henderson memo to Smith, Nov. 1, 1940, "Advisory Commission" folder, box 625, Stettinius papers. For Export Control's increasing activity in the area of economic warfare, see Anderson *Standard*, 191ff; Young memo to Morgenthau, Jan. 6, 1941, Morgenthau diary, 345:92–B,C; Turner letter to director, Fleet Maintenance Division, March 13, 1941, folder A2-A3, ser. 1, WPD, RG 38; numerous memos, letters, and minutes, Feb.–Apr., 1941, entry 88, box 698, RG 169.

19. Glover memo to CNO, June 5, 1941, folder A16-3/A7-3, ser. 1, WPD, RG 38. Morgenthau diary, 392:72.

20. "Conferences with the President" binder, May 2, Sept. 15, 1941, Smith papers.

21. For British concern about flow of supplies to Germany via Japan and Soviet Union see Butler, *Grand Strategy*, 2:406; Ministry for Economic Warfare memo, March 8, 1940, Steel minute, March 17, 1940, Lothian to FO, March 14, 1940, files 25073/W4414, W4518, W4516/8/49, FO circular, March 21, 1940, file 24249/A2373/434/45, FO 371. Growing American concern can be seen in G-2 memo to Walker (WPD), March 18, 1941, Area file, China 4810.50, G-2, RG 165; military attaché report, London, Apr. 30, 1941, file 2655-Z-17, G-2, RG 165; Kamarck (Foreign Funds Control Committee) memo to Harry D. White (Treasury), June 13, 1941, "Miscellaneous World War II Records and Studies: FFC" folder, box 66, RG 56. Initial American reluctance to cooperate is evident in Hickerson memo, Dec. 8, 1939, file 700.00116 M.E./8, précis of telegrams received by British Embassy, Nov. 1, 1940, file 811.20 (D) Regulations/720, RG 59; Lothian to FO, Oct. 23, 1940, FO to Washington Nov. 1, 1940, file 24710/F4888/193/61, FO to Washington, Nov. 29, 1940, file 24734/F5241/103/23, "Reports of the Far Eastern Committee" Dec. 18, 1940, file 24711/F5683/193/61, Ministry of Economic Warfare memo, "Restrictions on Japanese Trade," Dec. 19, 1940, file 24734/F5689/103/23, FO to Washington, Feb. 21, 1941, file 28921/W715/715/49, FO 371.

22. Trueblood memo, Nov. 12, 1940, *FR 40*, 4:615; European Affairs Division memo, Nov. 15, 1940, Green memo, Dec. 4, 1940, files 811.20 (D) Regulations/1007, 1008, Welles memo, Dec. 23, 1940, file 611.946/471, RG 59; Butler to FO, Nov. 7, 1940, file 24734/F4995/102/23, FO 371. On State being bypassed, see Green memo, Nov. 18, 1940, file 811.20 (D) Regulations/857, RG 59.

23. For pressure from within State to have restrictions imposed, see Feis memo, Nov. 18, 1940, file 811.20 Defense (M)/737, RG 59; Feis memo to

Jesse Jones, Nov. 19, 1940, "Nat. Defense, Strat. and Critical" folder, box 19, Federal Loan Agency/39-45, RG 234; Trueblood memo of meeting of Interdepartmental Strategic Materials Committee, Dec. 23, 1940, Bursley memo, Jan. 15, 1941, files 811.20 Defense (M)/865 1/2, 826, Yost memo, Jan. 11, 1941, file 811.20 (D) Regulations/2806, RG 59. FE objections are in FE memo (drafted by Ballantine for Hamilton), Jan. 21, 1941, file 811.20 (D) Regulations/2807, RG 59. Though the British were sincere in their belief that Japan was buying for Germany, the amount of aid Germany received from Japan was very small. See Meskill, *Hitler and Japan*, 128–37. A list of the items Britain wanted placed under license dated Dec. 11, 1940 is in file 811.20 (D) Regulations/2806, RG 59. To see how these items were treated see following blocks of files. Minutes of the subcommittee on Legislation, Proclamations, and Regulations, Jan. 18, Feb. 5, 21, 26, 1941, box 698, entry 87, Report on Beryllium, Feb. 12, 1941, reports on Lead and Jute, Feb. 18, 1941, entry 88, box 699, "Summary of Conclusions and recommendations, May 19, 1941, Commodities Committee, entry 88, box 698, RG 169; British embassy to FO Apr. 18, May 3, 1941, file 28921/W2783/715/49, 27920/F4288/122/23, FO 371; various memos, Dec. 9, 1940–Feb. 7, 1941, files 811.20 (D) Regulations/956, 958, 1009, 1016, 2125, Green memo, March 21, 1941, file 894.24/1315, RG 59.

24. Price memo, June 21, 1941, file 811.20 (D) Regulations/3066, RG 59; Morgenthau diary, 345:166. 458:268; 473:212.

25. Anderson, *Standard*, 159–65.

26. Hornbeck memo, Jan. 11, 1941, FE memo, Jan. 22, 1941, *FR 41*, 4:776–82; Feis memo, Jan. 21, 1941, file 811.20 (D) Regulations/2550, various memos beginning Jan. 1941, file 894.24/1200ff, RG 59; FE and Hornbeck memos, Jan. 21, 1941, "Secretary of State" folder, box 372, Hornbeck papers.

27. Butler to FO, Jan. 9, 1941, with attached minutes, file 28844/W412/54/49, FO to Halifax, Feb. 20, 1941, Halifax to FO, March 13, 1941, file 28845/W3058/54/49, FO 371; Hornbeck memo, March 6, 1941, box 372, Hornbeck papers; British memo, "Japanese Oil Situation," Feb. 8, 1941, file JJ7-3/EF37, CNO records, Ghormley to CNO, Feb. 11, 1941, file A16-3FF, ser. 1, WPD, British statement, Feb. 9, 1941, minutes of 6th joint Anglo-American staff meeting, Feb. 10, 1941, file 4402-89 B.U.S. (J) 12, WPD, RG 38.

28. The whole affair is briefly described in Land, *Winning the War*, 27–32. Hull wrote National Maritime Commission head Emory S. Land endorsing his actions on March 26, 1941. Prior to that, State seems to have played no role. See *FR 40*, 4:800. Anderson, *Standard*, 162–63 argues that it was Hull who initiated the request for tanker control, choosing that method to give the British what they wanted. Anderson mistakes Hull's formal approval of a decision already taken for his initiating the action. The level of tanker loss is shown in Abbazia, *Roosevelt's Navy*, 152ff. See also Langer and Gleason, *Undeclared War*, 416–18, Ickes, *Diary*, 3:453.

29. Anderson, *Standard* 181; Hornbeck memo, Jan. 15, 1941, "Secretary of State" folder, box 372, Hornbeck papers; Yost and Hornbeck memos, Feb. 19, 1941, file 811.20 (D) Regulations/2141, RG 59; Ministry of Econo-

mic Warfare draft to Halifax, March 27, 1941, Halifax to FO, file 28846/ W3642 and W4567/54/49, FO 371; Barnes memo, June 16, 1941, file 811.20 (D) Regulations/3648, RG 59.

30. Wallace letter, May 10, 1941, Hull to Grew, May 31, 1941, *FR 41,* 4:815–17. Wolthuis, *US and Netherlands Indies,* 200.

31. Green memos, Sept. 7, 17, 1940, Hamilton memos, Sept. 10, 23, 1940, Hickerson memo, Sept. 20, 1940, Yost memos, Sept. 23, 28, 1940, files 811.20 (D) Regulations/1798, 900, 904, 905, RG 59; Welles memo, Sept. 24, 1940, *FR 40,* 4:148.

32. Yost memo Apr. 9, 1941, *FR 40,* 4:805–9; Hornbeck memos, March 12, Apr. 1, 1941 "Secretary of State" folder, box 372, Hornbeck papers; Feis memo, Apr. 4, 1941, *FR 40,* 4:803–5; Green memo to Acheson, July 19, 1941, file 811.20 (D) Regulations/3884 1/2, RG 59. See also Apr. 4, 1941 memo drafted in Divisions of Commercial Policy and Agreements and Economic Affairs (Feis's division), *FR 40* 4:803–5. Anderson, *Standard,* 165 maintains that the suspension of granting new licenses was intended to provide time to develop a new system of rationing the flow of oil to Japan. This is certainly what Yost and others in State hoped, but there is no evidence this is what Hull intended and the fact that three months later such a quota system had still not been devised tells whose influence, Yost's or Hull's, was dominant.

33. Hamilton and Hornbeck memos, Apr. 14, 1941, *FR 41,* 4:150–52, 164–67; Morgenthau, *China,* 1:379. For evidence of Hull's interest in rationing Japan but always short of risking a confrontation, see Halifax to FO, March 4, 1941, file 28846/W3114, W3058/54/49, FO 371.

34. Subcommittee on Legislation, Proclamations, and Regulations, minutes Apr. 23, May 14, 1941, entry 87, box 698, RG 169.

35. The correspondence is included in file 811.6363/380 1/2, 381 1/2, RG 59. The presidential correspondence is in Ickes, *Diary,* 3:553–59. For Morgenthau's support of Ickes, see Morgenthau diary, 404:131, 405:311.

36. Hamilton memo, Apr. 9, 1941, file 694.119/361, RG 59; Navy shared this desire to restrict Japan's ability to stockpile oil while not provoking it. See 6th meeting minutes, Feb. 10, 1941, file 4402-89 B.U.S. (J), WPD, RG 165; Ullman memo to White, White memo to Morgenthau, Apr. 4, 1941, Morgenthau diary, 386:88–89.

37. Berle diary, Nov. 27, 30, 1940, box 212; FE memo, Nov. 28, 1940, file 890.00/230, RG 59; Morgenthau, *China,* 1:243, 282, 314–15; Ickes, *Diary,* 3:384–85; Morgenthau, *China,* 1:314–15; Cochran (Treasury) memo, Dec. 2, 1940, folder 141, box 48, Hull papers. See also Jones memo, Dec. 15, 1940, file 893.51/7167 1/2, RG 59; Arthur Young memo, Apr. 21, 1941, folder A, box 16, Young papers; Morgenthau, *China,* 1:345; Morgenthau diary, 390:121; press release, Apr. 25, 1941, *FR 41,* 5:633.

38. Schaller, "Air Strategy," 6–9; Knox letter to Hull, Oct. 19, 1940, State memo to Navy, Oct. 23, 1940, *FR 40,* 4:671, 677; Stimson memo, Nov. 1, 1940, "China" folder, box 2, Sec. Army (Stimson), oral statement to Chinese Embassy, Dec. 4, 1940, *FR 40,* 4:686, 697, 706.

39. Morgenthau diary, 342-A:10.

40. The meeting is described in minutes, Dec. 23, 1940, binder #6, box 888, OCS, RG 165; J. H. Burns memo, Dec. 23, 1940, file 4389-5, WPD,

RG 165; Morgenthau letter to Hull, Jan. 10, 1941, Morgenthau diary, 346:383A. For Army and Navy attitudes preceding this meeting see memo to files, Dec. 16, 1940, binder #6, box 888, RG 165; M. L. Deyo memo for Sec. of Navy, Dec. 20, 1940, file EF16/A21, CNO, RG 38.

41. Chennault, *Way of a Fighter*, 101–4; Hamilton memo, Dec. 23, 1940, *FR 40*, 4:713; WPD report, Nov. 1941, file 4510, WPD, RG 165. On the meager amount of support that the Flying Tigers received from the United States see Young, *China and the Helping Hand*, 148–53. Schaller, *Crusade in China*, 71–83, interprets this small support as a major commitment to stopping Japan.

42. Langer and Gleason, *Undeclared War*, 488–89; Morgenthau diary, 348:177; Roosevelt press conference, March 11, 1941, no. 725, 17:183–84, PPC, FDRL; Currie memo to Roosevelt, March 15, 1941, *FR 41*, 4:95.

43. Treasury memo, Apr. 21, 1941, "China (Pre-Pearl Harbor)" folder, Sherwood collection, box 305, Hopkins papers.

44. Currie memo to Roosevelt, Apr. 25, 1941, *FR 41*, 4:168; Gerow memo, May 29, 1941, file 4389-3, WPD, RG 165; Joint Planning Committee memo to Joint Board, July 9, 1941, J.B. no. 355, ser, 691, file AG 452, June 4, 1941, J.B. memo, July 14, 1941, file AG 452, July 14, 1942, AGO, RG 407. In his analysis of Currie's presentation and the Joint Board's subsequent approval, Michael Schaller emphasizes the value of a Chinese air force to strike at Japanese cities. The point was made by Currie but not stressed and the Joint Board approved a program of deterrence, not an offensive one. It was not China that interested most people in Washington by this time, but Southeast Asia and the South Seas. Schaller, "Air Strategy," 14–17. It should also be noted that the idea of sending American pilots to train Chinese was not original with this Joint Board proposal in July. Some pilots had already left to do just that in June. See memo of June 10, 1941, binder #1, Sec. of War Conference, box 887, OCS, RG 165.

45. Hornbeck memo, May 16, 1941, "Secretary of State" folder, box 372, Hornbeck papers; State memo, May 29, 1941, "China (Pre-Pearl Harbor)" folder, Sherwood collection, box 305, Hopkins papers; FE memo, May 29, 1941, *FR 41*, 5:651–56.

46. Gerow memo, June 13, 1941, file 4389-5, WPD, RG 165; Currie memo to Hopkins, July 13, 1941, file AG 400-3295, July 3, 1941, AGO, RG 407; Welles memo to Hopkins, July 7, 1941, "China (Pre-Pearl Harbor)" folder, Sherwood collection, box 305, Hopkins papers (a copy is also filed in file 4389-7, WPD, RG 165;) Hopkins memo to J. H. Burns, July 12, 1941, "China (Pre-Pearl Harbor)" folder, Sherwood collection, box 305, Hopkins papers (copy in file AG 400.3295 July 3, 1941, AGO, RG 407); Gerow memo to Moore, Aug. 1, 1941, file AG 400.3296, July 3, 1941, AGO, RG 407.

47. Tabulation of U.S. exports to Middle East, China, and Russia, Aug. 1941, "Defense Aid Reports" folder, box 138, Hopkins papers.

48. The War Department made it very clear that it was interested in China only as a means of tying down Japanese troops, not waging an offensive war against Japan. See WPD memo, Oct. 25, 1941, Thomas Handy memo, Oct. 28, 1941, file WPOD exec. #4, no. 12, folder 12, Miles memo, Oct. 21, 1941, Gerow memo, Nov. 1, 1941, Army Air Force memo,

Nov. 3, 1941, Magruder, Nov. 4, 1941, Bundy memo, Nov. 11, 1941, Stimson, Nov. 15, 1941, files 4389-33, 27, 29, 31, 32, 30 respectively, WPD, RG 165.

49. In *Flying Tigers* (Republic Pictures, 1942, David Miller director) John Wayne runs a wing of the Flying Tigers in which much combat—and virtually the entire film—is set before December 7, 1941. A more realistic portrayal is in Toland, *Flying Tigers.*

50. Hosoya, "Tripartite Pact," 214–57, "Miscalculations," 111; Butow, *Tojo,* ch. 8; Schroeder, *Axis Alliance,* 116–27.

51. Richardson testimony, *PHA,* pt. 1, 266.

Chapter 8

1. Abbazia, *Roosevelt's Navy,* 142ff.

2. Walsh memo to Roosevelt, Jan. 26, 1941, *FR 41,* 4:14ff. For the role of the John Doe associates throughout the negotiations of 1941, see Butow, *John Doe,* passim.

3. Butow, *John Doe,* 9–10.

4. For the importance of Japan showing a change of heart see Ballantine memo, Feb. 5, 1941, Hull memos to Roosevelt (drafted by FE), Feb. 5, 1941, *FR 41,* 4:20–27.

5. Butow, *John Doe,* 9–10.

6. Hull memo, Feb. 14, 1941, *FR Japan,* 2:387–89; Berle, *Navigating,* 359–60. For Nomura's view of this meeting see Nomura to Tokyo, Feb. 15, 1941, USDOD, *MAGIC,* 1:A-1.

7. Hull memos, March 8, 14, 1941, *FR Japan,* 2:389–98; Nomura to Tokyo, March 8, 14, 15, 1941, USDOD, *MAGIC,* 1:A11–A12, A16–A19.

8. On the John Doe associates, see Butow, *John Doe,* ch. 10. The proposal is in *FR Japan,* 2:398–402.

9. Both Dallek, *Roosevelt,* 261, and Reynolds *Anglo—American,* 198–99, maintain that Roosevelt reversed his fleet transfer decision because he decided not to engage in convoying at that time (certainly true) which was in turn caused by his fear of adverse public reaction (possibly true). Roosevelt was concerned about public support for his increasing involvement in the Atlantic, but he was also very much concerned about avoiding a two-front war. We cannot rely upon what Roosevelt gave as his reasons because he said different things to different people, claiming concern for public opinion to Stimson and the need to protect Hawaii when speaking to Marshall. See Stimson diary, April 23, 1941. For Navy's efforts to get ships transferred to the Atlantic see Turner memos to Stark, March 31, April 2 and 4, 1941, files A4-3/CV1, CNO, and folder A4, ser. 1, WPD, RG 38; Quinlan, "United States Fleet," 177–85.

10. Hull memos, April 14, 16, 1941, *FR Japan,* 2:402–10.

11. Hornbeck memos, April 5, 1941 to Grew and May 19, 1941 to Hull, Hornbeck papers; Hornbeck memo to Hull, April 8, 1941, folder 309, box 72, Hull papers; Hornbeck memo, May 6, 1941, letter to Grew, May 14, 1941, *FR 41,* 4:179, 189; Hull to Grew, May 26, 1941, Grew to Hull, May 27, 1941, *FR 41,* 4:228, 231–32. Hull insisted upon "clear-cut and une-

quivocal terms" in any agreement. See Hull memo, June 6, 1941, *FR Japan,* 2:466.

12. Butow argues convincingly that there was a fundamental misunderstanding that hurt the chances for successful talks. As mentioned earlier, however, so long as Hull insisted on sweeping terms for peace, there was virtually no chance for success with or without the fundamental misconception held in Tokyo (Butow, *John Doe,* 164–67). My argument that Nomura deliberately misrepresented the April 9 draft is admittedly speculative. It has been fashionable to assume that Nomura did not clearly understand Hull's English. Yet it seems improbable that a man of Nomura's experience, one who had been foreign minister, would not have been aware that had he sent back the April 9 draft as his own creation and not State's, the talks would have ended. As we shall see below, Nomura showed enough spunk to withhold a message from Foreign Minister Matsuoka when he did not think it served the purpose of peace. An on at least one occasion he had sought to salvage the talks by deliberately misleading his government to believe that American acceptance of a draft was assured. See memo of Hull-Nomura conversation, May 20, 1941, *FR Japan,* 2:434. To understand Nomura see USDOD, *MAGIC,* 1–4, especially Nomura to Tokyo, April 14, 15, 17, 1941, USDOD, *MAGIC,* 1:A33–A41. See also Conroy, "Nomura," "Strange Diplomacy." Butow's argument about Nomura's language problems is argued in Butow, *John Doe,* 354.

13. A memo describing how the talks were conducted is in *FR Japan, 1931–41,* 2:411–92. See also Ballantine, "Oral History Interview," 35, 42; Halifax to FO, June 26, 1941, file 27909/F5655/86/23, FO 371.

14. Various memos of conversation between Hull and Nomura, May 16–June 16, 1941, *FR Japan,* 2:429, 434–35, 442, 445, 477; Hackworth memo, May 29, 1941, *FR 41,* 4:239. While it was clear Japan desired to move south, the concensus in Washington was that Japan would wait and see how the next German offensive progressed. See Stark memo to Roosevelt, Feb. 5, 1941, folder #2, entry 50, ser. 7, Turner papers; Hornbeck memo, March 7, 1941, *FR 41,* 4:63.

15. Hull memo, April 16, 1941, *FR Japan,* 2:407; FE memos, April 9, 14, 1941, Hornbeck memo, May 24, 1941, *FR 41,* 4: 159, 219–21. Hull did not change as the months dragged by. See Stimson memo, Oct. 6, 1941, Stimson papers; Halifax to FO, Oct. 3, 1941, file 27910/F0329/86/23, FO 371.

16. Two historians who see Hull as a judge or preacher spouting idealistic principles are Butow, *John Doe,* 28–29, and Burns, *Soldier of Freedom,* 136. Schroeder, *Axis Alliance,* 206, attributes the American insistence on Japanese withdrawal from China to "a sentimental attitude."

17. Langer & Gleason, *Undeclared War,* 471–74; Toland, *Rising Sun,* 74–76; Schroeder, *Axis Alliance,* 126–36. Matsuoka's intransigence was revealed as early as March 4 when he cabled Nomura that in case the U.S. attacked Germany, Japan would go to war. A similar attitude is expressed in Matsuoka to Nomura, May 13, 1941. See USDOD *MAGIC,* 1:A10, A65–70, 2:A4-A6.

18. Stimson diary, May 15, 1941.

19. Hornbeck letter to Grew, May 14, 1941, *FR 41,* 4:189.

20. As early as Oct. 9, 1940, Hull had assured Asst. Sec. Breckenridge Long that Hornbeck would not be the spokesman for the department on delicate matters. See Long, *Diary*, 139. The British also recognized that Hornbeck had been kept at arm's length from the real activities in State. See Campbell to FO, Aug. 29, 1941, file 27910/F8643/86/23, FO 371. My judgment that Hornbeck was not part of the inner circle within State rests not on authority but from a reading of the mass of memoranda which appeared. Hornbeck remained vociferous but his recommendations were rarely followed. The tone of his memoranda became more strained. See Hornbeck memo to Welles, March 22, 1941, file 890.00/258, RG 59. Hornbeck memo to Berle, April 18, 1941, "Adolf A. Berle, 1938–1941" folder, Hornbeck papers. On one occasion, Hornbeck deliberately distorted a War Department report in order to make it appear Army supported his policy. Fortunately for all concerned, Hornbeck thought better of delivering his doctored document. See Hornbeck memo, "Better to give aid on two fronts and fight on one than to withhold aid on one and have to fight on both," May 6, 12, 14, 1941, forwarded to Stimson May 22, 1941, Marshall memo to Stimson, copy forwarded to Hornbeck, Hornbeck memo to Hull, June 10, 1941, Hornbeck papers.

21. For Navy's attitude see Stark letter to Hart, April 19, 1941, folder 14, Hart papers; Turner memo to Stark, April 29, 1941, folder #1, entry 50, ser. 8, Turner papers; Operation Order, Kimmel to Task Force Seven, May 15, 1941, file A4-3/FF12, CNO, RG 38; Draft of RAINBOW 5 war plan, May 1941, file J.B. no. 325 (ser. 642–5), JB, RG 165; Stark memo to Knox, June 10, 1941, folder #1, entry 50, ser. 7, Turner papers; Abbazia, *Roosevelt's Navy*, 142ff. For details of ship movements see memos "Organization of U.S. Pacific Fleet, April 3, June 27, 1941, file A2-11/FF12 (2), RG 38. For the civilian side see Ickes, *Diary*, 3:485, 491–92, 512–13, 523; Stimson diary, April 23, May 2, 5, 6, 8, 1941.

22. For British concern see Foulds and Clarke minutes, June 14, 16, 1941, file 27909/F5147/86/23, FO 371. For Hull's assurances and subsequent outburst, see Hull memo, May 16, 1941, *FR 1941*, 4:197–98; Halifax to FO, May 25, 1941, file 27908/F4430/86/23, FO 371. For British concern over the talks see Halifax to FO, May 18, 1941, FO to Halifax, May 21; 1941, files 27880, 27940/F4187/12/23, FO 371. Further evidence of Hull's tense state is in Ickes, *Diary*, 3:520–21.

23. Halifax to FO, May 17, 1941, file 27909/F4569/86/23, FO 371; Reynolds, *Ango-American*, 230–36. On Matsuoka's problems see Schroeder, *Axis Alliance*, 134–36.

24. Hull memo of phone conversation with Willkie, May 15, 1941, folder 309, box 72, Hull papers.

25. Memos of Hull-Nomura conversations, April 14, May 2, 7, 11, 1941, extracts from Hull address of April 24, 1941 handed to Nomura May 16, 1941, *FR Japan*, 2:405, 411, 413–14, 417–18, 430–32.

26. Hosoya, "Tripartite Pact," 233–55; Meskill, *Hitler and Japan*, 3–22; Sommer, *Deutschland und Japan*, 436–46; Schroeder, *Axis Alliance*, 124–25.

27. Ballantine memos, June 4, 9, 1941, *FR Japan*, 2:457, 469.

28. Woods memo, undated but post–World War II, folder 184, box 56, Hull papers; Long, *Diary*, 206.

29. Hull memo and oral statement, June 21, 1941, *FR Japan*, 2:483–86. Matsuoka was furious with Hull's statement. See Matsuoka to Nomura, July 14, 1941, USDOD, *MAGIC*, 1:A76–A78.

30. Butow, *John Doe*, 225–26; Langer & Gleason, *Undeclared War*, 639; Toland, *Rising Sun*, 96–98.

31. Langer & Gleason, *Undeclared War*, 640; Ike, *Japan's Decision*, 80–98. Nomura to Tokyo, July 16, 1941, USDOD, *MAGIC*, 2:A84–A85.

32. Hamilton memo of phone conversation with Hull, July 17, 1941, *FR 41*, 4:325.

33. Turner memo, July 19, 1941, file A11–A15, ser. 1, WPD, RG 38.

34. As seen in ch. 7, there had been some talk during the spring of restricting Japan to prewar amounts of vital materials. There had also been some talk among military planners of building up the Philippines. What Roosevelt decided on, therefore, was the logical action given the alternatives before him and what had been discussed in the previous months. For army talk of fortifying the Philippines, see Gerow memos, Dec. 26, 1940, Jan. 25, Feb. 5, 1941, file 3251-39, 34, 42, Anderson memo, Apr. 14, 1941, file 3251-42 WPD, RG 165; G-2 memo, Apr. 28, 1941, file "Jap Empire," box 958, Far East Branch, G-2, RG 165.

35. Langer & Gleason, *Undeclared War*, 647–49; Halifax to FO, July 19, 1941, file 27972/F6472/1299/23, FO 371.

36. Halifax to FO, FO to Halifax, July 21, 1941, files 27972/F6588, F6599/1299/23, FO 371; Foley (Treasury) memo of July 19 conversation, dated July 21, 1941, Foley memo, July 24, 1941, Morgenthau diary, 423:194–95, 424:153–54.

37. Bell (Treasury) memo, July 24, 1941, Morgenthau diary, 424:155.

38. Bell memo, July 25, 1941, Morgenthau diary, 424:155; Halifax to FO, July 24, 1941 and Butler letter to FO, July 25, 1941, files 27972/F6728, F7664/1299/23, FO 371.

39. Welles memo, July 31, 1941, *FR 41*, 4:846–48. Roosevelt's approval is noted on the copy in the Morgenthau diary, 426:151. A copy of the directive is also filed in the "Japan: Oil Shipments To" folder, FFCC, RG 56.

40. Subcommittee on Legislation, Proclamations, and Regulations, minutes, Aug. 1, 1941, RG 169; Yost memo, Aug. 16, 1941, file 811.20 (D) Regulations/4148 2/3, RG 59.

41. Burns, *Soldier of Freedom*, 109–10; Pratt, *Hull*, 2:492; Langer & Gleason, *Undeclared War*, 655; Feis, *Road*, 242–48. For a more detailed discussion of how historians have misinterpreted the nature of the freeze, see Utley, "Upstairs, Downstairs," 25–26.

42. Ickes, *Diary*, 3:588; Ickes letter to Josiah Wedgwood, M. P., July 28, 1941, file 27976/F8016/1299/23, FO 371; memo, Aug. 5, 1941, Morgenthau diary, 428:126; memo of conference between Treasury and Export Control, Aug. 6, 1941, FFCC, RG 56; Ickes, *Diary*, 3:591; Hiss memo to Hornbeck, Aug. 16, 1941, Hornbeck papers. At a meeting on July 29, three days before Export Control granted any licenses, Acheson announced that Welles had said it would be best for FFCC simply not to act on Japanese

applications for a "week or so." Presumably it would take Export Control that long to make its calculations or perhaps Welles just wanted the Japanese to worry for a while. In any case, Acheson carried his inaction beyond "a week or so" (Morgenthau diary, 426:19). The full amount of oil Japan would be permitted to buy under Roosevelt's plan was not apparent until mid-August. See Yost memo, Aug. 16, 1941, file 811.20 (D) Regulations/ 4148 2/3, RG 59.

43. See various memos in "Japan: Oil Shipments To" folder, FFCC, RG 56, especially, Aug. 9, 12, 1941, Jan. 13, 1942; Acheson memo, Aug. 15, 1941, file 840.51 Frozen Credits/3302, RG 59.

44. In a phone conversation with Welles on Aug. 2, 1941, Hull spoke of what "would have" happened if oil had been cut off entirely; that is, he used the conditional voice (*FR41*, 4:359). Acheson commented on the opposition within FE in a phone conversation with J. W. Pehle of Treasury, see Pehle memo, Aug. 9, 1941, FFCC, RG 56. See also Towson memo, Sept. 6, 1941, minutes of senior meeting, Oct. 1, 1941, FFCC, RG 56.

45. Acheson memo to Welles, Aug. 16, 1941, *FR 41*, 4:859. Nomura suggested that pending a final agreement each nation would "permit export to the other of commodities in amounts up to the figures of usual or pre-war trade" excepting only commodities restricted as part of the defense program. Since Hull believed that was the formula already in existence he was probably curious why Nomura had submitted it as a proposal. Though on the next day Hull learned how far the embargo had proceeded, Acheson apparently convinced him that it was Treasury that was responsible, because Hull had Acheson contact Treasury to find out what it was doing. Japanese proposal, Sept. 4, 1941, *FR Japan*, 2:600; Acheson memo, Sept. 5, 1941, *FR 41*, 4:868–69; Yost memo, Sept. 5, 1941, Hornbeck papers; Acheson, *Present*, 26; Hamilton memos, Oct. 7, 8, 1941, file 811.20 (D) Regulations/ 989, RG 59. See also White memo, Aug. 11, 1941, file 825.635/16, Luthringer memo, Aug. 25, 1941, file 840.51 Frozen Credits/3187 1/2, RG 59.

46. Berle, *Navigating*, 381. By this time, Acheson already had a public reputation as a "hawk" who was appointed to offset the "appeasement" faction within State. See Janeway, "Trade Currents," 400. If Acheson had been privy to highly secret MAGIC material, he would have seen that as early as July 23, the foreign ministry was warning Normura that a freeze of Japanese assets that cut off trade would bring about "an exceedingly critical situation." Given his mood and that of those around him, Acheson would probably have brushed aside such warnings as merely signs of Japanese weakness. Tokyo to Nomura, July 23, 1941, USDOD, *MAGIC*, 2:A91. A further discussion of Acheson's role in this affair is in Utley, "Upstairs, Downstairs," 28. Anderson, "de facto Embargo" argues that the actions of Acheson and the FFCC were more the result of bureaucratic reflexive action than any intention to change policy.

Chapter 9

1. Brune, "Considerations of Force," 396–97, believes Hull had given up on diplomacy and only reluctantly agreed to continue the talks. I think it

more reasonable to conclude that while Hull was not optimistic about the chances for success, he showed no reluctance to reopen the talks and took the initiative in doing so. Had he not done so, certainly neither Welles nor Roosevelt would have taken the lead.

2. Wilson, *First Summit*, 87–93, 112–17, 163–67; Welles memo, Aug. 9, 1941, *FR 41*, 1:346–54; Bundy memo to Gerow, Aug. 9, 1941, file WPD exec. #4, no. 10, WPD, RG 165; Churchill to FO, Aug. 12, 1941, file 27847/F7882/4366/61, FO 371. For British attitude see Reynolds, *Anglo—American*, 213–19, 238–39; Clarke minute, July 24, 1941, file 27972/F6693/1299/23, War Cabinet minute, July 28, 1941, file 27975/F7457/1299/23, FO memo, Aug. 15, 1941, file 27847/F7812/4366/61, Clarke minute, Aug. 20, 1941, file 27909/F7985/76/23, FO 371; Ballantine memo, June 12, 1944, *FR 41*, 4:375ff; Ballantine, 1941, oral history interview, 207; Knox letter to Annie Knox, Aug. 17, 1941, Knox papers; Wilson, *First Summit*, 243. For FO response to American reneging, see Clarke minute, Aug. 25, 1941, Bennett minutes, Aug. 23, 25, 1941, file 27909/F8218/86/23, FO 371.

3. Butow, *Tojo*, chs. 9–10; Tokyo to Nomura, Aug. 7, 1941, USDOD, *MAGIC*, 3:A8–A9; Butow, "Backdoor Diplomacy," 48–59.

4. Memo of Roosevelt Nomura conversation, Aug. 28, 1941, *FR Japan*, 2:572. See also Langer & Gleason, *Undeclared War*, 698–702. Dallek, *Roosevelt*, 301–2, portrays Roosevelt as being much less enthusiastic about a leaders' conference.

5. Long, *Diary*, 215; Hull's recollection of this entire episode is in Hull, *Memoirs*, 2:1016–27.

6. Ballantine memo to Hull, Aug. 28, 1941, *FR 41*, 4:404; Miles memo to Roosevelt, Stimson, Hull, and others, Sept. 5, 1941 file 4510, G-2, WPD, RG 165; memo of Stimson conversation with Hull, Oct. 6, 1941, Stimson papers. My view of Hull differs from the conventional portrayal of Hull as an idealist unaware of the realities of power. See, for example, Schroeder, *Axis Alliance*, 206–8.

7. Ballantine, oral history interview, 45; Hull statement, *PHA*, pt. 2, 407–825; Stimson diary, Aug. 8, 1941; Butow, *Tojo*, 142–66.

8. For Japanese proposals see various documents in *FR Japan*, 2:573–75, 608–9, 623–24, 633, 637–45. The American reactions are in *FR Japan*, 2:616, 675, 614–15, 656–66, *FR 1941*, 4:428–29, 432–34, 449, 470–75, 493–97. See also Hull testimony, *PHA*, pt. 2, 424. Butow, "Backdoor Diplomacy," 60–72, believes that the behind-the-scenes maneuvering of the John Doe associates was instrumental in blocking the Roosevelt—Konoye meeting. Certainly nothing they did helped, but Hull was motivated by reasons and attitudes that went far beyond anything the John Doe associates did.

9. Heinrichs, *Ambassador*, 343–48; Grew to Hull, Sept. 29, 1941, *FR Japan*, 2:602–3, 646–48; Grew diary, 149:5334, 150:5584–89, 151:5629, 5643, Grew letter to Roosevelt, Sept. 22, 1941, vol. 112, Grew letter to Roosevelt, Aug. 14, 1942, file Fms AM 1687.1, Grew papers.

10. Tokyo to Nomura, Aug. 26, Sept. 4, 1941, USDOD, *MAGIC*, 3:A45, A71.

11. Tokyo to Nomura, Oct. 4, 1941, USDOD, *MAGIC*, 3:A139; Ballan-

tine memo, Sept. 23, 1941, Hull memo to Roosevelt, Roosevelt response, Sept. 28, 1941, *FR 41*, 4:472–75, 483; memo of Roosevelt conversation with Nomura, Sept. 3, 1941, *FR Japan*, 2:588; Ballantine, oral history interview, 208.

12. Toland, *Rising Sun*, 127; Butow, *Tojo*, 270–94.

13. For the pessimism see Nomura to Tokyo, Nov. 16, 1941, USDOD, *MAGIC*, 3:A158–61; Hull memo, Oct. 16, 17, 1941, *FR Japan*, 2:689; Stimson diary, Oct. 16, 1941. For the fatalism see Hornbeck memo, Oct. 20, 1941, Hornbeck papers; Japanese to Nomura, Oct. 12, 1941, USDOD, *MAGIC*, 4:A3; Schuirman memo, Oct. 17, 1941, folder 14, Hart papers. For optimism see Grew to Hull, Oct. 25, 1941, *FR Japan*, 2:697–98 and Oct. 26, 1941, *FR 41*, 4:553; Hamilton memo to Hull, Oct. 18, 1941, Langdon memo, Oct. 25, 1941, *FR 41*, 4:523, 549. Hull's emotions seem to have been rising and falling with the news of the day. Just a few days before he showed any optimism he confided to the British ambassador that he was "pretty near the end of his tether" and that he did not see what else could be done. See Halifax to FO, Oct. 15, 1941, file 27910/F10885/86/23, FO 371.

14. Grew to Hull, Nov. 3, 1941, *FR Japan*, 2:700–701; Japanese to Nomura, Nov. 4, 1941, USDOD, *MAGIC*, 4:A15.

15. Grew diary, 152:5816, 153:5935. Grew did not use the blunt language of his diary in his telegrams.

16. Gerow memo, July 11, 1941, file 4510, G-2; Gerow diary entry, July 31, 1941, file Exec. #10, no. 1, Miles memo, Sept. 5, 1941, file 4510, G-2, WPD, RG 165; Hayes, *Joint Chiefs of Staff*, 1:19; Weigley, "War Department," 181–84. Talk of building up the Philippines had been circulating for some time. See Manchester, *American Caesar*, 191–95; Marshall memo, undated (c. March 18, 1941), file 2449-12, COS, Miles memo, May 14, 1941, file "Jap Empire" box 958, G-2, Far East Branch, RG 165. For the Army view of the Philippine role see Gerow memo, Oct. 1941, file 4510, Gerow memo, Oct. 2, 1941, file WPD Exec. #8, book A, WPD, RG 165. See also Brune, "Considerations of Force," 395.

17. Memo of conference, July 28, 1941, Sec. War Conferences, binder #1, box 887, Marshall memo to Stark, Sept. 12, 1941, file 18136–56 1/2, OCS, RG 165; Gerow memo, Oct. 8, 1941, file 3251–60, WPD, RG 165; Joint Board minutes, Sept. 19, 1941, RG 225; Manchester, *American Caesar*, 195–98. Harrington, "Careless Hope," attributes this attitude to a combination of a longing for peace and a need to restrain Japan. While these factors were present, these army officers also needed to convince themselves that they were not engaged in a futile effort. In the spring, they had argued it was folly to try and make the Philippines impregnable. Now they had presidential orders to do just that. No wonder they placed their faith in B-17s.

18. Stimson letter to Roosevelt, Oct. 21, 1941, file "White House Conference," box 11, Sec. Army (Stimson) subject file, RG 107; Stimson diary, Oct. 21, 1941. When Stimson met with Hull on Oct. 6, he stressed the absolute importance of the talks continuing and avoiding a breach that would lead to war. Stimson memo, Oct. 6, 1941, Stimson papers.

19. Bundy memos, Nov. 1, 1941, file 4389–27, Scobey memo, Nov. 2,

1941, Executive File #8, book A, WPD, RG 165; Hornbeck memo, Nov. 2, 1941, Hornbeck papers. Stark's concern had been evident in September when he urged Hull to continue the talks with Japan even if there was little chance of reaching an agreement. See Stark letter to Hart, Sept. 22, 1941, Stark letter to Kimmel Sept. 23, 1941, folder 14, Hart papers.

20. Miles memos, Sept. 18, 23, 1941, file "Jap Empire," box 958, General Staff memo, Oct. 1941, file 4510, Wyman memo to Gerow, Oct. 25, 1941, Exec. #4, no. 12, folder 12, Rogers memo to Gerow, Nov. 7, 1941, file 4389-32, Gerow memo, Nov. 8, 1941, file 4389-30, WPD, RG 165. The conclusions of the November 3 conference which were forwarded to the president with Hull's concurrence are in Gerow memo, Nov. 3, 1941, file 4389–29, Marshall and Stark memo to Roosevelt, Nov. 4, 1941, Executive #8, book A, WPD, RG 165. Most of this is printed in *PHA*, pt. 2, 328, 649, 652.

21. Feis, *Road*, 302–3; Langer & Gleason, *Undeclared War*, 852, 860; Toland, *Rising Sun*, 146–51. See also Tokyo to Nomura, Nov. 4, 1941, USDOD, *MAGIC*, 4:A12–A16.

22. Stimson diary, Nov. 6, 1941, printed in *PHA*, pt. 11, 5420; Langer & Gleason, *Undeclared War*, 852.

23. Ballantine memo, Nov. 1941, Hull memo Nov. 10, 1941, *FR Japan*, 2:706–10, 715–17.

24. FE comments on Nomura's proposal, Nov. 10, 1941, file "FE Files, U.S.-Japanese conversations/41," RG 59. Toland has demonstrated that Plans A and B were translated through MAGIC in such a manner as to make Japan appear less interested in a settlement than it actually was (see Toland, *Rising Sun*, 153–56). The point is well taken, but at such a late stage of negotiations the mistranslation made little difference. Besides, FE objections to the Japanese proposal were based on the text Nomura submitted, not the MAGIC translations. For the Japanese telegraphic traffic available to American policy managers at this time see USDOD, *MAGIC*, 4:A10–A93.

25. In the week of October 15–21, for example, Hornbeck sent Welles alone twenty-one memos all saying essentially the same thing. See also Hornbeck memo, Aug. 16, 1941, Hornbeck papers; Hornbeck memo, Sept. 2, 1941, *FR 41*, 4:419.

26. Ballantine memos, May 9, July 8, 1941, *FR 41*, 4:181, 296. See also Japanese statement, Aug. 28, 1941, *FR Japan*, 2:574; For other examples of this Japanese feeling see Nomura to Tokyo, Apr. 14, Aug. 2, 8, 1941, USDOD *MAGIC*, 1:A33, 2:A117, 3:A13; Grew memo, Nov. 10, 1941, *FR Japan*, 2:714.

27. Ballantine and Schmidt memo, Nov. 11, 1941, Hawkins memo, Nov. 10, 1941, *FR 41*, 4:576–84. Langer & Gleason *(Undeclared War*, 871) suppose that the memo was the result of a Hull inquiry, which in turn was the result of presidential interest. While Roosevelt was interested in a modus vivendi, there is no evidence that Hull requested this study, and Ballantine would not have used the language he did if he had been submitting something at the request of the secretary.

28. Grew to Hull, Nov. 10, 12, 1941, Ballantine memos, Nov. 10, 12, 13, 1941, *FR Japan*, 2:719–29.

29. Ballantine memo, Nov. 15, 1941, *FR Japan*, 2:731–34.

30. Morgenthau diary, 405:471ff. The memo was originally drafted in May and completed June 6, 1941.

31. The changes were nominal. Compare the original draft in the Morgenthau diary with the version submitted to state on Nov. 18 and that drafted by FE on Nov. 19, 1941. *FR Japan*, 2:606–13, 623–25. See also Hornbeck memo to Hull, Nov. 19, 1941, Hornbeck papers.

32. Japanese draft proposal, Nov. 20, 1941, *FR Japan*, 2:755–56.

33. Roosevelt memo, undated, *FR 41*, 4:626. Before Roosevelt acted, Ballantine had urged action along similar lines. Ballantine memo, Nov. 19, 1941, *FR 41*, 4:621–22.

34. It is probable that Roosevelt's undated memo proposing a modus vivendi was written on November 21 because the State Department draft of that date does not contain a modus vivendi while the one on Nov. 22 does. See these documents in *FR 41*, 4:627–30, 635–40.

35. These documents are printed in *FR 41*, 4:623–26, 627–30, 635–40.

36. The Nov. 24, 1941 draft is in *FR 41*, 4:643–44.

37. Stimson diary, Nov. 26, 1941. For the text of the final statement, see *FR Japan*, 2:768–70. Hull made up his mind not to deliver the modus vivendi on the morning of November 26 and told Stimson. It was after this that Stimson told Roosevelt of Japanese troop movements in the South Pacific. Stimson records that Roosevelt "fairly blew up—jumped up in to the air, so to speak, and said . . . that changed the whole situation." Though it was Roosevelt's final decision to make, clearly he would endorse Hull's recommendation not to offer the modus vivendi. Stimson diary, Nov. 26, 1941.

38. For Hull's meeting with Nomura and Kurusu on Nov. 26, see Ballantine memo, Nov. 26, 1941, *FR Japan*, 2:764–67; Nomura, Nov. 26, 27, 1941, USDOD, *MAGIC*, 4:A97–A105.

39. Hull made no secret of the fact that he thought diplomacy had ended, though he did claim never to have said he washed his hands of the matter. Stimson diary, Nov. 27, 1941; Ballantine testimony, International Military Tribunal of the Far East, "Proceedings," 10, 952–53; Ballantine, oral history interview, 214; Berle, *Navigating*, 378; Hornbeck memo, Nov. 27, 1941, *FR 41*, 4:675; Halifax to FO, Nov. 29, 30, 1941, file 27913/F12993, F13003/86/23, FO 371; Roosevelt press conference no. 787, Nov. 28, 1941, 18:326, PPC, FDRL. During the debate prior to November 26, public opinion was not mentioned. Compared with the importance of avoiding war, the problems of satisfying the public were insignificant, a point Hull made to Halifax when he said he was aware of American public opinion but also felt that it would be negative if negotiations broke down over "a few barrels of oil" (Halifax quoting Hull). See Halifax to FO, Nov. 26, 1941, file 27912/F12766/86/23, FO 371. On the general question of Hull's suceptibility to public pressure see Utley, "Diplomacy in a Democracy."

40. Stimson diary, Nov. 7, 1941; Hull testimony, *PHA*, pt. 2, 433; Ballantine memo, July 3, 1942, *FR 41*, 4:374.

41. Hull memo, Nov. 22, 1941, *FR 41*, 4:640; Halifax to FO, Nov. 23, 1941, file 27912/F12654/86/23, FO 371.

42. Japanese to Nomura, Nov. 22, 1941, USDOD, *MAGIC,* 4:A89. Roosevelt to Churchill, Nov. 24, 1941, *FR 41,* 4:649.

43. Hull memo, Nov. 24, 1941, *FR 41* 4:646–47.

44. Hull memo, Nov. 25, 1941, *FR 41,* 4:654–55; Reynolds, *Anglo-American,* 243–46; London to Halifax, Nov. 21, 1941, Churchill minute, Nov. 23, 1941, FO minute, Nov. 24, 1941, files 27912/F12475, F12813, F12655/86/23, FO 371. The Chinese made their point to State, Roosevelt, and the War Department. See various documents, Nov. 24, 25, 1941, *FR 41,* 4:650–61. Stimson diary, Nov. 26, 1941; Hull memo, Nov. 27, 1941, *FR 41,* 4:668; Clarke minute, Nov. 27, 1941, Halifax to FO, Nov. 29, 1941, files 27913/F12959, F12992/86/23, FO 371; Ballantine memo, July 1, 1943, file 711.94/2087, RG 59; Ballantine, oral history interview, 203. The material sent to the War Department, however, was forwarded to Hull after he had already made his decision. See "China" folder, box 2, Sec. Army (Stimson) subject file, RG 107.

45. Stimson diary, Nov. 25, 1941; Current, "'Maneuver' the Japanese" passim. For Hornbeck's contribution to this mood see Hornbeck memo, Nov. 23, 1941, Hornbeck papers. Ballantine recalled that at this late date they still wanted peace and were working sixteen hours a day to find it. Ballantine, oral history interview, 44, 204; Berle, *Navigating,* 379, 381; Halifax to FO, Nov. 27, 1941, file 27913/F12939/86/23, FO 371; Hull memos, Nov. 22, Dec. 1, 1941, *FR Japan,* 2:760–61, 775–77. For a detailed narrative of the events during these days see Langer & Gleason, *Undeclared War,* ch. 27.

Chapter 10

1. Stimson, Knox, and Hull memos to Roosevelt, Nov. 27, 29, 1941, *FR 41,* 4:675–80, 688–98; Stark memo, Nov. 29, 1941, folder 1, entry 50, ser. 7, Turner papers, OA; Hornbeck memo, Nov. 30, 1941, "Far East" folder, box 4, Sec. Army (Stimson) subject file, RG 107; Halifax to FO, Dec. 1, 1941, file 27914/F13115/86/23, FO 371; Berle, *Navigating,* 380.

2. Stimson diary, Dec. 1, 1941; Hamilton memo, Dec. 2, 1941, *FR 41,* 4:710; Esthus, "Roosevelt's Commitment;" Halifax to FO, Nov. 30, Dec. 1, 5, 1941, Churchill to Roosevelt, Nov. 30, 1941, Butler minute, Dec. 3, 1941, files 27913/F12994, F13114, F13053/86/23, and 27914/F13280/86/23, FO 371.

3. Hornbeck memo, Dec. 1, 1941, Hornbeck papers. He also sent a copy to Stimson, "State Dept." folder, box 10, sec. Army (Stimson) subject file, RG 107.

4. Historians who argue that Hull ignored military factors while emphasizing moral, diplomatic, and political ones are Brune, "Considerations of Force," 401–3; Wolthuis, *U.S. and the Netherland Indies,* 298–99; Morison, *Turmoil,* 440; Schroeder, *Axis Alliance,* 179–80.

5. Paul Schroeder's older but still influential book eloquently condemns Hull for his devotion to the sanctity of treaties, sentimental attachment to China, and insistence on a liberal commercial world order. He is right that Hull insisted on a liberal commercial world order. See Schroeder, *Axis Alliance,* 210–12.

BIBLIOGRAPHY

A Note on Sources

Much on policy has been published, but the struggle within the State Department to determine and to implement policy is not generally revealed in the published sources. The single most important source is the department's decimal file, RG 59. Even better in this respect are the personal papers of State Department officers. Moffat's diary is excellent for earlier years—Hornbeck's papers are an absolute treasure. Hugh Wilson's small collection and the manuscript version of the Berle diary are both very helpful, the one for the earlier period, the other for the final year or so before war. While the published Berle diary is good, many interesting references were not included and the manuscript version should be consulted.

The papers of Nelson Johnson and Joseph C. Grew reflect the characters of the two men. Johnson's papers are most useful for revealing how his mind operated. Grew's papers are an excellent source for understanding both the man and the mood in Washington, at least as seen from Tokyo. Perhaps the most interesting observations on Japanese feelings as well as Washington attitudes are in the Department of Defense publication of the MAGIC intercepts. An excellent perspective can be gained from reading Hull's summary of his conversation with Nomura, then Nomura's summary cabled back to Tokyo.

Hull remains something of an enigma to historians. The existing biographical studies are inconclusive, and his papers are disappointing. Though large in bulk, they tell very little about Hull or about the State Department. His *Memoirs,* while more revealing, are not always reliable.

War Department records are extensive and generally helpful. RG 165 and RG 107 proved the most useful. Secretary of War Stimson's diary is vital to any research in this area, though it reveals less about the War Department than it does about the cabinet-level operations. Navy Department files, especially RG 38, proved useful; but as is usually the case, the real feelings of naval officers are found in less official sources, notably Stark's letters published in *Pearl Harbor Attack* and the Leahy diary.

Sources for the course of economic pressure on Japan are almost all unpublished. Morgenthau's diary (actually a transcript of his office conversations) is the place to start. Treasury records in RG 56 are not very helpful except for one thin file in the Division of Foreign Funds Control that reveals how the freeze was administered, a story not available from any other source. RG 169, a massive collection of Export Control records housed in Suitland, Maryland, is worth looking at, as is RG 179 for the NDAC. Perhaps the best source for NDAC activities is the Stettinius papers at the University of Virginia.

Finally, there is the problem of Franklin Roosevelt. His presidential files are extensive but they reveal less about the man than do many of his press conferences. This is a greater problem for those interested in the man than in the entire story of policy because to understand policy we must look far beyond the president and study the people who comprised the Washington bureaucracy. For them, the records are massive.

Unpublished U.S. Official Records

FO 371, records of the British Foreign Office, Public Record Office, London, England.

International Military Tribunal for the Far East, "Proceedings," LC.

Kittredge, Tracy B. (Captain USN), "United States British Naval Relations, 1939–1942," typescript, ComNavEu file, OA.

RG 38, records of the Chief of Naval Operations. Pre-1940 files in NA, all other files in OA.

RG 40, U.S. Department of Commerce, general records, NA.

RG 56, records of the Secretary of the Treasury, NA. Records of the Division of Foreign Funds Control, accession #67A2435, (which house the 1941 FFCC files), are available through the Division of Foreign Assets Control but are in the possession of the Office of Alien Property, Civil Division, Department of Justice, Washington, D.C.

RG 59, Department of State decimal file and FE Division office file, 1941, entry 730, NA.

RG 80, records of the Secretary of the Navy, NA.

RG 94, records of the Office of the Adjutant General, pre–1940, NA

RG 107, Secretary of War, general correspondence; Secretary of the Army (Stimson) subject file; Office of the Assistant Secretary of War, classified decimal file; Office of the Assistant Secetary of War for Air, classified decimal file, NA.

RG 151, records of the Bureau of Foreign and Domestic Commerce, Department of Commerce, NA.

RG 165, records of the War Department: War Plans Division (WPD); Office of the Chief of Staff (OCS); Joint Board (JB); Military Intelligence Division (G-2) military attaché reports through June 1941, NA. G-2 military attaché reports after June 1941, regional file, and subject files in Washington National Records Center, Suitland, Md.

RG 169, records of the Office of the Administrator of Export Control, part of the records of the Foreign Economic Administration, entries 87 and 88, Washington National Record Center, Suitland, Md.

RG 179, records of the Advisory Commission to the Council on National Defense, some filed in NA and some in FDRL.

RG 225, records of the Army and Navy Munitions Board; records of the Joint Army-Navy Board, NA.

RG 234, records of the Federal Loan Agency and the Metals Reserve Company, part of the records of the Reconstruction Finance Corporation, NA.

RG 253, records of the Petroleum Coordinator for National Defense, part of the records of the Petroleum Administration for War, NA.

RG 330, records of the Secretary of Defense, NA

RG 353, records of the Standing Liaison Committee, NA.

RG 407, records of the Adjutant General's Office, 1940–41, NA.

Unpublished Manuscript Collections

American Committee for Non-Participation in Japanese Aggression, office files, Littauer Library, Harvard Univ.

Joseph W. Ballantine, oral history interview, Columbia Univ.

Adolf A. Berle papers, FDRL.

William L. Clayton papers, Fondren Library, Rice Univ.

Norman H. Davis papers, LC.

Felix Frankfurter papers, LC.

Joseph Coy Green papers, Firestone Library, Princeton Univ.

Roger Sherman Greene papers, Houghton Library, Harvard Univ.

Joseph C. Grew papers, Houghton Library, Harvard Univ.

Thomas B. Hart papers, OA.
Thomas B. Hart, "Narrative of Events, Asiatic Fleet, Leading Up to War and from 8 December 1941 to February 1942," unpublished typescript, OA.
Leon Henderson papers, FDRL.
Harry Hopkins papers, FDRL.
Stanley K. Hornbeck papers, Hoover Institution on War, Revolution and Peace, Stanford, Calif.
Cordell Hull papers, LC.
Royal E. Ingersoll, oral history interview, Columbia Univ. and OA.
Nelson T. Johnson papers, LC.
Jesse H. Jones papers, LC.
Alan G. Kirk, oral history interview, Columbia Univ. and OA.
Alan G. Kirk papers, OA.
Frank Knox papers, LC.
William D. Leahy papers, LC.
Breckinridge Long papers, LC.
John VA. MacMurray papers, Firestone Library, Princeton Univ.
Jay Pierrepont Moffat papers, Houghton Library, Harvard Univ.
R. Walton Moore papers, FDRL.
Henry Morgenthau Jr., diary, FDRL.
Robert P. Patterson papers, LC.
William Phillips papers, Houghton Library, Harvard Univ.
Key Pittman papers, LC.
Franklin D. Roosevelt papers, President's Secretary's File (PSF), President's Personal Files (PPF), Presidential Press Conferences (PPC), FDRL.
Francis Bowes Sayre papers, LC.
Whitney Shepardson papers, FDRL.
Harold D. Smith papers, FDRL.
Edward R. Stettinius papers, Univ. of Virginia Library.
Henry L. Stimson papers, Sterling Library, Yale Univ.
Arthur Sweetzer papers, LC.
Richmond K. Turner papers, OA.
Harriet Welling papers, Harper Library, Univ. of Chicago.
Harry Dexter White papers, Firestone Library, Princeton Unv.
Hugh Wilson papers, Herbert Hoover Library, West Branch, Iowa.
Harry E. Yarnell papers, LC and OA.
Arthur N. Young papers, Hoover Institution, Stanford Univ.

Printed Primary Sources

Advisory Commission to the Council of National Defense, *Minutes, June 12, 1940 to October 22, 1941* (Washington: GPO, 1946).
ACNPJA, *America's Share in Japan's War Guilt* (New York: np, 1938).
Atwater, Elton. *American Regulation of Arms Exports.* Washington: GPO, 1941.
Berle, Adolf A. *Navigating the Rapids, 1918–1971: From the Papers of Adolf A. Berle.* Edited by Beatrice B. Berle and Travis B. Jacobs. New York: Harcourt, Brace, Jovanoich, 1973.

Cadogan, Alexander. *The Diaries of Sir Alexander Cadogan. O.M., 1938–1945.* Edited by David Dilks. New York: Putnam, 1972.

Douglas, Henry H. "A Bit of American History—Successful Embargo Against Japan, 1918," *Amerasia* 4 (1940): 258–60.

———. "America Finances Japan's 'New Order,' " *Amerasia* 4 (1940): 221–24.

———."The Japanese Navy and the United States," *ASIA* 41 (1941): 162–65.

Gallup, George N., ed. *The Gallup Poll: Public Opinion, 1935–1971,* vol. I. New York: Random House, 1972.

Ickes, Harold L. *The Secret Diary of Harold L. Ickes,* vols. II, III. New York: Simon and Schuster, 1954.

Ike, Nobutaka, ed. and trans. *Japan's Decision for War, Records of the 1941 Policy Conference.* Stanford: Stanford Univ. Press, 1967.

Janeway, Eliot. "Japan's New Need: American Steels, Machines and Oils," *ASIA* 38 (1938): 338–40.

———. "Japan's Partner: Japanese Dependence Upon the United States," *Harpers* 177 (June 1938): 1–8.

———. "Trade Currents," *ASIA* 41 (1941): 400.

Long, Breckinridge. *The War Diary of Breckinridge Long, Selections from the Years 1939–1941.* Ed. Fred L. Israel. Lincoln: Univ. of Nebraska Press, 1966.

National Munitions Control Board. *Second Annual Report of the National Munitions Control Board.* House Doc. no. 465, 75th Cong., 3rd sess., 1938.

Morgenthau, Henry Jr. *From the Morgenthau Diaries,* vols. I, II. Ed. John Morton Blum. Boston: Houghton Mifflin, 1959, 1965.

Morgenthau, Henry, Jr. *Morgenthau Diary (China).* Ed. Anthony Kubek, prepared by the Internal Security subcommittee of the Judiciary committee, U.S. Senate, 89th Cong. 1st sess., vol. I. Washington: GPO, 1965.

Roosevelt, Franklin D. *Roosevelt and Churchill: Their Secret Wartime Correspondence.* Eds. Francis L. Loewenheim, Harold D. Langly[1], and Manfred Jonas. London: Dutton, 1975.

"Town meeting of the Air," Feb. 23, 1939.

U.S. Congress, Joint Committee on the Investigation of the Pearl Harbor Attack. *Hearings.* Washington: GPO, 1946.

U.S. Department of Defense. *The "MAGIC" Background of Pearl Harbor.* Washington: GPO, 1978.

U.S. Department of State. *Bulletin.* Washington GPO, 1937–41.

———. *Papers Relating to the Foreign Relations of the United States, Japan 1931–1941,* 2 vols. Washington: GPO, 1943; *1937–1941,* multiple volumes, Washington: GPO, 1954–56.

Secondary Sources: Books

Abbazia, Patrick, *Mr. Roosevelt's Navy: The Private War of the U.S. Atlantic Fleet, 1939–1942.* Annapolis, Md.: Naval Institute Press, 1975.

Acheson, Dean G. *Morning and Noon*. Boston: Houghton Mifflin, 1965.
————. *Present at the Creation: My Years at the State Department*. New York: Norton, 1969.
Anderson, Irvine H., Jr. *The Standard-Vacuum Oil Company and United States East Asian Policy, 1933–1941*. Princeton: Princeton Univ. Press, 1975.
Barron, Gloria M. *Leadership in Crisis: FDR and the Path to Intervention*. Port Washinton, N.Y.: Kennikat, 1973.
Borg, Dorothy. *The United States and the Far Eastern Crisis of 1933–1938, from the Manchurian Incident through the Initial Stage of the Undeclared Sino-Japanese War*. Cambridge, Mass: Harvard Univ. Press, 1964.
Borg, Dorothy, and Shumpei Okamoto, eds. *Pearl Harbor as History: Japanese-American Relations, 1931–1941*. New York: Columbia, 1973.
Buhite, Russell D. *Nelson T. Johnson and American Policy Toward China, 1935–1941*. East Lansing: Michigan State Univ. Press, 1968.
Burns, James MacGregor. *Roosevelt, the Lion and the Fox*. New York: Harcourt, Brace & World, 1956.
————. *Roosevelt: Soldier of Freedom*. New York: Harcourt, Brace, Jovanovich, 1970.
Burns, Richard Dean, and Edward M. Bennett. *Diplomats in Crisis: United States-Chinese-Japanese Relations, 1919–1941*. Santa Barbara: ABC Clio, 1974.
Butler, J. R. M. *Grand Strategy, September 1939–June 1941*. London: HMSO, 1957.
Butow, Robert J. C. *Tojo and the Coming of the War*. Princeton: Princeton Univ. Press, 1961.
————. *The John Doe Associates: Backdoor Diplomacy for Peace, 1941*. Stanford: Stanford Univ. Press, 1974.
Chennault, Claire. *Way of a Fighter; The Memoirs of Claire Lee Chennault*. New York: Putnam, 1949.
Clifford, Nicholas R. *Retreat From China: British Policy in the Far East, 1937–1941*. Seattle: Univ. of Washington Press, 1967.
Cohen, Warren I. *America's Response to China: An Interpretative History of Sino-American Relations*. New York: Wiley, 1971.
————. *The Chinese Connection: Roger S. Greene, Thomas W. Lamont, George E. Sokolsky and American-East Asian Relations*. New York: Columbia Univ. Press, 1978.
Cole, Wayne S., *Roosevelt & the Isolationists, 1932–45*. Lincoln: Univ. of Nebraska Press, 1983.
Craigie, Robert. *Behind the Japanese Mask*. London: Hutchison, 1945.
Craven, Wesley F. and James L. Cate, eds. *The Army Air Forces in World War II*, vol. I: *Plans and Early Operations: January 1939 to August 1942*. Chicago: Univ. of Chicago Press, 1948.
Crowley, James B. *Japan's Quest for Autonomy: National Security and Foreign Policy, 1930–1938*. Princeton: Princeton Univ. Press, 1966.
Dallek, Robert. *Franklin D. Roosevelt and American Foreign Policy, 1932–1945*. New York: Oxford Univ. Press, 1979.
Divine, Robert A. *The Illusion of Neutrality*, Chicago: Univ. of Chicago Press, 1962.

————. *The Reluctant Belligerent: American Entry into the Second World War*, 2d. ed. New York: Wiley, 1979.

————. *Roosevelt and World War II*. Baltimore: Johns Hopkins Univ. Press, 1969.

Drummond, Donald F. *The Passing of American Neutrality, 1937–1941*. Ann Arbor: Univ. of Michigan Press, 1955.

Eden, Anthony. *The Eden Memoirs, Facing the Dictators*. Boston: Houghton Mifflin, 1962.

Esthus, Raymond A. *From Enmity to Alliance: U.S.-Australian Relations, 1931–1941*. Seattle: Univ. of Washington Press, 1964.

Farley, James A. *Jim Farley's Story: The Roosevelt Years*. New York, Whittlesey House, 1948.

Fehrenbach, T. R. *F.D.R.'s Undeclared War, 1939–1941*. New York: McKay, 1967.

Feis, Herbert. *The Road to Pearl Harbor: The Coming of the War Between the United States and Japan*. Princeton: Princeton Univ. Press, 1950.

Friedman, Donald J. *The Road From Isolation: The Campaign of the American Committee for Non-Participation in Japanese Aggression, 1938–1941*. Cambridge: Harvard East Asian Research Center, 1968.

Gardner, Lloyd C. *Economic Aspects of New Deal Diplomacy*. Madison: Univ. of Wisconsin Press, 1964.

Griswold, A. Whitney. *The Far Eastern Policy of the United States*. New Haven: Yale Univ. Press, 1937.

Hayes, Grace P. *The History of the Joint Chiefs of Staff in World War II: The War Against Japan*. Annapolis: Naval Institute Press, 1982.

Heinrichs, Waldo H., Jr. *American Ambassador: Joseph C. Grew and the Development of the United States Diplomatic Tradition*. Boston: Little, Brown, 1966.

Herzog, James H. *Closing the Open Door: American-Japanese Diplomatic Negotiations, 1936–1941*. Annapolis: Naval Institute Press, 1973.

Hinton, Harold B. *Cordell Hull, A Biography*. Garden City, N.Y.: Doubleday, 1942.

Hull, Cordell. *The Memoirs of Cordell Hull*. 2 vols. New York: Macmillan, 1948.

Iriye, Akira. *Across the Pacific: An Inner History of American-East Asian Relations*. New York: Harcourt, Brace & World, 1967.

————. *Power and Culture: The Japanese-American War, 1941–1945*. Cambridge: Harvard Univ. Press, 1981.

Jonas, Manfred. *Isolationism in America, 1935–1941*. Ithaca, N.Y.: Cornell Univ. Press, 1966.

Koginos, Manny T. *The Panay Incident: Prelude to War*. Lafayette, Ind.: Purdue Univ. Studies, 1967.

Land, Emory S. *Winning the War with Ships: Land, Sea, and Air—Mostly Land*. New York: McBride, 1958.

Langer, William L., and S. Everett Gleason. *The Challenge to Isolation, 1937–1940*. New York: Harper, 1954.

————. *The Undeclared War, 1940–1941*. New York: Harper, 1953.

Lee, Bradford A. *Britain and the Sino-Japanese War, 1937–1939: A Study in in the Dilemmas of British Decline.* Stanford: Stanford Univ. Press, 1973.

Leutze, James R. *Bargaining for Supremacy: Anglo-American Naval Relations, 1937–1941.* Chapel Hill: Univ. of North Carolina Press, 1977.

Lowe, Peter. *Great Britain and the Origins of the Pacific War: A Study of British Policy in East Asia, 1937–1941.* New York: Oxford Univ. Press, 1977.

Lu, David J. *From the Marco Polo Bridge to Pearl Harbor: Japan's Entry into World War II.* Washington: Public Affairs Press, 1961.

Manchester, William. *American Caesar: Douglas MacArthur, 1880–1964.* Boston: Little, Brown, 1978.

Matloff, Maurice, and Edwin M. Snell. *Strategic Planning for Coalition Warfare, 1941–1942.* Washington: Office of the Chief of Military History, Department of the Army, 1953.

McIntire, Ross. *White House Physician.* New York: Putnam, 1946.

Medlicott, William N. *The Economic Blockade,* 2 vols. London: H.M. Stationery Office, 1952, 1959.

Meskill, Johanna Menzel. *Hitler and Japan: The Hollow Alliance.* New York: Atherton, 1966.

Morison, Elting E. *Turmoil and Tradition: A Study of the Life and Times of Henry L. Stimson.* Boston: Houghton Mifflin, 1960.

Pelz, Stephen E. *Race to Pearl Harbor: The Failure of the Second London Naval Conference and the Onset of World War II.* Cambridge: Harvard, 1974.

Perry, Hamilton D. *The Panay Incident: Prelude to Pearl Harbor.* New York: Macmillan, 1969.

Pogue, Forrest C. *George C. Marshall: Ordeal and Hope, 1939–1942.* London: MacGibbon & Key, 1968.

Prange, Gordon W. *At Dawn We Slept: The Untold Story of Pearl Harbor.* New York: McGraw-Hill, 1981.

Pratt, Julius W. *Cordell Hull, 1933–1944,* 2 vols. New York: Cooper Square, 1964.

Range, Willard. *Franklin D. Roosevelt's World Order.* Athens: Univ. of Georgia Press, 1959.

Rauch, Basil. *Roosevelt From Munich to Pearl Harbor.* New York: Creative Age Press, 1950.

Reynolds, David. *The Creation of the Anglo-American Alliance, 1937–41: A Study in Competitive Co-operation.* Chapel Hill: Univ. of North Carolina Press, 1982.

Richardson, James O., with George C. Dyer. *On the Treadmill to Pearl Harbor: The Memoirs of Admiral James O. Richardson.* Washington: Naval History Division, Dept. of Navy, 1973.

Roosevelt, Eleanor. *This I Remember.* New York: Harper, 1949.

Rosen, S. McKee. *The Combined Boards of the Second World War: An Experiment in International Administration.* New York: Columbia Univ. Press, 1951.

Russett, Bruce M. *No Clear and Present Danger: A Skeptical View of the U.S. Entry into World War II.* New York: Harper, 1972.

Schaller, Michael. *The U.S. Crusade in China, 1938–1945.* New York: Columbia Univ. Press, 1979.

Schroeder, Paul W. *The Axis Alliance and Japanese-American Relations, 1941.* Ithaca, N.Y.: Cornell Univ. Press, 1958.

Shai, Aron. *Origins of the War in the East: Britain, China and Japan, 1937–39.* London: Helm, 1976.

Shepardson, Whitney O. *The United States in World Affairs, 1937.* New York: Council on Foreign Relations, 1938.

Sommer, Theo. *Deutschland und Japan Zwischen den Mächten. 1935–40: Vom Antikominternpakt zum Dreimächtepakt; eine Studie zur diplomatischen Vorgeschichte des Zweiten Weltkriegs.* Tübingen: Mohr, 1962.

Stimson, Henry L. *The Far Eastern Crisis: Recollections and Observations.* New York: Harper, 1948.

Toland, John. *The Flying Tigers.* New York: Dell, 1963.

———. *The Rising Sun: The Decline and Fall of the Japanese Empire.* New York: Random House, 1970.

Van Mook, H. J. *The Netherlands Indies and Japan: Battle on Paper, 1940–41.* New York: Norton, 1944.

Varg, Paul A. *Closing the Door: Sino-American Relations. 1936–1946.* East Lansing: Michigan State Univ. Press, 1973.

Watson, Mark Skinner. *Chief of Staff: Prewar Plans and Preparations.* Washington: GPO, 1950.

Welles, Sumner. *The Time for Decision.* New York: Harper, 1944.

Wheeler, Gerald. *Prelude to Pearl Harbor: The United States Navy and the Far East, 1921–1931.* Columbia: Univ. of Missouri Press, 1963.

Wilson, Theodore A. *The First Summit: Roosevelt and Churchill at Placentia Bay, 1941.* Boston: Houghton Mifflin, 1969.

Wilson, Hugh R. *Disarmament and the Cold War in the Thirties.* New York: Vantage, 1963.

Wolthuis, Robert K. *United States Foreign Policy Toward the Netherland Indies, 1937–1945.* Baltimore: Johns Hopkins Univ. Press, 1968.

Young, Arthur N. *China and the Helping Hand, 1937–1945.* Cambridge: Harvard Univ. Press, 1963.

Dissertations and Periodical Literature

Adams, Frederick C. "The Road to Pearl Harbor: A Reexamination of American Far Eastern Policy, July 1937–December 1938," *JAH* 58 (1971): 73–92.

Anderson, Irvine H., Jr. "The 1941 *de facto* Embargo on Oil to Japan: A Bureaucratic Reflex," *PHR* 44 (1975): 201–31.

Bader, Ernest. "Some Aspects of American Public Reaction to Franklin D. Roosevelt's Japanese Policy, 1933–1941." Ann Arbor: Univ. Microfilms, 1958.

Barclay, Glen St. John. "Singapore Strategy: The Role of the United States in Imperial Defense," *Military Affairs* 39 (1975): 54–61.

Brune, Lester H. "Considerations of Force in Cordell Hull's Diplomacy, July 26 to November 26, 1941," *Diplomatic History* 2 (1978): 389–405.

Burns, Richard Dean. "Cordell Hull: A Study in Diplomacy, 1931–1941." Ann Arbor: Univ. Microfilms, 1960.

———. "Stanley K. Hornbeck: The Diplomacy of the Open Door." In Burns and Bennett, *Diplomats in Crisis*, 91–117.

Butow, Robert J. C. "The Hull-Nomura Conversations: A Fundamental Misconception," *American Historical Review* 55 (1960): 822–36.

———. "Backdoor Diplomacy in the Pacific: The Proposal for Konoye-Roosevelt Meeting, 1941," *JAH* 59 (1972): 48–72.

Clauss, Errol MacGregor. "The Roosevelt Administration and Manchukuo, 1933–1941," *The Historian* 32 (1970): 595–611.

Conroy, Hilary. "Nomura Kichisaburo; the Diplomacy of Drama and Desperation." In Burns, *Diplomats in Crisis*, 297–316.

———. "The Strange Diplomacy of Admiral Nomura," *Proceedings of the American Philosophical Society* 114 (1970): 205–16.

Current, Richard N. "How Stimson Meant to 'Maneuver' the Japanese," *MVHR* 40 (1953): 67–74.

Distretti, Joseph P. "The American Military and Naval Attachés and the Sino-Japanese War: 1937–38." Unpublished MA thesis, Univ. of Tennessee, Knoxville, 1981.

Doyle, Michael K. "The U.S. Navy and War Plan Orange, 1933–1940: Making Necessity a Virtue," *Naval War College Review* 32 (May–June 1980): 49–63.

Esthus, Raymond A. "President Roosevelt's Commitment to Britain to Intervene in a Pacific War," *MVHR* 50 (1963): 28–38.

Feis, Herbert. "Some Notes on Historical Record-keeping, the Role of Historians, and the Influence of Historical Memories During the Era of the Second World War." In Francis L. Loewenheim. *The Historian and the Diplomat: The Role of History and Historians in American Foreign Policy.* New York: Harper, 1967, pp 91–122.

Haight, John McVicker, Jr. "Franklin D. Roosevelt and a Naval Quarantine of Japan," *PHR* 40 (1971): 203–26.

———. "Roosevelt and the Aftermath of the Quarantine Speech," *Review of Politics* 24 (1962): 233–59.

Harrington, Daniel F. "A Careless Hope: American Air Power and Japan, 1941," *PHR* 48 (1979): 217–38.

Heinrichs, Waldo H. "The Role of the United States Navy." In Borg and Okomato, *Pearl Harbor as History*, 197–223.

Herzog, James H. "Influence of the United States Navy in the Embargo of Oil to Japan, 1940–1941," *PHR* 35 (1966): 317–28.

Hosoya, Chihiro. "Miscalculations in Deterrent Policy: Japanese-U.S. Relations, 1938–1941," *Journal of Peace Research* 5 (1968): 97–115.

———. "The Tripartite Pact, 1939–1940." In James W. Morely (ed.). *Deterrent Diplomacy: Japan, Germany and the USSR, 1935–1940.* New York: Columbia Univ. press, 1976, 191–257.

Iriye, Akira. "The Role of the United States Embassy in Tokyo." In Borg and Okamoto, *Pearl Harbor as History*, 107–26.

Jacobs, Travis Beal. "Roosevelt's Quarantine Speech," *The Historian* 24 (1964): 483–502.

Leonard, Thomas M. "Stanley K. Hornbeck: Major Deterrent to America-

Japanese Summitry, 1941," *Towson State Journal of International Affairs* 8 (1974): 113–21.

Libby, Justin. "The Irresolute Years: American Congressional Opinion Towards Japan, 1937–1941." Ann Arbor: Univ. Microfilms, 1971.

McCarty, Kenneth G., Jr. "Stanley K. Hornbeck and the Far East, 1931–1941." Ann Arbor: Univ. Microfilms, 1970.

Miner, Deborah Nutter. "United States Policy Toward Japan, 1941: The Assumption That Southeast Asia Was Vital to the British War Effort." Ann Arbor: Univ. Microfilms, 1979.

Morton, Louis. "War Plan ORANGE: Evolution of a Strategy." *World Politics* 11 (1959): 221–50.

Potter, David M. "Why the Republicans Rejected Both Compromise and Secession." In George H. Knoles, ed. *The Crisis of the Union, 1860–1861.* Baton Rouge: Louisiana State Univ. 1965.

Pratt, Julius W. "The Ordeal of Cordell Hull," *Review of Politics* 28 (1966): 76–98.

Quinlan, Robert J. "The United States Fleet: Diplomacy, Strategy and the Allocation of Ships (1940–1941)." In Harold Stein, ed. *American Civil Military Decisions: A Book of Case Studies.* Birmingham: Ala., 1963, pp. 153–201.

Schaller, Michael. "American Air Strategy in China, 1939–1941: The Origins of Clandestine Air Warfare," *American Quarterly* 28 (1976): 3–19.

Utley, Jonathan G. "Diplomacy in a Democracy: The United States and Japan, 1937–1941," *World Affairs* 139 (1976): 130–40.

———. "Upstairs, Downstairs at Foggy Bottom: Oil Exports and Japan, 1940–41," *Prologue* 8 (1976): 17–28.

Weigley, Russell F. "The Role of the War Department and the Army." In Borg and Okamoto, *Pearl Harbor as History,* 165–188.

Welles, Sumner. "Roosevelt and the Far East," *Harpers* 202 (Feb., March 1951): 27–38, 70–80.

INDEX

Going to War with Japan, 1937–1941 was composed into type on the Mergenthaler Linotron 202N Phototypesetter in ten point Sabon with two points of spacing between the lines. The book was designed by Jim Billingsley, typeset by Williams of Chattanooga, printed offset by Thomson-Shore, Inc., and bound by John H. Dekker & Sons. The paper on which the book is printed is designed for an effective life of at least three hundred years.

The University of Tennessee Press : Knoxville